The Best European Travel Tips

The Best European Travel Tips 1994–1995

John Whitman

HarperPerennial
A Division Of HarperCollins*Publishers*

My special thanks to these readers who have added a tip or corrected information in the previous guide: Lou Aleksich, Jr., Margaret Antonopoulos, Carol Antonow, J. Bell, Jean Bullock, R. Butler, Dawn Carmack, Heather Cowap, Vivian J. Cummings, Marcia Daszko, Mike Dewey, Andrew Dorio, John A. Elling, Gwen and Davey Farrington, Sue Ferer, Tony Freeman, Albert Furtwangler, Elizabeth Gilbert, Josephine Gillis, R.L. Goodale, Leo J. Goode, Jason Gow, Jackie and Jim Haeston, Tony Harkin, Rasamond Haverstock, John R. Hayden, Joe Hodge, Jane H. Holzherr, Stephen S. Johnson, Donald King, Harry O. Knowles, Glynis J. Laing, Linda D. Little, Linda L. Lorenz, Kate MacDonald, Eloise McGinnis, Rachel McLean, Betty Mendolia, Lydia Morgan, Christopher and Marie North, Jan O'Rourke, Joy Owen, Marc Parsont, Mary Lou Dunn-Rankin, Marge Ritenhouse, Marvin L. Saltzman, Floyd D. Seele, J. T. Shim, Ruth L. C. Simms, William Skiff, Steve Snowden, William Speck, Doris W. Suthers, James T. Swearingen, Lynne Terrell, David C. Trautvetter, Gail Ann Williams, Betty M. Wilson, Harry P. Wilson, Kenney Wright.

HarperCollins books may be purchased for educational, business, or sales promotional use. For information, please write: Special Markets Department, HarperCollins Publishers, Inc., 10 East 53rd Street, New York, NY 10022.

FIRST EDITION

Library of Congress Cataloging-in-Publication Data

Whitman, John.
    The best European travel tips, 1994–1995 /by John Whitman.
       p.   cm.
    Includes index.
    ISBN 0-06-273267-6
      1. Europe—Guidebooks.   I. Title.
D909.W537 1994
914'.04559—dc20   93-27138

94 95 96 97 98 ◆/RRD10 9 8 7 6 5 4 3 2 1

Contents

PART II: THE TRIP

APPENDIXES

Foreword

This is the first edition of this guide to include Eastern Europe. As a foreword, I am including some special tips aimed at that region, which has some of the most spectacular scenery, cities, and cultural attractions on the Continent. Please note that things are changing so rapidly in this region that many of these tips may be obsolete, or true one day, not the next, and then true again. The emphasis on the negative is not meant to discourage travel to this fascinating area. I simply believe that forewarned is indeed forearmed. Many additional tips are included throughout the book.

The Countries

- Hungary is most prepared for tourism. Czechoslovakia* is popular, but rooms are truly a problem, especially in Prague during the peak season. Poland is developing. Travel to Bulgaria and Romania must be viewed as adventure travel, although some of the things to see and do there are outstanding. Yugoslavia has been deleted from the guide for the time being.

Visas

- Find out ahead of time whether visas are needed for travel to a specific Eastern European country. Most are dropping the requirement for stays of less than 30 days. When visas are required, where, how, and when they will be issued can be confusing. Check months ahead of your planned trip for current information by contacting the appropriate tourist office (pp. 247–250). Where visas are presently required, the need for one is often dropped if you take a state-run tour. Hopefully, the concept of visas for limited stays will be completely outdated by the time you read this book.

*Please note that throughout this guide we refer to Czechoslovakia as one country, although it is now divided into two independent Czech and Slovak countries: the Czech Republic and Slovakia.

What to Bring with You

- What we take for granted may be hard or impossible to find. Medicine, batteries, radio, personal items from tampons to toiletries (including soap), toilet paper, and a towel—bring all of these, if needed. If any medication contains a controlled substance, carry a doctor's prescription with you. Never remove it from its original container. Bring matches and several disposable lighters (the latter make an excellent gift).

When to Travel

- The best time to travel is in late spring, before the tourist invasion of summer. The weather is good, most places are open, and crowds are down. September is also highly recommended along the Adriatic, which has fine resorts and equally fine fall weather. Off-season travel cannot yet be recommended, although cultural events are at their peak at this time. Pollution (smog) is bad during winter months. Many places close down. In some areas food becomes hard to find. Again, this situation will change, but for the time being put the odds in your favor.

Getting There

- Air travel to Eastern Europe may still be more expensive than flying to a Western European city close to your final destination combined with train travel to complete your trip. Study options carefully if money is a major consideration.
- Study tours available. For information on these contact the appropriate tourist offices (pp. 247–250) or agencies (p. xxi).

Important Facts About Money

- Prices in Eastern Europe vary greatly by the way you travel and how experienced you are. Rates for foreigners are often much higher than for locals, both by regulation and by subtle manipulation of prices not posted (the locals know what to pay, you don't). Bulgaria offers the best value for the travel dollar.

Poland is relatively inexpensive overall. In Romania prices are high for what you get. Czechoslovakia and Hungary are quickly getting close to Western European prices and in some cities are even higher because of the room shortage.

- Money generally must be carried in dollars or German Deutschmarks (referred to as hard currency in most publications). As strange as it sounds, local money often cannot be used to buy international train or plane tickets, goods in special shops, rooms in many hotels, and so on. In short, local currency is often useless. Bring lots of hard currency into Eastern Europe.

- Avoid large denomination bills. Bring as many $1 bills for petty exchanges and tips (no less than 100, more if possible).

- You may be asked to declare the exact amount of money you're bringing into a country. When you leave the country, any amount over the declared amount could be confiscated. Keep the declaration form—don't lose it!

- It has been illegal to import or export local currency except in extremely small amounts. Check on present laws, since it is helpful to have some of the local currency on arrival, especially at local airports where exchange lines are horrendous. *Note:* you can often buy currencies at a better rate outside the country (for example, Romanian money may be sold at a better rate in Poland than on the black market in Romania). However, this is of little value if the money can be confiscated upon entry into the country—check carefully about currency import and export regulations. Obviously, money has been crossing borders illegally, right?

- Exchange rates vary daily and by location. Private exchange offices, travel agencies, major hotels, post offices, and private individuals may give you better rates of exchange than banks or traveler's check offices. Compare before exchanging large amounts of currency. The source for the best rate of exchange varies by country and day. In Bulgaria travel agencies (Balkantourist offices) often offer better rates than banks. In Czechoslavakia banks are generally preferred. In Hungary post offices are often the best place. In Poland a private exchange office (*kantor*) often offers the best rate. In Romania you'll make far more money by exchanging with private parties (the black market).

- When exchanging money, the rate is important, but so is the commission. Always ask what the commission will be before exchanging money.

- Exchange only the amount you plan to use, since the local currencies are worthless outside the country itself.

- Banks will often give you large denomination notes. Refuse these and ask for smaller notes. You want to pay for everything with as close to the exact amount as possible.
- It is often difficult or impossible to exchange local currency back into dollars. Try once right away just to see whether this is the case. If you cannot get dollars, there is probably a thriving black market.
- When you exchange currency, you may be given a form showing the amount exchanged. Keep this. It may have to be stamped at each place you stay as proof that you were not making exchanges on the black market. Hold onto the form or forms until you have left the country. Hopefully, this will have changed by the time you travel.
- Exchanging money with private parties may still be illegal. Ask locally about regulations. In some instances, you'll get a much higher rate on the black market. Be extremely wary of exchanging money in this fashion. Thievery is common in a number of ways. You may be given obsolete bills, the amount given may seem to be more than actually given through sleight of hand, or you may be robbed. Your safest bet is to exchange money with waiters, desk clerks at hotels, owners of small boardinghouses, and so on. These people aren't suddenly going to disappear into the night. Tourists leaving a country and foreign business people also are eager to unload otherwise useless currency.
- Before exchanging currency on the black market, get samples of different denomination bills. Study these carefully. Note that some bills look similar, although they vary greatly in value. Finally, some scam artists are producing fake money on color photocopy machines. Feel the notes as well as checking on size, color, and artwork.
- Credit cards are just beginning to be accepted. Do not rely on them. If they can be used, expect to pay a surcharge of up to 10 percent. And always ask whether there will be a surcharge before using them.
- Traveler's checks can be hard to exchange, especially in larger denominations (take many $20 checks). American Express checks are the most widely accepted. The service fee for cashing checks can be exorbitant. If you plan to travel to East Germany, buy Deutschmark traveler's checks, since these are easy to exchange in this one area and help you avoid the stiff commission paid for all hard currency exchanges (presently a major rip-off).
- Often the barter system for service or goods is better than money. Many goods are scarce. A small portable radio might be

worth a small fortune. A package of cigarettes may be worth a long taxi ride. A chocolate bar may be worth its weight in gold (all right, not quite). In fact, one of the tricks of hitchhikers is to hold up a package of Kents or a chocolate bar to entice drivers to stop. In Eastern Europe you're expected to pay a little for every ride anyway, at least the equivalent of bus fare.

- *Important tip:* Use a money belt, a pouch (hangs from your neck or belt and stays under your clothes), or both to conceal money. Avoid keeping all of your money in one place—split it up (see pp. 136–140).
- If you buy expensive items in Eastern Europe, get a receipt indicating that you have paid in hard currency. Keep the receipt. Border guards may insist on seeing it. Otherwise, you may have to pay a fee. For refunds of the Value Added Tax (VAT) get forms stamped at the German border. Get refunds for Czechoslovakia at Cedok offices. Get refunds for Hungary from Ibusz offices. Note that a number of items are not allowed to be exported at all (see p. 205), even though they are often sold within the country anyway.

Where to Stay

- Finding a room during the peak season without advance reservations can be extremely difficult. Prague is notorious for its shortage of rooms. Hotels in Czechoslovakia and Hungary can be very expensive. Hotel rooms in Poland are more affordable. Note that payment in advance for rooms in Bulgaria and Romania can result in substantial discounts. This can be done through foreign travel agents in Europe, at the border, at auto clubs, and in other locations of the National Tourist Office abroad. Contact the appropriate tourist information office (pp. 247–250) for current information on exactly where to buy these coupons or vouchers (if they still exist at the time). This will save you up to 50 percent on all but the most luxurious hotels. Also contact youth-oriented organizations (see p. 8) and ask about vouchers for really inexpensive places to stay if you're on a tight budget. Some of these vouchers must be purchased in advance.
- However, in general, you pay much more for a room if a reservation is made from abroad rather than locally. Paying more may be worth it for short trips or for peace of mind in cities such as Prague in peak season.

- As in other countries, there are boardinghouses, dormitories, and private homes where rates are more reasonable. Networking with other travelers is often the best way to know about inexpensive and just-opened places to stay. Mark names and addresses down in a little black book. This information is invaluable. Exchanging information is critical to successful independent travel. *Special tip:* When you stay in a place you really like, ask the owner whether there is a similar place in the next town or city you plan to visit. If so, have the owner call ahead to make a reservation for you. The right person making a call works magic. Pay for the call—it's worth it.
- *Special note:* in many Eastern European countries (Hungary excepted) there is a two-tier pricing system—one for foreigners, one for locals. Locals may pay as little as one-tenth what you pay for the same room. You can sometimes beat this system by offering to pay the clerk directly for the room in dollars (although some hotels will only take dollars anyway). Naturally, you try to figure out what the locals are paying and pay an equivalent amount in dollars converted from the "unofficial" or black market rate prevailing at the time. This may or may not work, but if it does, you'll save a lot. Yes, the system stinks, but I didn't create it.
- Many hotels are inferior by Western standards. Such things as heat, light bulbs, hot water, toilet paper, and food are often lacking. In more remote areas rooms may be abysmal and bug-infested. Other places are just fine. Check rooms out carefully before handing over any money.
- Camping in motor homes (caravans), mini vans, or in a tent is generally an economical alternative. The quality of campgrounds in Bulgaria varies. There are over 100, but they are often hard to find. Some won't take in foreigners (again, this may change). "Organized" camping is not recommended in Romania. In other Eastern European countries there is little problem.
- Sleeping out or freelance camping is illegal in Eastern Europe and must be done extremely discreetly. In theory, the police are supposed to know where you are at all times, although this policy may be changing rapidly as regulations loosen. If you see locals camping out, try to camp with them. At the very least, get far away from any road so that you are totally inconspicuous. Note that in some areas foreigners are such a novelty that you might be invited to stay in someone's home. Always give a gift of some kind for such hospitality if any offer of

money is refused. Gifts most highly appreciated are utilitarian, such as cigarettes, scented soaps, candy bars, coffee, spices (pepper), cosmetics, packets of vegetable seeds, tea bags— you've got the idea. Gifts should be light, inexpensive, and easy to pack.

- About youth hostels: In Bulgaria have a Pirin travel agent call ahead to make a reservation for you if you find getting into hostels is still difficult. Otherwise, you may not get in, although this too is changing rapidly. Hostels in Czechoslovakia are often as good as modest hotels. Hostels in Hungary are excellent and may be student housing converted for use during the summer months. Youth hostels are good in Poland and most closely resemble those of Western Europe. Romania doesn't have hostels (surely some will open in the near future). *Tip*: Even if you are carrying your own sleeping sheet or sack, you may still have to rent one in some hostels (no sense arguing). *Special tip*: do not trust publications on hostels. These are often inaccurate.

- Note that in both Czechoslovakia and Hungary there are dormitories known as "tourist hostels," which are not truly youth hostels and are often open to tourists of any age. Ask about these at local tourist offices, because they are a real bargain.

- Check locally about youth-oriented rooms, generally with student organizations or local travel agencies. Older travelers should note that you can often get into many inexpensive places despite your age. Local travel agents and tourist offices often have information on rooms in private homes.

Getting Around

- Airports and train and bus stations can be chaotic and extremely confusing because of the language barrier and the systems themselves. Although some major routes are relatively easy to handle, trips to minor destinations can be extremely difficult. However, buses and trains may be the most economical way to get to certain locations. Note, however, that some buses are open only to locals (this too may soon change). The reason? The prices are extremely low, and the foreign countries don't want you taking advantage of this. I'm convinced that this may soon be obsolete.

- Using a local travel agent to help with train travel or other travel may be practical, saving you time and money. They are less likely to sell you an invalid ticket or reserve a seat that has already been reserved (both happen enough to be frustrating).

- If a train requires reserved seats, get them in advance or you will pay a substantially higher fee on the train for the reservation.

- Also, ticketing may be done in local branches of the railway system rather than in a crowded station itself. Go to these offices as early in the day as possible to buy tickets or make reservations (which may be required for specific trains). Again, if you have any questions about the existence or location of such offices, ask in a major hotel where someone at the front desk will help you. If they spend a lot of time with you, give them a tip unless you're staying in the hotel. If they do something truly special, give them a tip automatically.

- *Special tip:* Although Czechoslovakia and Poland are not yet part of the Eurail system, a number of travelers have reported being able to use Eurailpasses in these countries. Whether this is oversight or ignorance on the part of conductors or a way to encourage tourism, no one seems to know. However, these countries have their own passes, which are certainly a safer bet. In general, bus and train travel in Eastern Europe is so inexpensive that passes of any kind may not be worth buying.

- *Important tip:* International train tickets are much more expensive than tickets for travel within each individual Eastern European country. They also must be purchased in hard rather than local currency (at least, at present). If your money is extremely tight, buy tickets to a border station, cross the border by foot, and then buy tickets in the next country. Ask locally about stations that are extremely close to each other, so that the walk is as short as possible between the adjoining countries. Crossing borders by foot is one of the fastest ways to get from one country to the next, and some experienced travelers do it routinely for this reason alone. In other words, border crossing by train or car can take hours. By foot, minutes.

- *Important tips:* Conductors often try to scam foreigners by claiming that there is something wrong with a ticket. If you're fined, demand a receipt. Then take the ticket and the receipt to a local branch of the National Tourist Office and find out whether the fine was a rip-off or justified. If you purchase a round-trip ticket, do not give it to the conductor, even if he insists he'll give it back to you later. You may never see him again. The only exception to this is if you rent a *couchette* (bunk bed) or sleeper. The conductor needs your ticket so that he doesn't have to wake you up every time there is a ticket check. Frankly, I'd skip the bed, sleep sitting up, and hang onto the ticket.

- Local trams, buses, and subways are usually excellent, but again, ticketing may cause confusion. Ask at a hotel about where to buy tickets and how to use them. Watch the locals and follow their lead. Always buy more tickets than you think you'll need. Occasionally, an additional ticket is required if you're carrying luggage. If you don't do what the locals do and have not had your ticket stamped properly, you will often be fined.

- Traveling with a tour is highly recommended, even for the more independent type of traveler, since tours lock up rooms and restaurants in advance. Some tour operators are listed with the National Tourist Offices (pp.247–250). Some of the Eastern European countries essentially operate their own tours. In most instances this will be more expensive than totally independent travel.

- Only the most adventuresome with plenty of time and energy should travel on their own. Things do and will go wrong. This is what the euphemistic term "adventure travel" means. It separates the traveler from the tourist. There is no implication that one is better than the other. They are just different. The traveler will find that it is possible to go anywhere and do anything anyone else could do on a guided tour, as long as the trade-off of time and energy is clear.

- If economically possible, the independent traveler should travel by car. Bring a steering wheel lock with you (some agencies insist you rent one). Rent cars in Eastern Europe, since they are manufactured with local gas (leaded) in mind. Ask about deductible amounts for collision insurance and any other potential snags in advance. Get everything in writing. Never sign any agreement that you can not understand. Have all dents and dings noted on the rental agreement in advance to avoid being charged for them and possibly accused of leaving the scene of an accident. Check the car out thoroughly, making sure that everything works. Always know ahead of time what borders you are allowed to cross with the rented car and the exact border crossings open to foreigners (some are for locals only). Always get a map showing the exact location of gas stations in each country. Always top off at each gas station, since they may close for no apparent reason or not have any gas. Occasionally, you may have to wait in line for several hours to get gas, so bring a good book. Note, however, that it is customary for foreigners with vouchers to go to the head of the line (see below). Carry extra gas in a metal container for those times when gas becomes next to impossible to find. Check ahead of time to see whether vouchers are necessary for the purchase of gas. Never drink and drive—never! Never drive at night. Always carry a red triangle to put out on the road in case of a breakdown. Pay to have the car placed in a protected area overnight. If this is not possible, place it in a conspicuous location and remove the windshield wipers (ask how to do this when renting the car). Note that it may still be illegal to sleep in your car overnight. If you do, do it as discreetly as possible to avoid problems with the police. Get further information from the individual national tourist offices or travel agencies (pp. 247–250).

Where to Eat

- Do not take food for granted. In some areas, tour operators reserve all tables in hotel and other restaurants far in advance. In other instances, food is simply hard to find at all.
- Note that food in hotels is the same price for foreigners and locals alike, and therefore it's usually reasonably priced in all but the most luxurious hotels. It is particularly recommended for women traveling alone, who are often hassled in local restaurants, cafeterias, and bars.
- In most Eastern European countries the concept of a private table is totally foreign. You will share a table with as many people as can get around it.
- Give all tips directly to waiters (never leave money on a table) if a service charge is not included with the meal. The concept of service is just beginning to be understood in more remote areas. Be patient.
- Carry bottled water with you at all times, especially onto trains. Carrying food is also a good idea, since it will often be exorbitant where it is least likely to be found and most likely to be needed.

Communicating

- Ease of communication varies by country. Have letters sent to your embassy if an American Express office is not available (see

p. 198). *Poste restante* (General Delivery) to major post offices is generally unreliable.

- Outgoing calls to the West are often difficult. Consider sending a telegram and having your party call you at a specific time if getting through from a pay phone or central post office does not seem to work.

Staying Healthy

- Read the chapter on health carefully. The more adventuresome you are, the more important reading that chapter will be (pp. 219–229). Pay special attention to the information on encephalitis, giardia, and Lyme disease. Be wary of swimming pools, since these are often poorly maintained. This is true worldwide. Pools can be the source of many highly contagious diseases, especially ones related to the eyes.

Photography

- When taking photos of people, ask them if it's okay. Simply lift your camera and nod your head. If they indicate with sign language that it's okay, go ahead. Note that nodding in Bulgaria (as in Greece) means "no." In some areas you'll be fined if you stop on major highways to take photos, so don't dawdle if a great scene is simply irresistible. Also, be careful not to take photos of so-called sensitive or security areas. Although the cold war is essentially over, indiscriminate photo-taking is ill advised. You could lose film, and your camera, and potentially face a fine or time in jail for inadvertently taking photos of such strategic targets as bridges. Again, Eastern Europe will lighten up, but be aware that regulations do exist which prohibit photo-taking in specified areas. When in doubt about local customs, ask.

Potential Hassles

- Places often are closed for no apparent reason. This includes just about everything, even tourist sights and gas stations (as mentioned earlier).

- Getting accurate information can be almost impossible. This is often clearly intentional, forcing you to rely on locals for services at inflated prices.
- Travel books simply can not keep up with the changes taking place in these countries. Information is often dated. Travel to Eastern Europe should be viewed as adventure. It can be fun. It can also be tiring, frustrating, and difficult. Border crossings (as into Romania) can be interminable (presently taking 18 hours). Keep expectations in line with reality.
- Street names in some countries are changing daily. The political climate is not certain. Political and social undercurrents are often difficult to predict or understand. For obvious reasons, Yugoslavia has not been included in this edition of the guide, although it was once a very fine tourist destination and may be again in the future.
- Travel agents familiar with Eastern Europe emphasize that there is an increasing number of scams for unwary tourists. These vary from phony room-finding services to "travel agencies" that are no more than fronts for con artists. Separating honest companies and services from ones that aren't is not easy. The object of every rip-off is to take your money, preferably hard currency (your dollars or Deutschmarks). Again, networking is extremely important. Ask as many people as you can about their experiences, whom they've dealt with, who has ripped them off, and, more importantly, who hasn't. This is especially important for the independent traveler.
- Racism exists. It is a real problem. Having confirmed reservations at hotels helps. Traveling with a tour may be your best option.
- Carry your passport at all times. Secret police still exist. You may be asked for identification. Have it.
- Petty theft and pickpocketing are rampant as is overcharging in restaurants. Tips on avoiding these are included throughout the guide.
- Don't even think about carrying or using illegal drugs.
- Expose yourself only to the same degree as the locals. Partial to full nudity is tolerated in some areas, absolutely forbidden in others.

Information

Contact the tourist or travel offices on pp. 247–250 for additional information. Each Eastern European country often runs what amounts to its own travel agency. Ask about its trips. Ask too for a list of other agencies offering trips to that same country. The following are two agencies specializing in Eastern Europe, offering trips to Czechoslovakia, Hungary, Poland, and Romania. Note that few agencies presently recommend travel to Romania because of the food shortage and other major problems.

Fugazy International
770 US-1
North Brunswick, NJ 08902
Tel: (800) 828-4488

Hungarian Travel
1603 Second Avenue
New York, NY 10028
Tel: (212) 249-9342

Lotus
5455 Garden Grove Boulevard, Suite 100
Westminister, CA 92683
Tel: (800) 675-0559
(714) 850-9876

Magyar Tours
27 Occident Avenue
Staten Island, NY 10304
Tel: (718) 816-6828

Please note that many additional tips for Eastern Europe are included throughout the guide. However, Eastern Europe is such a new destination for most North American travelers that I look forward to hearing from you with any additional tips to include in future revisions:

John Whitman
P.O. Box 202
Long Lake, MN 55356

Charts

Part I
Preparations

Travel Documents

You'll need certain documents to travel freely through Europe or to avoid potential problems. Here are some tips to make the whole process of getting these documents less costly and more enjoyable.

Passports

If you are planning a trip to Europe, you must obtain a passport. If you already have one, check the expiration date to see whether the passport will be valid for the entire length of your trip. If it will expire during your stay in Europe, you must apply for a new one.

Kinds of Passports

- Each person in your party must have a passport.
- If you plan to travel extensively, ask for the special 48-page passport when you apply. It costs no more than the standard document and provides added space for the visas you may need.

When to Apply for a Passport

- Apply for a passport as far in advance as possible since they can take many weeks to be processed during peak travel periods.
- The situation on visas changes frequently, and you may have to apply for them far in advance. This is another reason to get your passport early.
- Note that it is possible to get a passport in as little as a day in the event of an emergency. Contact the nearest passport office for exact information on the procedure. The following agencies specialize in handling quick turnarounds of both passports and visas for a fee:

Travisa
2122 P Street NW
Washington, DC 20037
Tel: (800) 222-2589

Washington Passport and
  Visa Service
2318 18th Street NW, Suite 200
Washington, DC 20009
Tel: (800) 272-7776

Applying for a First Passport

- To get your first passport, you must apply in person at the appropriate agency. So must all members of your family who are 12 years of age or older. Younger children need not appear in person.
- The passport agency is listed in your telephone directory under U.S. Government Offices. If there is no passport agency in your town, the service may be handled at a federal, state, or probate courthouse or at a designated post office. Call the listed number for hours.
- Ask the clerk about the least busy hours to come in and apply for a passport.

What to Bring When You Apply

- *Passport application.* You will need to fill out a passport application in person at the appropriate passport agency. Your social security number is critical.
- *Proof of U.S. citizenship.* For proof of U.S. citizenship, come armed with a birth certificate or certified copy (look for a raised seal imprinted on the copy) or a certificate of naturalization or citizenship. If you don't have any of these, you can get by with a certificate of baptism or circumcision; hospital birth records; documentary evidence from census, school, or insurance companies; or affidavits. No proof, no passport!
- *Proof of identity.* If you're known to the clerk or if you have a certificate of naturalization or citizenship, that's all the proof of identity you'll need. Otherwise you must produce a valid driver's license, a government identification card or pass, or a witness. The witness must have valid identification (passport, driver's license, government pass, or certificate of naturalization or citizenship) and must have known you for at least 2 years. All identification must bear signatures and photos.
- *Two passport photos.* You'll need two passport photos, taken within the last 6 months. Each should be signed as indicated on the application (the procedure changes occasionally). Note that photos taken in a photo booth will not be acceptable. Passport photos must be 2 by 2 inches. They should be clear, front-view shots of your head and shoulders only, taken against a white background. No hats or sunglasses allowed! Prints must be on thin, nonglossy paper. Photos can be either in color or in black-and-white.

Passport Photos

- Agencies no longer allow passports with a dark background, and this has caused some resentment and confusion. Have your photos taken with a white background.

- Many agencies issuing passports now offer a passport photo service as well. Call ahead to see whether such a service is available in your area. Ask what the fee will be and the cost of extra prints. Then call several passport photo shops and passport photo studios listed in the yellow pages, as well as the local branch of the American Automobile Association (AAA), for cost comparison. A separate trip might save you several dollars if you're so inclined.
- You will need two photos for your passport. You should always carry two spare copies for emergencies. And you will need extra photos for visas (see p. 6).

Passport Fees

- You will be charged a standard passport fee and an execution fee for each passport. The execution fee varies from one area to the next. Call ahead to see what the total charges will be.
- When you call, ask how the payment should be made. Some offices refuse to take cash and may insist on a bank draft, money order, or check (personal, traveler's, certified, or cashier's). Avoid this situation: "What do you mean you won't take cash?" You've been warned!

Applying if you Have Had a Passport Before

- If you have had a passport during the last 12 years and were older than 16 when you received your last passport, you may apply for your new passport by mail. This will save you a trip and the execution fee. But you have to pay for mailing the passport, which can now cost more than the execution fee you pay when making an application in person.
- Call the nearest passport agency and ask for a Passport Office Form DSP-82, "Application for Passport by Mail." When this form arrives in the mail, fill it out, sign it, and date it. Attach your old passport, two up-to-date passport photos signed as instructed, and a check or money order to cover the passport fee.
- If your name has changed, include the original or a certified copy of your marriage certificate or the change-of-name papers when making an application by mail.
- Send the passport by registered mail and hold on to the receipt until the new passport arrives.
- *Note:* If you were under 16 when you applied for your old passport, you'll have to apply for the new one in person.
- Naturally, you can always apply for a passport in person if you prefer. But in that case you must pay the execution fee.

Protecting Yourself and Your Passport

- When your passport arrives in the mail, check it for correctness before signing. If there is an error in any of the information, you must return the passport to have it corrected. Never write in, alter, or mutilate any portion of the passport, as this will make it invalid.
- Make two photocopies of information in the passport. These photocopies will be invaluable if your passport is lost or stolen. File one of the photocopies in a safe place and take the other with you to Europe. Don't carry it with your passport! Reduce it on a photocopy machine to take up less space.

If You Lose Your Passport in the United States

- If your passport is lost or stolen in the United States, contact the Passport Office, Department of State, Washington, DC 20524, immediately. You'll need the information that you recorded on a photocopy of the original passport.
- Canadian citizens should report lost or stolen passports to the closest Canadian passport office. You'll find one in each province.

Visas

Visas are special notations and stamps, added to your passport by officials of foreign countries, that allow you to enter and leave these countries. Most Western European countries do not require visas from American visitors, except for long-term stays (over 3 months).

Most Eastern European countries used to require visas, but many are no longer doing this. However, check with the appropriate tourist office listed on pp. 247–250 before traveling to a specific country. Good travel agents also are familiar with the most recent visa requirements. As mentioned earlier, visa requirements change. Never assume anything.

Where to Get Visas

- Visa information is outlined in a government leaflet entitled "Visa Requirements of Foreign Governments" (Passport Office Publication M-264). You can get the leaflet from most passport agencies, and it will tell you what countries require visas. You'll then have to write the embassy or consulate of the foreign country to get a visa application form with information on fees and procedures. You'll generally have to send passport photos along with a completed application and payment for the service.

- Canadians should contact a travel agency or the nearest passport office. Visa information is outlined in the Travel Information Manual, which good agents should have. If your agent doesn't have one, ask him or her to order one from the following address: Travel Information Manual, P.O. Box 7627, 1117 vj Schipol Airport, The Netherlands.

Special Tips on Getting Visas

- If you want to get visas in advance for extended stays or for a country requiring a visa, mail your passport with the appropriate application to the appropriate foreign consulate or embassy. Note that even in countries requiring visas for short-term stays, it may be possible to get them at border crossings or airports. In some areas they are not available at train stations. If you plan train travel, then getting a visa in the United States may make sense.
- Use registered mail and keep the receipt until your passport has been returned.
- You are expected to include a check for the visa, as well as enough money to cover return postage. Ask the consulate or embassy to return the passport by registered mail. Make sure you've included enough money to cover the fee for such a service.
- Always apply for visas at the foreign consulate or embassy in your city or the city nearest you. Most embassies and consulates are located in Chicago, New York, San Francisco, and Washington, DC. You'll find the addresses in individual city directories or in the Congressional Directory, found in most major libraries.
- In Canada, refer to the Travel Information Manual previously mentioned, which you'll find at many travel agencies and in a few libraries.
- If you intend to travel to areas requiring visas, allow an extra 3 to 6 weeks for each necessary visa. Obtaining visas can be a long—disturbingly long—process. You may want to start the process months ahead of your planned trip!

International Driver's Licenses

If you plan to drive at all in Europe, you should get an International Driver's License. It's required in most countries, helps you avoid hassles with the police, and occasionally gets you out of a fine.

How to Get Licensed

- To get a license, you must be 18 years of age or older and you must hold a valid driver's license.
- You can get a license from the local branch of the American Automobile Association (AAA) without being a member.
- You'll need two photo booth photos; keep the extras. Make sure they are as similar to your passport photos as possible. Note that many branches of AAA offer a photo service, but the cost is higher than in photo booths.
- You'll be asked to sign the photos.
- You may have to return or have the license sent to you. Such a license is not valid until you sign it. It's good for one year from its issue date.

Stick Shifts

- If you don't know how to operate a stick shift, you should learn. Even if you reserve a car with an automatic shift, there's no guarantee that you'll get one. Furthermore, in an emergency you should be able to drive any car that's available. A competent driving instructor can teach you how to use a stick shift in 6 hours or less—from the basics to starting on a 45-degree incline.

International Student and Youth ID Cards

If you're a full-time student or young person, get an International Student Identification or Youth Card. Each brings reductions on inter-European charter flights; on all forms of other transportation; in hotels and hostels; at museums, movies, galleries, and special events; and in many shops. This can save you hundreds of dollars.

To Get a Card

The following organizations have many branch offices and specialize in both youth and student travel. Contact them for current regulations. You'll probably need one photo (similar to a passport photo), a copy of your fee statement as proof of full-time student status (for the student card), and a check for the present fee for whichever card you choose. Note that many universities have branch offices of these constantly growing organizations:

Council on International
Educational Exchange (CIEE)
205 East 42nd Street
New York, NY 10017
Tel: (212) 661-1450

Travel Cuts
187 College Street
Toronto, ON M5T 1P7
Canada
Tel: (416) 979-2406

STA
17 East 45th Street, Suite 805
New York, NY 10017
Tel: (800) 777-0112

Checks and Credit Cards

Each year, more than a million travelers lose cash in Europe due to theft and negligence. For this reason, you should rely on traveler's checks as a way of carrying money throughout Europe, and you can extend your purchasing power by using credit cards.

Traveler's Checks

- Traveler's checks are available from American Express, Bank of America, Barclay's Bank, Citibank, Deak International, Ltd., Thomas Cook, and many other institutions.
- Normally, you'll pay a 1 percent service fee when buying these checks.
- You can purchase foreign currency traveler's checks in the United States. For example, you can buy French franc traveler's checks for a trip to France. As strange as it may sound, these are often more difficult to cash than traveler's checks in dollars!

Fee-free Traveler's Checks

Offers come and go, but if you look around, you'll find that you can buy traveler's checks without paying the 1 percent fee. Barclay's Bank and Deak International frequently do not charge the fee. It's worth the effort.

- Auto clubs and banks often offer traveler's checks free of any fee to members or preferred customers. You may have to pay for them with cash, a cashier's check, or a bank money order.

When you Buy Traveler's Checks

- Count them because they're usually sold in packets containing a specific amount in specific denominations. Very rarely will a check be missing, but it doesn't hurt to be sure.

- Sign them as instructed. If you lose an unsigned check, it's gone forever.
- Couples should carry individual checks requiring only one signature. Note that there is now a modern version of check made out to two people requiring only one signature, but this might cause confusion in a foreign bank. In short, the bank might insist that both persons be present to cash them. So buy individual checks.
- Get checks of varying denominations to avoid the currency exchange rip-off. You should exchange only the amount of money you really need.
- Buy all traveler's checks in the United States. If you buy them in Europe, your currency will go through two exchanges before being converted into checks. You might lose 5 percent of your money just on the exchange, not to mention the 1 percent service fee.
- Keep a written record of all the checks you've used. The simplest way to do this is to write all the numbers down in a safe place and to strike the number of each check cashed. This will be essential information if you lose the checks!
- Don't carry this record in the same place as your checks. If your checks get ripped off or lost, you'll lose the record as well.

Letters of Credit, Bank Money Orders, or Cashier's Checks

- You may have heard of letters of credit. Well, forget about them. Banks abroad rarely honor them without horrendous arguments. Do not attempt to travel with letters of credit!
- The same goes for bank money orders and cashier's checks. Although perfectly legitimate, they're next to impossible to cash. Your time is too valuable to waste in dismal corridors of foreign banks.

Personal Checks

- You may not believe it, but it is a good idea to take some personal checks with you. Bring about half a dozen. You'll be surprised at the number of hotels, restaurants, and shops that will take them. Use them only for big-bill items.

Credit Cards

They're as good as gold in much of Western Europe. There is very little suspicion of credit cards there. In Eastern Europe their use is lim-

ited and often a surcharge of up to 10 percent will be added to the bill.
- The best credit cards are American Express, Carte Blanche, Diners Club, MasterCard, and Visa.

Advantages of Credit Cards

- Credit cards are safer to carry than cash, because if they're lost or stolen, you have limited liability, and you have no liability at all if you report the loss before they're used.
- With a credit card there's very little hassle renting a car or signing in at a hotel. You don't need to carry large amounts of cash at any time to pay for these big-expense items. Your signed receipt is all that's needed—even if you choose to pay with cash later (the receipt is then destroyed).
- When you use credit cards, you have excellent records of your expenses. This is good for trip planning and for the IRS at tax time.
- Credit card companies allow you to use their money on a float— you may not have to pay the bill for a month or two. This ends up being an interest-free loan.
- Companies automatically convert all charges to dollars at the rate of exchange prevailing when the charges are posted, not on the day the service or goods were purchased. This means you can avoid much of the currency exchange hassle by using the card frequently. Surveys indicate that most companies give you a 6 percent edge over typical bank exchanges. Occasionally, you may lose a little money if the charges are posted on a day the dollar's value has gone down.
- Credit cards are easy to carry and honored in many shops, restaurants, car rental agencies, and hotels. Request from your credit card company a pamphlet outlining the establishments that honor the card.
- Many credit cards allow you to get cash in a pinch. The regulations and fees for such a service change frequently, so check with your credit card company for current information.
- Credit cards may cover flight insurance and collision insurance on car rental. Check to be sure.
- Credit cards are useful in avoiding the Value Added Tax (VAT) on goods purchased abroad (see p. 205). Have clerks record both charges for goods and credit for VAT at time of purchase (no waiting for refunds this way), although you may have to send the purchase home through the mail at the time of purchase. Shops vary on how strictly they adhere to local regulations regarding VAT refunds to tourists.

- *Note:* You should not have to pay a surcharge on a bill paid with a credit card except in Eastern Europe.

Insurance

If you carry any insurance at all, it will probably cover part of your trip. Exceptions to this general rule and additional information on the subject are detailed below.

Accident Insurance

- Check to see whether your policy is valid in Europe.
- Accident insurance often excludes so-called hazardous activities. If you are into motorcycling, hot-air ballooning, kayaking, and other strenuous or potentially dangerous activities, make sure the policy has no such exclusion. Even skiing is excluded in some policies.

Baggage Insurance

- Read your homeowner's or renter's policy. In most instances it will cover your baggage up to a specific value. But don't assume this. Ask your agent to be sure.
- If you must bring along any expensive articles, such as furs, jewelry, and cameras, pay a small fee to have a *personal articles floater* added to your policy.
- Find out whether your policy will cover new purchases made abroad for a specified grace period.
- If you don't have a homeowner's or renter's policy, you can buy special baggage insurance, which is available from most insurance companies and can be obtained directly from the airline at check-in time.
- Do some comparison shopping over the phone to come up with the least expensive coverage. Don't assume the costs will be comparable.
- To protect yourself, keep a list of all the clothes and personal belongings packed in each bag. Also note the value of each article.
- Note that even without insurance, if your bags are lost or damaged during a flight, the airline will reimburse you up to a specified limit. However, all items will be depreciated, and you may have to produce receipts. I have yet to meet a person able to do this for every article packed in a suitcase.
- If you travel light and with very few valuables, most of this worry and expense is eliminated!

Bankruptcy Insurance

In recent years airlines, travel agencies, and tour operators have sometimes folded, leaving passengers who had already paid for travel footing the bill. This insurance protects you from such an occurrence. Note that this insurance can be included in some trip cancellation policies (check with the company to be sure). Information on trip cancellation insurance follows.

Car Insurance

• Your car insurance is invalid in Europe (see pp. 59 and 172 for full details on car insurance). Get a letter from your insurance agent indicating an accident-free record if you have one. This may entitle you to a substantial discount.

Health Insurance

• As of January 1991, Medicare and Medicaid don't cover you in Europe. However, check to see whether the law has changed recently.
• Most health policies do cover you worldwide, but ask to be sure. Generally, you'll have to pay for all expenses and be reimbursed when you return home.
• Carry your insurance card, your agent's telephone number, and your insurance company's telephone number when you travel. This way you can always get in touch with them for advice in an emergency. In some European countries you will be covered, at least partly, by national health insurance; in most countries, however, you'll have to pay for all services—a good reason to have that information about your plan at hand.

Home Insurance

• Since your home may not be covered if you are away for more than 30 days, check with your agent for advice if you plan an extended trip.

Life Insurance

• If you already carry a reasonable amount of life insurance, you won't need any extra for the vacation. Flight insurance is basically a rip-off. Statistically, flying is incredibly safe.
• Some policies are written with a double-indemnity clause for accidental death.
• Travel and auto clubs often provide life and accident insurance to members. Check on the most recent offerings.

- Many banks, credit card companies, and travel clubs now offer *free* flight insurance if you charge the flight to the card.
- Some travel agencies offer *free* flight insurance to their customers.

Trip Cancellation Insurance

- Some flights are sold on a restricted basis and have stiff cancellation charges. If you must cancel the flight because of an emergency—such as illness or death in the immediate family—trip cancellation insurance can remove the sting.
- Note that this insurance is not valid when the illness has been in existence during the previous year.

Documents for a Trusted Friend

Following is a list of things you should leave with a trusted friend. Although your trip may go without a hitch, this simple precaution could save you an incredible amount of trouble and time.

- *Itinerary.* Provide your friend with the most accurate places and dates you can. Leave exact mailing addresses (see advice on mail, pp. 195–198).
- *List of traveler's check numbers.* You should carry a list of these numbers separate from your checks, but it's a good idea to leave another list with your friend—just in case you lose everything, including your duplicate list.
- *Numbers of credit cards.* Leave your friend a photocopy of all of your credit cards and keep one copy for yourself separate from your credit cards.
- *Number, date, and place of issue of passport.* You should memorize this information as soon as you get the passport. You'll need it when checking in at hotels. If you lose a passport, it will be essential information. Leave your friend a reduced photocopy and keep one for yourself separate from your passport.
- *Number, date, and place of issue of airline tickets.* Leave your friend photocopies of your tickets and keep copies for yourself separate from your tickets. To get reimbursed for lost or stolen tickets with a minimum of hassle, have this information readily available.

Medical Precautions

For more medical information, read the section on what to do about problems that occur while you're in Europe. This is outlined in detail in Chapter 18.

Medical Documents

Most travelers don't experience major medical problems abroad. However, be prepared for them just in case. Keeping a record of your vaccinations is a good start.

International Certificates of Vaccination

At one time everyone traveling to Europe was required to show proof of smallpox vaccination. The proof consisted of a doctor's signature and official stamp in a yellow card. Since smallpox has been officially eradicated, such proof is no longer necessary, but these yellow cards, called International Certificates of Vaccination, are still available.

Although yellow cards are no longer necessary for travel to Europe, it doesn't hurt to have one. By having all of your immunizations listed in this official document, you have an accurate record of them. In case of an unusual outbreak of a specific disease, you can be immunized abroad and have that noted in the yellow card. This will allow you to cross the border into and out of a disease zone. Such an occurrence is rare, but it does happen, particularly in the case of cholera.

Most passport agencies, health service offices, and medical clinics have copies of the yellow card, which is given out free of charge.

Medical Information

Never ask travel agents for medical information, since they're usually behind the times on health problems.

In the United States

Check with a *public health office*. State headquarters keep up-to-date bulletins on disease outbreaks worldwide. For useful, current bulletins on disease, contact:

The Centers for Disease Control
1600 Clifton Road
Atlanta, GA 30333
Tel: (404) 639-3311

In Canada

The *Travel Information Offices of Health and Welfare* in Canada can give you current information and health bulletins. You'll find these offices in Edmonton, AB; Gander, NF; Halifax, NS; Montreal, PQ; Ottawa, ON; Prince George, BC; Prince Rupert, BC; Regina, SK; Saint John, NB; Saint John's, NF; Sydney, NS; Thunder Bay, ON; Toronto, ON; Vancouver, BC; Victoria, BC; and Winnipeg, MB.

Inoculations

No two doctors agree on the shots that travelers should have before going abroad. However, follow commonsense guidelines. The longer you travel and the more remote your destination, the more protection you need.

- Many inoculations are given free of charge or for a token charge at public clinics.
- Get shots well ahead of your trip. Some must be given in a series over weeks or even months.
- Some have side effects that could affect your trip if you wait until the last minute!

Cholera

- A vaccination against cholera is needed only if you're traveling to an area where there is an outbreak. Cholera outbreaks are rare.
- Cholera shots are not reliable in preventing the disease at all. Have one only if *officially* required.

Encephalitis

A vaccine for tick-borne encephalitis is made in Austria and Germany. It is not available in the United States. See p. 224 for further information.

Hepatitis A

- Gamma (immune) globulin can be effective in preventing hepatitis A. The dosage is related to the length of your trip and your weight.
- Because the shot provides only short-term protection, it is worth getting only if you'll be traveling to remote areas with poor sanitation. Backpackers and explorer types should get it.

Hepatitis B

- Hepatitis B serum is roughly 96 percent effective against hepatitis B, which can be debilitating at best, deadly at worst.
- Unfortunately, hepatitis B is becoming more common, although only 5 to 10 percent of the population in the United States has been exposed to it. In other countries the rate is much higher.
- Hepatitis B serum is given in three doses over a 6-month period. It is very expensive.
- If you plan to travel extensively in remote areas, the cost is worth it. It is doubly important if you have frequent sexual contact.
- Some doctors recommend that you have a blood test before getting the serum. If the cost of the blood test is low and the test shows that you have already been exposed to hepatitis B, you won't need the serum, and you might save yourself a great deal of money. However, if the test is expensive, skip it. According to the laboratory that makes it, there are no adverse reactions to the serum even if you have already been exposed to hepatitis B.

Polio

- All doctors agree that this is essential. You may need a booster.

Tetanus/Diphtheria

- Doctors agree that this one is essential, too. You may be due for a booster.

Typhoid

- Typhoid shots are somewhat controversial. Their value can only be related to risk, which in most areas is low. Again, if you'll be traveling to remote areas, it may well be worth the cost of this "insurance."
- Initially, you'll get two typhoid shots. After that, boosters are effective.

Getting Set to Go

A few routine steps can help take the worry out of travel if you have a medical problem of any kind. Here are some suggestions.

Medical Preparations for Travel

- Before going on a trip, see both a doctor and a dentist for a quick checkup.
- Have your doctor fill out the yellow card with a complete history of your immunizations.
- Get the immunizations suggested for the kind of travel you'll be doing. To confirm your doctor's recommendations, write the Centers for Disease Control in Atlanta (see p. 16), or write or call your state department of health, which receives updates from Atlanta.
- Get a prescription for a good drug to combat both diarrhea and insomnia (for jet lag).
- *Special note:* It is illegal to import medications containing codeine into some countries. Greece is especially intolerant of this controlled substance, even when prescribed by a doctor. If carrying a controlled medication, always have a doctor's prescription with you and ask ahead of time whether it is prohibited in areas you plan to visit.
- If you're pregnant, you'll want to get recommendations from your doctor before going abroad. Note too that airlines may refuse passage after a certain month of pregnancy. Ask ahead of time.

Chronic Health Problems

- If you have a chronic health problem, take with you all the drugs you'll need for the entire trip. Include enough to cover a week or two extra in case of an unexpected extended stay.
- If you have heart or respiratory problems, be wary of high altitude travel.

Diabetics

- Consider signing up with one of the organizations listed below that provide help and identification abroad—they can save your life. Also consider subscribing to:

Diabetic Traveler
P.O. Box 8223 RW
Stamford, CT 06905
Tel: (203) 327-5832

- Carry urine-testing equipment, regular and long-lasting insulin, oral drugs or syringes, extra carbohydrates (your schedule will get fouled up), and a doctor's note stating that your are a diabetic. This note helps you explain syringes when you cross borders.
- Becton-Dickinson disposable syringes are available in most European pharmacies abroad, but may require a doctor's prescription. In Eastern European countries they are not uniformly available, especially in less developed countries or areas.
- If you intend to buy insulin abroad, learn about the variations in strengths and how to deal with them before going.

Useful Medical Organizations

If you have a chronic illness or medical problem, you may be interested in contacting the following organizations for information on their services:

Access America
P.O. Box 90315
Richmond, VA 23286
Tel: (800) 284-8300

Assist-Card International
1001 South Bayshore Drive,
  Suite 2302
Miami, FL 33131
Tel: (305) 381-9959

Carefree
P.O. Box 310
120 Mineola Boulevard
Mineola, NY 11501
Tel: (800) 645-2424

International Association of
  Medical Assistance to
  Travelers (IAMAT)
417 Center Street
Lewiston, NY 14092
Tel: (716) 754-4883

International SOS Assistance,
  Inc.
8 Neshaminy Interplex,
  Suite 207
Trevose, PA 19053
(mailing address):
P.O. Box 11568
Philadelphia, PA 19116
Tel: (800) 523-8930
(215) 244-1500

Medic Alert Foundation
P.O. Box 1009
Turlock, CA 95381
Tel: (800) 344-3226

TravMed
P.O. Box 10623
Baltimore, MD 21285
Tel: (800) 732-5309
(410) 296-5225

Worldwide Assistance Services
1133 15th Street N.W.
Washington, DC 20005
Tel: (800) 821-2828

Prescription Items

A few precautions are useful here:

Drugs

- Bring fresh drugs with you. If you're not sure about the value of older medications, call your pharmacist.
- Carry enough of any prescription to last a week or two beyond your expected stay, just in case you get delayed for some unforeseen reason.
- Always keep all prescription drugs in the original containers. Some of these containers are huge, so ask the pharmacist to divide the amount into two smaller containers, both clearly labeled. These are easier to carry, and you can throw them away as they're used up.
- If your drugs contain narcotics, bring along a doctor's prescription.
- Ask your doctor or pharmacist for the generic name of any drug you're using. Write it down. This name will probably be familiar to a foreign druggist if you lose or run out of pills.
- Never put drugs into luggage that will be checked on a plane. Carry them with you.

Eyeglasses

- Either bring with you a spare pair of glasses in a hard case or the prescription itself. Note that a lens can be duplicated from the pieces of a broken lens (in case you forget to bring a prescription).

Itineraries

Determining what countries you'll visit and what spots in each country you'll see is obviously a crucial step in planning your itinerary. This chapter will give you many hints for planning the best trip possible.

Where to Go

You may know from the start where you want to go, or you may be open to suggestions. Either way, the more care you take in picking the places you go, the more fun you'll have abroad.

Basic Considerations

- If you and any potential travel partner can't agree on where to go, plan to travel independently. You can still arrange to meet to do the things you can agree on during your trips.
- If you'll be traveling with kids, give them some say about where to go. They'll be much better travelers for it.
- If *money* is a major consideration in your plans, you may wish to restrict your itinerary to southern Europe. Greece, Portugal, and Spain are the least expensive countries to travel in. Austria, Belgium, Great Britain, Italy, Luxembourg, the Netherlands, and Norway are moderately expensive. Denmark, Finland, France, Germany, Sweden, and Switzerland are expensive. Eastern Europe will be expensive until more hotels and restaurants open up, creating competition in the market.
- If *time* is a problem, plan your trip to the minute. If you've only got a week, you don't want to waste even an hour.
- And if your own *energy* is limited, save it by joining a tour that is going to places you want to see. Tours are especially valuable for those going to Eastern Europe. The amount of energy saved is enormous.

Fine-tuning your Choices

- Browse in travel books and magazines at the library or a bookstore to get an idea of the possibilities (see p. 22).
- Look at newspaper travel sections as well, especially the *New York Times* Sunday travel sections, for more up-to-date news of attractions.

- Try to get copies of newspapers from cities you might visit in Europe (newsstands and libraries may have them). Check out concerts, plays, and sporting events you may want to attend.

Sources of Information

The more you know, the better you'll plan; the better you plan, the more fun you'll have on your trip.

Airlines

- Call various airlines and ask for any free brochures or pamphlets they may have that cover destinations on your trip.

National Tourist Offices

- For good general background information and some helpful tips, write to the National Tourist Office of each country you think you want to visit. You can ask for hotel and restaurant guides; sightseeing information; lists of gardens, castles, museums, spas; travel maps; and so on. Write at least 2 months in advance, 4 if possible.
- Note that tourist offices shy away from questions of comparison. (Is one hotel better than another? Should we go here instead of there?) The more specific your question, the more difficult it may be for a country's tourist office to answer. Include a return address in your letter. A stamped, self-addressed envelope is not required, but often will speed up a reply. Tourist offices in both the United States and Canada are listed in Appendix B (pp. 247–250).

Magazines, Books, and Reports

- Check the following magazines for travel suggestions and information: *Condé Nast, European Travel and Life, Gourmet, Holiday, National Geographic Traveler,* and *Travel and Leisure.*
- Plan your own itinerary (if you are so inclined) by using these specialized books: *Official Airline Guide, Official Hotel and Resort Guide, STAR (Sloane Travel Agency Reports),* and *World Travel Directory.* These extremely expensive volumes are used in the travel industry. You can find them in the travel section of a few major libraries or at a travel agency.
- There are now over 70 bookstores in the United States specializing only in travel books. These are excellent sources of information if just the right travel book eludes you in regular bookstores.
- Travel reports can help with trip planning. To find out which of

these reports suits your personality, write to each of them asking for a sample copy.

Consumer Reports Travel Letter
P.O. Box 53629
Boulder, CO 80322
Tel: (800) 999-7959

Entree Travel
P.O. Box 5148
Santa Barbara, CA 93150
Tel: (805) 969-5848.

Travel Smart
Communications House
40 Beechdale Road
Dobbs Ferry, NY 10522
Tel: (800) 327-3633
(914) 693-8300

Auto Clubs

You should comparison shop when looking for an automobile club. Compare membership fees, emergency road services, emergency travel expenses, accidental death and dismemberment payoff amounts, arrest and bail bond, legal defense fees, and routing maps.

• Read the fine print. Make sure the club has reciprocal agreements with auto clubs abroad.

Allstate Motor Club
1500 West Shure Drive
Arlington Heights, IL 60004
Tel: (800) 255-2582

American Automobile
   Association
1000 AAA Drive
Heathrow, FL 32746
Tel: (800) 336-4357

Amoco Motor Club
P.O. Box 9046
Des Moines, IA 50368
Tel: (800) 334-3300

Chevron Travel Club
P.O. Box P
Concord, CA 94524
Tel: (800) 222-0585

Exxon Travel Club
P.O. Box 3633
Houston, TX 77253
Tel: (713) 680-5723

Montgomery Ward Auto
   Club
200 Martingale Road
Schaumburg, IL 60194
Tel: (800) 621-5151

Shell Motorist Club
P.O. Box 60199
Chicago, IL 60660
Tel: (800) 621-8663

Agents and Agencies

Good agents work hard to find super bargains amidst the garble of airline and tour brochures. Nevertheless, it's a customer's responsibility to do reading and research before going to a travel agent. This will make your relationship more beneficial.

- If you're a free spirit, if you're aggressive and resourceful, and if you're ready to study up on alternatives in transportation, food, and lodging, you can probably save yourself some money by planning and arranging your own trip.
- Even if you fit that description, an agent may know of tour packages that are so reasonably priced that you can't afford not to take advantage of them. So never rule out travel agencies before checking to see what they have to offer. Use them as an ally to get what you want. Agencies are especially helpful in travel to Eastern Europe. Some of the finest are listed on p. xxii and with the National Tourist Offices (pp. 247–250). Travel to this area is still highly specialized and difficult.
- If you don't want to plan and arrange your own trip, a well-chosen agent can be a fine resource. But don't walk in and say, "I want to go to these twelve cities. Book me flights and rooms." If you do, you'll pay through the nose! Instead, ask for tours to match your interests and then have the agent alter them if necessary.
- In short, shop around. Compare what an agent can do with what you can do, balance the benefits and costs, and act accordingly.

What Good Agents Can Do

- They can find the cheapest airfare from A to B, saving you the hassle. If an airline goes bankrupt, the agency is still responsible to get you to your destination. Unfortunately, this is a possibility these days.
- They can get you on a cruise or tour that matches your personality. You pay nothing extra for their service.
- They can make appropriate reservations for hotels, car rental, and sporting activities. None of these services should involve a charge if you're booking a tour or making all your travel arrangements through them. Some agencies are beginning to charge for these services, so shop around.
- They can give you access to expensive books with excellent information on hotels. Many agencies also have a library of offbeat or unusual books, which you can look through to help you make decisions.

What Agents Can't Do

- Travel agents can't read minds. Be as specific as possible in telling an agent what you want. The more specific you are, the better your chances of getting what you want.

Picking an Agency

- Larger agencies tend to have more clout than smaller ones. It may be more personal and more convenient to go to a neighborhood agent, but what happens if something goes wrong? Find out whether the agency has representatives abroad, just in case something does go wrong.
- Ask the agency what kind of travel it specializes in. If it doesn't match your travel plans, ask the agency to refer you to another one specializing in your brand of travel.
- In special cases, you may want to work with agents in other cities. If the best agency for skiing tours happens to be in New York, conduct your business over the phone and through the mail.

Recognizing a Good Agent

Good travel agents are harder to find than the American Society of Travel Agents would like to admit. Unfortunately, many of them are in the business more for the low-cost travel benefits than for their clients' interests.

On the other hand, some agents are outstanding. Most of the good ones specialize in some way: low-cost tours, luxury travel, study groups, ski vacations, incentive travel, business, and so on.

- Most travel agents are members of the American Society of Travel Agents (ASTA), so be wary of those who are not. ASTA maintains a file of complaints. You can write or call them at 1101 King Street, Alexandria, VA 22314, Tel: (703) 739-2782.
- Look for the initials CTC (Certified Travel Consultant) after an agent's name. This designation signifies that the agent is a person of good reputation who has been through a specialized course.
- Find out whether someone in the agency is familiar with the specific area you plan to visit. Such a person will not only be able to reserve flights, make reservations, and book you into tours, but will be able to provide you with valuable information.

Maps

Good maps appropriate to the kind of traveling you'll be doing can make a trip far less frustrating and more enjoyable. For most travel you can get free maps that are adequate for your purposes. Detailed maps are expensive, but essential for off-the-beaten-path travel.

Where to Get Good General Maps (Free)

- *National tourist offices*. Request a *free* map from the government tourist office nearest you (see pp. 247–250).
- *Travel agents*. Ask any agent you deal with to provide a *free* map for your travels.
- *AAA and other auto clubs*. If you belong to an auto or travel club, have them give you a *free* map. These clubs should also provide route maps and related services. Request these as far in advance as possible!
- *Insurance companies*. If you'll be traveling by car, get *free* maps from the agency.
- *Note:* Every person in your party should have a map (see p. 177). It makes travel more exciting, makes kids feel special, divides the responsibility—and it costs nothing!

When to Go

A great deal of fiction has been written about the wonderful weather in Europe. Don't be conned by this propaganda, which is more wishful thinking than fact. The bikini-clad women in travel brochures were photographed in the August heat, not in the dead of winter, as promoters would have you believe. The guidelines below cover the best times to visit various parts of Europe. The Climate Chart in Appendix A has more details (see pp. 241–246).

Travel Seasons

- Travel to *Scandinavia* during the summer, which lasts from mid-May to early October. Not only is the weather good during this period, but you will also be able to take advantage of the long days. Just the opposite is true during the winter, which is snowy and dark—so dark that sightseeing becomes a joke.
- Visit *Central Europe* (including the British Isles) from late April to late October if you're concerned about good weather. Much of this area experiences heavy rainfall, so bring a good umbrella and the

best raincoat you can afford. You'll find some of Europe's most fascinating cities in this belt, however—and if you see them during the off-season (November through mid-April), you can take advantage of smaller crowds and lower prices.

- Winters in *Southern Europe* are not as mild as some people would like you to believe. True, you'll run into sunny winter days. But don't expect to brave the chill of Mediterranean or Atlantic waters. Furthermore, summers can get so hot in the South that you will want to do what the natives do from noon until late afternoon— sleep in a cool place. If you're traveling to Southern Europe in the summer, you may want to stay on a beach by the sea—an alternative chosen often by French, Greeks, Italians, and Portuguese, young and old.
- Some places do offer fair-to-excellent off-season weather. In the fair-to-good category: the Balearics (Majorca, Menorca, and Ibiza), Corsica, Madeira, and Sardinia. Just a little better: Malta and Sicily. Better yet: Crete, Cyprus, Rhodes, and Turkey. And the most reliable for warm winter sun: the Canaries.

How Long to Stay

The length of your trip may be predetermined by the time you have available for your vacation, leaving you little leeway. However, if it's at all possible, try to schedule your trip to Europe for at least 3 weeks. This will give you the time to enjoy and savor the European scene.

- Subtract 3 days from the overall length of your trip. The first, and probably the last, day of any trip will be wasted, and you may have to spend the second day recuperating somewhat from your transatlantic flight.
- Write off at least part of any day spent traveling long distances, such as from one city to the next.
- Fight the urge to see all of Europe in 10 days, and arrange to spend more time in fewer places. If you slow down, your trip will be more enjoyable.

The following chart indicates the minimum recommended lengths of stay in European countries. Periods are given in days, and do not include the time needed for transportation in and out of the country. All that you possibly can get in a minimum stay is a "feel" for the country, no more. And that's all that this chart implies.

Minimum Recommended Stays in European Countries and Islands

Country	Length of Stay
Andorra	1 day
Austria	5 days, with 3 days in Vienna
Azores	3 days
Belgium	3 days, with 2 days in major cities
Bulgaria	3 days
Canaries	3 days
Czechoslovakia	4 days
Corsica	2 days
Crete	2 days
Cyprus	2 days
Denmark	3 days, with 2 days in Copenhagen
Finland	2 days
France	10 days, with 5 days in Paris
Germany	4 days, with 2 days in Munich
Gibraltar	1 day
Great Britain	10 days, with 5 days in London
Greece	7 days, with 3 days on mainland
Hungary	4 days
Iceland	2 days
Ireland	3 days
Italy	10 days, with 4 days in Rome, 3 in Florence, 1 in Venice
Liechtenstein	Half a day
Luxembourg	1 day
Madeira	2 days
Majorca	2 days
Malta	1 day
Netherlands	3 days, with 2 days in Amsterdam
Norway	3 days
Poland	3 days
Portugal	5 days, with 2 days in Lisbon
Romania	3 days
Sardinia	1 day
Sicily	1 day
Spain	10 days, with 3 days in Madrid and Toledo combined
Sweden	3 days
Switzerland	4 days
Turkey	4 days

How Far and How Fast

If this is your first trip to Europe, you may be inclined to travel fast and far to give yourself a sneak preview of trips to come. It is totally natural to want to do this, and high-speed travel can be exhilarating. The trouble is, it's also exhausting and costs a bundle.

The more you try to see, the less you will really see, and you'll find yourself experiencing the "today-is-Tuesday-this-must-be-Brussels" syndrome. Many tours operate on this kind of plan, giving you a smattering of many cities rather than a deeper profile of several.

Planning Trip Mileage

- To help you enjoy your trip more fully, use the mileage chart on the following page and a map to plan your itinerary. Decide which cities you'd like to see. You might trace your route in red with a felt-tipped pen. Now add up the mileage to see just how far you plan to go.
- Divide the total mileage by the number of days you'll be in Europe. (Don't count the first and last days.)
- If you are traveling by train or car, don't plan to cover more than 150 miles per day. The same rule applies to traveling on a tour bus. Naturally, you will sometimes travel farther than this average distance. If you consistently cover much more than 150 miles per day, however, your trip will turn out to have been too expensive and time-consuming, as well as too tiring.
- If you will be flying between two points, ignore the mileage between them—simply write off one full day. Do this for each plane trip you'll be taking. Subtract these days from the total number of days you'll be abroad (minus the first and last days). This will give you a good idea of how many days you'll have left to enjoy Europe.
- If you find that you'll be traveling too far in too short a time, admit it. Here are some options: cut down on the number of cities to be seen, extend your trip to make your travel time more enjoyable, or plan a second trip for a later date. With the possible exception of Venice, most European cities will still be there in years to come.

Mileage Between Western European Cities

Distances are given between each pair of cities. Each city (row) lists its mileage to the cities that follow it, in the column order: Barcelona, Berlin, Bordeaux, Brussels, Calais, Copenhagen, Dublin, Florence, Geneva, Hamburg, Helsinki, Lisbon, London, Madrid, Marseilles, Milan, Munich, Naples, Nice, Oslo, Paris, Rome, Stockholm, Venice, Vienna.

Amsterdam: Barcelona 950, Berlin 450, Bordeaux 660, Brussels 125, Calais 235, Copenhagen 590, Dublin 565, Florence 775, Geneva 545, Hamburg 290, Helsinki 1025, Lisbon 1365, London 305, Madrid 1145, Marseilles 800, Milan 670, Munich 535, Naples 1160, Nice 815, Oslo 865, Paris 315, Rome 955, Stockholm 920, Venice 740, Vienna 820

Barcelona: Berlin 1215, Bordeaux 405, Brussels 810, Calais 800, Copenhagen 1355, Dublin 965, Florence 730, Geneva 490, Hamburg 1135, Helsinki 1865, Lisbon 785, London 725, Madrid 385, Marseilles 355, Milan 650, Munich 830, Naples 1055, Nice 420, Oslo 1645, Paris 685, Rome 915, Stockholm 1760, Venice 825, Vienna 1155

Berlin: Bordeaux 1015, Brussels 490, Calais 620, Copenhagen 465, Dublin 950, Florence 810, Geneva 690, Hamburg 185, Helsinki 970, Lisbon 1690, London 690, Madrid 965, Marseilles 700, Milan 375, Munich 1135, Naples 920, Nice 805, Oslo 665, Paris 995, Rome 865, Stockholm 700, Vienna 625

Bordeaux: Brussels 535, Calais 555, Copenhagen 830, Dublin 815, Florence 440, Geneva 905, Hamburg 1685, Helsinki 755, Lisbon 570, London 440, Madrid 415, Marseilles 740, Milan 755, Munich 1110, Naples 515, Nice 1565, Oslo 350, Paris 1580, Rome 930, Vienna 1055

Brussels: Calais 130, Copenhagen 655, Dublin 460, Florence 415, Geneva 370, Hamburg 1185, Helsinki 1245, Lisbon 200, London 965, Madrid 675, Marseilles 635, Milan 495, Munich 1320, Naples 690, Nice 1030, Oslo 185, Paris 1080, Rome 1180, Stockholm 875, Venice 750

Calais: Copenhagen 780, Dublin 330, Florence 880, Geneva 470, Hamburg 505, Helsinki 1285, Lisbon 1260, London 70, Madrid 945, Marseilles 690, Milan 620, Munich 510, Naples 1145, Nice 790, Oslo 1160, Paris 210, Rome 1005, Stockholm 1180, Venice 890

Copenhagen: Dublin 1115, Florence 1215, Geneva 985, Hamburg 215, Helsinki 500, Lisbon 1895, London 1235, Madrid 1060, Marseilles 775, Milan 1540, Munich 1255, Naples 380, Nice 835, Oslo 1400, Paris 395, Rome 1105, Vienna 1030

Dublin: Florence 1215, Geneva 800, Hamburg 785, Helsinki 1615, Lisbon 1595, London 260, Madrid 1275, Marseilles 1000, Milan 950, Munich 900, Naples 1475, Nice 1010, Oslo 1490, Paris 505, Rome 1335, Stockholm 1510, Venice 1125, Vienna 1175

Florence: Geneva 495, Hamburg 970, Helsinki 1715, Lisbon 1455, London 935, Madrid 1110, Marseilles 415, Milan 200, Munich 440, Naples 325, Nice 1590, Oslo 745, Paris 185, Rome 1610, Stockholm 170, Venice 550

Geneva: Hamburg 705, Helsinki 1485, Lisbon 1190, London 540, Madrid 680, Marseilles 265, Milan 230, Munich 320, Naples 795, Nice 300, Oslo 1370, Paris 325, Rome 650, Stockholm 1380, Venice 405, Vienna 645

Hamburg: Helsinki 720, Lisbon 1690, London 525, Madrid 1335, Marseilles 970, Milan 770, Munich 480, Naples 1190, Nice 1090, Oslo 510, Paris 550, Rome 1060, Stockholm 615, Venice 815, Vienna 565

Helsinki: Lisbon 2395, London 1355, Madrid 2115, Marseilles 1735, Milan 1560, Munich 1275, Naples 2040, Nice 1785, Oslo 445, Paris 1335, Rome 1900, Stockholm 105, Venice 1115, Vienna 1305

Lisbon: London 1335, Madrid 408, Marseilles 1190, Milan 1430, Munich 1675, Naples 1830, Nice 1145, Oslo 2240, Paris 1105, Rome 1700, Stockholm 2290, Venice 1650, Vienna 1945

London: Madrid 1015, Marseilles 740, Milan 690, Munich 640, Naples 1215, Nice 750, Oslo 1230, Paris 245, Rome 1075, Stockholm 1250, Venice 865, Vienna 915

Madrid: Marseilles 705, Milan 1050, Munich 1415, Naples 1435, Nice 805, Oslo 1995, Paris 780, Rome 1295, Stockholm 2010, Venice 960, Vienna 1700

Marseilles: Milan 355, Munich 610, Naples 730, Nice 120, Oslo 1615, Paris 480, Rome 590, Stockholm 1630, Venice 550, Vienna 930

Milan: Munich 310, Naples 615, Nice 220, Oslo 1440, Paris 560, Rome 390, Stockholm 1455, Venice 175, Vienna 505

Munich: Naples 765, Nice 535, Oslo 1155, Paris 495, Rome 625, Stockholm 1170, Venice 325, Vienna 255

Naples: Nice 595, Oslo 1920, Paris 1060, Rome 130, Stockholm 1935, Venice 460, Vienna 955

Nice: Oslo 1660, Paris 580, Rome 465, Stockholm 340, Venice 370, Vienna 730

Oslo: Paris 1215, Rome 1780, Stockholm 340, Venice 995, Vienna 1180

Paris: Rome 930, Stockholm 1230, Venice 690, Vienna 815

Rome: Stockholm 1795, Venice 355, Vienna 820

Stockholm: Venice 1010, Vienna 1200

Venice: Vienna 380

Travel Partners and Tours

Should you make a trip by yourself, with a friend or spouse, with a group of people you like, or as part of a tour group? Should you take the kids or a baby? There's no easy answer, although the answer is often taken for granted, especially in the case of couples. The hints in this chapter should be helpful to you, not only in making your decision, but also in living with it!

Solo Travel

There are many advantages to traveling alone: you can do as you damn well please, when you damn well please, at your own pace, with or without someone else along, as you choose. In short, you have total freedom.

On the other hand, you pay for such freedom. If you go on a tour, you may be socked with a surcharge. If you're totally on your own, you will have no way of sharing bills at mealtime, in the hotel, and for personal transportation. It's all out of your pocket and your pocket only.

You may also be lonely—but you can convert loneliness to your advantage, as it will force you to get to know Europeans and other travelers.

Traveling Alone and Liking It

- Take advantage of short and inexpensive tours to popular tourist sights. You'll not only meet people, but you'll keep your costs down.
- Be willing to share the cost of a room. If you are concerned about sharing a room with a stranger, put anything of value in the hotel safe.
- When faced with the prospect of eating alone, bring a newspaper, a book, or writing paper with you to the restaurant. If you meet someone interesting, fine; if not, you will catch up on your reading.
- Go to restaurants before or after the peak dinner hour, to avoid running into the poor treatment at the hands of waiters that solo travelers sometimes experience.

Single but Looking for Company

- Cruises are a natural for someone looking for a travel partner.
- So are resorts and tours designed for single travelers. The following organizations cater to single travelers:

Club Med (Head Office)
40 West 57th Street
New York, NY 10019
Tel: (800) 258-2633
(212) 977-2100

Gramercy Singleworld
401 Theodore Fremd Avenue
Rye, NY 10580
Tel: (800) 223-6490

Odyssey Network
455 Washington Street
Wellesley, MA 02181
Tel: (617) 237-2400

Partners in Travel
11660 Chenault Street, Suite 119
Los Angeles, CA 90049
Tel: (310) 476-4869

Travel Companion Exchange
P.O. Box 833
Amityville, NY 11701
Tel: (516) 454-0880

Women Traveling Alone

Most people can travel alone without a hitch, women included. Just add a little common sense to your spirit of adventure and you'll get by almost anywhere! Read the section on personal safety (see pp. 136–143).

- Womantour is a travel agency offering both group and individual tours for women traveling alone. Rainbow Adventures is not an agency, but organizes groups of women over 30 for travel to varying destinations, some of which are in Europe.

Rainbow Adventures
1308 Sherman Avenue
Evanston, IL 60201
Tel: (708) 864-4570

Womantour
5314 North Figueroa Street
Los Angeles, CA 90042
Tel: (213) 255-1115

Twosome and Family Travel

The big advantages of traveling with a companion are shared company and shared costs. A room for a couple may cost only a few dollars more than it would for a solo traveler. In many instances, the same savings apply to food and transportation. In short, it costs far less for two people to travel together than to go independently. But savings mean nothing unless you're both doing what you really want to do.

Traveling as a Twosome

- If you and your partner cannot agree on the purpose of a trip, consider traveling independently. You may prefer completely different destinations, so why not go your separate ways?
- Meet again in places you'd both like to visit.
- Carry your own bags, unless you're willing to pay someone else to do it for you. It is unfair to ask a partner to carry your luggage.
- Share all responsibilities with your partner. The one who has to make most of the decisions shoulders the burden for any mistakes. That burden should be equally divided.
- Iron out all money matters before you start. Good reckoning makes good friends.
- Each partner in a couple should have control of part of the money, including "mad money" for special occasions. You should both be responsible for handling part of the payment for everyday expenses.

Family Travel

The more people involved in a European trip, the more complex the planning is going to be. You can't expect to suit all tastes at all times when working with a group.

- Make sure that each person in the family has a say in planning the trip.
- Gear the trip to the pace of the youngest family member.
- Agree that all responsibilities will be shared.
- Since each person will carry his or her own luggage, make sure that the size of the bag matches the size of the person.
- Give each member of your group a "get unlost" card explaining exactly what to do if he or she gets lost. Getting lost can be extremely frightening.
- Note that younger children can appreciate cathedrals, churches, and art galleries—in small doses. Children tend to be activity oriented, which means that they'd rather go to a beach than to the cathedral at Chartres—or would rather combine the two, preferably in a period of 20 minutes!
- Allow for the option of splitting up the party from time to time, so that those primarily interested in cultural attractions can have adequate time to appreciate them.

- Remember that families of all nationalities congregate in campgrounds, which makes them very enjoyable for most children.

Traveling with a Baby

- When making reservations for air travel, try to schedule departure and arrival times so that they do not coincide with the baby's feedings. Avoid the peak or rush hours as well, choosing less popular flight times. Note that the earlier the flight, the less likely it is to be delayed, especially if it originates in the city from which you are flying.
- Contact the airline well in advance if you wish to reserve a bassinet. Ask about preboarding privileges.
- Bring milk if you're feeding the baby from a bottle. Ask an available flight attendant to warm it up.
- Have something for the baby to drink during takeoff and landing: the sucking will relieve the pressure that builds up in the baby's ears.
- Bring a towel to cover you during feeding and to place under the baby at changing time.
- Bring a small blanket, plastic bags for disposable diapers, small toys for the baby to play with, and a folding (umbrella) stroller. The stroller will make it much easier for you both to get around, and you can lift it into a booth or chair in a restaurant without waking the baby up.
- Because many European restaurants welcome children at noon but look upon them coldly in the evening, plan larger meals for the middle of the day and have snacks at night.
- If you are traveling by car, you must buy or bring some sort of safety harness that will fit into the back seat, as it is against the law in most European countries for small children to ride in the front seat of a car.

For Older People

The following organizations have information for older travelers.

American Association of
    Retired Persons
601 East Street NW
Washington, DC 20049
Tel: (202) 434-2277

Elderhostel
75 Federal Street
Boston, MA 02110
Tel: (617) 426-7788
(please write)

Golden Companions
P.O. Box 754
Pullman, WA 99163
Tel: (208) 858-2183

Mature Outlook
6001 North Clark Street
Chicago, IL 60660
Tel: (800) 336-6330

National Council of
  Senior Citizens
1331 F Street NW
Washington, DC 20004
Tel: (202) 347-8800

Younger Travelers

Young travelers usually have more time, less money, and more energy than other travelers—a potent combination.
* Take more money than you think you're going to need. Europe's not that cheap.
* Pick up an International Student Identification Card (see p. 8).
* Try to give friends and relatives a vague itinerary. They can get in touch with you in an emergency through:

Citizens Emergency Center
U.S. Department of State
2201 C Street NW
Washington, DC 20520
Tel: (202) 647-5225

* No itinerary? Then register with consulates as you make your vagabond way through Europe—if you can stand the inconvenience.

Traveling with a Disability

The following organizations have information and tours for disabled travelers:

Evergreen Travel Service
4114 198th Street S.W.
Lynnwood, WA 98036
Tel: (206) 776-1184

Flying Wheels Travel
P.O. Box 382
143 West Bridge Street
Owatonna, MN 55060
Tel: (507) 451-5005

Mobility International/USA
P.O. Box 3551
Eugene, OR 97403
Tel: (503) 343-1284

Tours

A tour can be the answer to a traveler's prayers or a form of temporary damnation. The most important question to ask yourself when
considering a tour is whether you are a good prospect for one. People who prefer to be alone should not take tours. People who get
impatient standing in lines will not like tours. Impulsive, free-spirited
people often regret traveling on tours.

On the other hand, people who dislike unplanned weekends, who
are not very aggressive, who lead scheduled lives, and who don't
speak foreign languages find tours an excellent way to travel. For
those in poor health, joining a tour may be more attractive than traveling alone. Tours are also highly recommended for travel to Eastern
Europe, since tour operators often book all hotel rooms and restaurant seats in advance. They also have knowledge on how to cut
through much of the red tape that still exists in this area. In short, it's
a question of personality. If you do decide to join a tour, its goals
and yours should be similar.

Advantages of Tours

- Tours can save you money. You're joining a group that buys
  everything as a block, which ensures substantial price reductions
  across the board.
- Tours can be prepaid, so you will know in advance how much the
  trip is going to cost. You can also put off payment by financing the
  trip.
- Tour packages, which include all your major expenses, allow you
  to pay in dollars and avoid the currency exchange rip-off.
- You can find tours that are tailored to your needs or interests, from
  skiing to bird-watching.
- Tours offer companionship for travelers prone to loneliness.
- Tours help less-aggressive travelers cope with the language barrier
  and avoid embarrassing situations.
- Tours have clout, including the ability to get you into hotels and
  restaurants in peak tourist seasons.
- Tours save you time and energy by preventing potential hassles.
- Tours are organized by experts who know the most interesting
  sights to see. They generally hire competent travel guides in each
  city to help you understand its beauty, history, and traditions.

Disadvantages of Tours

- Tours herd people together. To find out how you react to this
  experience, take a group tour of a local museum or industrial

plant. If you enjoy yourself, you may also enjoy taking a tour abroad. If you can't stand going on a local tour, avoid foreign tours!

- Tours can be hurried, impersonal, and flavorless. Throughout the trip you will have to follow a prearranged schedule that is oriented to a group and its needs. It may take the travail out of travel, but it can also wring the lust out of wanderlust.
- Most tour groups in Europe travel by bus. Although convenient and usually comfortable, buses can be boring and confining.
- You pay for a tour sight-unseen, which is something like marrying the same way. There's no real chance for a refund if things go awry.
- Tours are made up of groups of people—people whom you may or may not like. But they'll be your companions regardless.
- The words in tour brochures are just that—words. A "first-class" hotel may end up being, well, second-rate, even in Soho!
- Most tour contracts squirm with loopholes and catches.
- Tours isolate you from contact with local people by taking care of everything for you.
- If you don't like the hotels chosen for you or the restaurants' bland fare, you might not be able to do anything about it.
- From a financial standpoint, you are sometimes better off planning your own trip. The luxury tours are a good example—Jason could have picked up a bucketful of golden fleece sheared from wealthy tour-goers!

Protecting Yourself from Defaults

Occasionally tours, cruises, and travel agencies go belly up. Here are some precautions you can take:
- Pay the least down possible.
- Use a credit card for payment. Do not pay the bill until satisfied that all is well.
- If paying by check, find out the name of the escrow company retaining funds. Make the check payable to that company.
- Buy trip cancellation insurance.

Tour Package Checklist

If you take the trouble to consult tour brochures or agents and find answers to the following questions, you will be in a much better position to judge the quality of any tour package you're considering.

☐ Is the tour operator a member of the United States Tour Operators' Association? (Most of these operators are reliable.)

☐ How much will the tour cost altogether?

☐ Will a service charge be added? If so, how much will it be? Often you'll find a service charge outlined in very fine print at the end of the brochure. Look out for words like "extra," "optional," and "bonus."

☐ What extra or supplemental charges will apply to you? What will optional packages cost you? How much is the advance deposit?

☐ What are the penalties for cancellation?

☐ Are substitutions allowed on the passenger list?

☐ Can the dates of the tour be changed arbitrarily?

☐ Can the schedule or itinerary be rearranged for any reason?

☐ Can the tour be canceled? How much notice must be given?

☐ Does the tour include transportation to and from the airport? (Many tours don't.)

☐ Does the tour cost include the full price of airfare to and from Europe? What are the dates and times of flights? Are the flights nonstop?

☐ Does the tour price cover all airport departure taxes?

☐ Is there a supplemental charge if you want a room to yourself? How much?

☐ Which hotels will you be staying in? Get the names.

☐ Can other hotels be substituted arbitrarily? If so, get the names.

☐ What's included in the room? Bath or shower? Two beds? Get details.

☐ Where are the hotels located? Ask to see them on a map.

☐ Are all tips and taxes included in the room price?

☐ Is there any charge whatsoever that's not included?

☐ Are all meals included in the price of the tour? Is any meal not included? If not, why not and where not?

☐ Where will you be eating? In hotels? In restaurants? What restaurants?

☐ What's included with the meal? Is wine included? Is coffee included? Is dessert included? Is anything excluded? If so, how much will it cost?

☐ Do you have a choice from the menu at each meal? Can you make substitutions at no extra charge?

☐ Are all tips and service charges for meals included in the tour price?

☐ Who pays the entrance fee to museums, galleries, and events?

☐ What kind of transportation is provided?

☐ Does the cost include all transfers from airports and train stations? Does it include transportation to meals and nightlife?

☐ What kind of intercity transportation is provided: bus, train, air?

☐ If it's a bus, is it air-conditioned or "air-cooled" (a tour-brochure expression meaning that the windows can be opened)?

☐ How many nights' accommodation are included in the tour price? Are there any nights on which the cost of a room has been left out?

☐ What is the pace of the tour? Does it leave you any free time?

☐ Does the tour spend enough time in each city to let you get anything out of the visit?

☐ Will the tour have an escort? Will the same escort be with the tour for the whole time? (It's disconcerting to have a new escort in every city.)

☐ Will you have tour guides for each city?

☐ Does the tour include insurance for accidents, health, baggage, etc? If so, how much? Any deductible? Any exclusions?

☐ Who takes care of the baggage? Is there any extra cost? Are all tips to porters included in the cost of the hotel room?

Transportation to Europe

By Plane

Almost everyone flies to Europe today because air travel is faster and cheaper than ocean travel. Yet, on every flight, some passengers wind up paying as much as three or four times what others pay. Smart travelers know this and learn strategies to keep costs down.

Comparison Shopping: Scheduled Airlines

- Spend some time on the phone getting different quotes for comparable flights on various airlines. Since the market has opened up competitively, prices do vary along identical routes.
- Watch for introductory fares or special coupon offers. As airlines open up new routes, they offer incentives to new customers in the form of reduced fares.
- Compare fares from Canada. Can you save money by taking advantage of the weak Canadian dollar?
- Use the toll-free or 800 numbers (listed in your phone book) when you call the airlines.

Asking the Right Questions

- Let the person on the other end of the phone know immediately that you're bargain hunting by asking for the lowest fare from A to B.
- Ask whether there are any incentive fares.
- Find out whether there are reductions for mid-week or night flights.
- Ask whether you can save money by flying to a less popular city near your final destination.
- Even after you've arranged for a flight, continue to watch for better deals. If a bargain pops up, turn in your ticket and go with the better fare. In some cases you'll save money, even if you have to pay a penalty for canceling!
- If you buy a ticket with a credit card and then have to cancel or change your travel plans, ask for a *refund receipt* when you return the ticket for credit. Note the ticket number and the date and place

you bought it so that you can contact the credit card company if the credit does not show up on your bill.

Special Tour Rates on Scheduled Airlines

In most areas, you can find specialized tour companies that buy blocks of seats on regularly scheduled airlines. In some cases, these seats are sold at rates far below those offered by the airline itself.

- Get familiar with the companies in your area that specialize in low-cost airfare. They tend to advertise heavily in Sunday papers.
- Call and ask them about any upcoming offerings to Europe.

Maverick Scheduled Airlines

- After comparison shopping the major airlines, check the fares of maverick lines such as Icelandair, Tel: (212) 967-8888, or Virgin Atlantic, Tel: (212) 206-6612. These airlines provide an accurate barometer of prevailing low rates, which come and go, as do a number of maverick airlines. If you fly Icelandair, you'll stop off in Iceland and continue on to Europe. The inconvenience may be worth the extra savings. That's for you to decide.

Comparison Shopping: Charters

Tour and charter companies rent planes to take passengers to specific destinations. These rented planes are called charters. In a few cases, the company actually owns the planes and runs a sort of mini-airline.

- Charters often leave at weird times and are rarely on a tight schedule, but if you're trying to save a buck, they can really make sense.
- On any contract with a charter company the escrow bank and bonding company must be clearly stated.
- Charter companies must clearly state what the itinerary will be and stick to it.
- Charter companies cannot cancel a flight within 10 days of the intended departure—they used to do this regularly, leaving passengers stranded.
- There are stiff cancellation penalty clauses on most charter airlines. You can take out cancellation insurance, available from charter companies and independent brokers.
- The following are a few companies offering charters to Europe. Tickets may only be available through travel agents, but write for information on available flights and schedules to see whether any of these make sense. Read the section on consolidators (p. 43) for additional information:

American Trans Air
P.O. Box 51609
Indianapolis, IN 46251
Tel: (317) 243-4150

GWV International Weekends
1170 Commonwealth Avenue
Boston, MA 02134
Tel: (617) 449-5450

Balair
608 Fifth Avenue
New York, NY 10020
Tel: (212) 581-3411

Tower Air, Inc.
Hangar 8
JFK Intl. Airport
Jamaica, NY 11430
Tel: (718) 553-8500

Comparison Shopping: Clearinghouses and Clubs

Clearinghouses and special airline travel clubs offer reduced tickets to countless places in the world. They pick up spaces on tours and flights that are not sold out.

- To get information on available flights and tours, you pay a service fee to a clearinghouse or club.
- These clubs are geared to spur-of-the-moment travel. You may have to make up your mind to go to Europe with only a few days to spare—at a discount, of course.
- Once you pay your money, there's no time to cancel. If you "get on the boat," you go!
- Also, you have to get to the point of origin of the charter, cruise, or tour that's being offered.
- Many of these clubs have a hot line with long, detailed, and boring recorded messages. Make sure the club has a toll-free number for its clients.
- Below is a list of discount travel clubs:

Discount Travel International
114 Forrest Avenue
The Ives Building, Suite 203
Narberth, PA 19072
Tel: (215) 668-7184

Hotline Travel
3001 East Pershing Boulevard
Cheyenne, WY 82001
Tel: (800) 543-0110

Encore's Short Notice
4501 Forbes Boulevard
Lanham, MD 20706
Tel: (800) 638-0930
(301) 459-8020

Last Minute Travel Club
1249 Boylston Street
Boston, MA 02215
Tel: (800) 527-8646
(617) 267-9800

Moment's Notice
425 Madison Avenue
New York, NY 10017
Tel: (212) 486-0503

Spur of the Moment
  Tours & Cruises
411 North Harbor Boulevard,
  Suite 302
San Pedro, CA 90731
Tel: (800) 343-1991
(310) 521-1070

Traveler's Advantage
3033 South Parker Road,
Suite 900
Aurora, CO 80014
Tel: (800) 548-1116

Vacations to Go
1502 Augusta Drive, Suite 415
Houston, TX 77057
Tel: (800) 338-4962
(713) 974-2121

Worldwide Discount Travel
  Club
1674 Meridian Avenue,
  Suite 206
Miami Beach, FL 33139
Tel: (305) 534-2082

Consolidators or Bucket Shops

- These companies or individuals sell tickets at wholesale prices. Look for them in travel sections of Sunday newspapers. Large cities, such as New York, often have the largest number of consolidators (bucket shops). London has had them for years.
- Although there are many consolidators throughout the United States, here are a few for you to start with:

Consumer Wholesale Travel
34 West 33rd Street, Suite 1014
New York, NY 10001
Tel: (800) 223-6862
(212) 695-8435

TFI Tours
34 West 32nd Street, 12th Floor
New York, NY 10001
Tel: (800) 745-8000
(212) 745-1140

Unitravel
1177 North Warson Road
St. Louis, MO 63132
Tel: (800) 325-2222
(314) 569-0900

- The following publication specializes in information on low-cost flights. Ninety percent of its information is on consolidators. The rest is on charters:

Jax Fax
397 Post Road
Darien, CT 06820
Tel: (203) 655-8746

Using Travel Agents

It costs no more to buy a ticket through a travel agent than to buy one directly from the airline. Unfortunately, though, many agents do not like working with discounted fares, because they make a commission on the total dollar value of tickets sold.

- Don't be afraid to comparison shop with travel agents. Make it clear to each one that you want to know the best deal to get you from A to B.
- A few agencies (not many) now guarantee that they will come up with the lowest possible rate or refund any overpayment you've made.
- Sometimes a good agent will come up with a tour fare that will cost you less than comparable airfare. This is getting very hard to do now, but it does happen.

Agencies Specializing in Cutting Airline Costs

The following are two travel agencies specializing in airfare cost reduction. Travel Avenue charges a set fee per person, so the more complicated your total itinerary, the more valuable the service. However, it rebates from 5 to 23 percent of the fare as a way of covering this expense. It also searches for the lowest possible fares, including charters for your trip. Travel For Less specializes in keeping costs down for travelers who have to travel on a specific schedule but do not know how to jump through all of the hoops to make substantial savings.

Travel Avenue
641 West Lake Street, Suite 201
Chicago, IL 60606
Tel: (800) 333-3335
(312) 876-1116

Travel For Less
1301 47th Street
Brooklyn, NY 11219
Tel: (800) 223-6045

Student Discounts

- All students (and teachers) should contact CIEE (see p. 9) for information on inter-European plane travel. It can save you 40 to 75 percent off regular fares.

Barter or Trade Exchanges

In most Sunday papers there is a section dealing with the sale of plane tickets. Many of these come from individuals who can't use up their frequent flyer coupons. The legality of all this is highly questionable, yet thousands of people have bought tickets in this manner. Be wary. Only buy a ticket if it can be issued in your name.

Free Travel Through Courier Services

- Approximately 900 companies use transatlantic couriers. Look for Air Courier Service in the Yellow Pages. These companies pay for part or all of your fare. Many magazines, books, and newsletters have named specific companies, only to have these inundated with inquiries. The companies then have no need for additional couriers. Note that major libraries have Yellow Page directories for most major cities. Librarians can help you get the addresses of courier companies. Write as many as you have the patience and stamina to try. Getting a job as a courier is not easy.
- Additional tip: many couriers are hired for one-way travel to the United States from Europe.

Money-Saving Strategies

No matter how you decide to travel, whether by tour, scheduled airline, or charter, you can usually save money by following certain strategies.

Buying Tickets in the United States

- Buy all your tickets for transatlantic travel in the United States. If you buy tickets abroad, you'll have to pay for them in foreign currency at a preset rate of exchange, which may cost you extra money.
- Note that the airline cannot raise the price of a ticket once you've paid for it. However, simply making a reservation does not guarranty the price.
- Hard to believe, but true: A round-trip ticket may be less than a one-way fare. Always ask about this if you're traveling only in one direction.
- When getting a quote on an airline ticket price, ask if it includes all fees and taxes for international travel, including inspection fees and departure taxes on all legs of the flight.

Buying Tickets in Advance

- Since only a certain number of seats are allotted for highly reduced fares on any given flight, you can save hundreds of dollars by buying a ticket far in advance of a planned trip. In short, the early bird does get the worm. The exceptions to this have already been noted in the section on travel clubs and clearinghouses (pp. 42–43), where the last in may get the best buy. Also, risk takers can often pick up steals on charters by waiting until the last minute to buy a ticket in the off-season (see below).

Keeping Flexible About Travel Dates

- Be as flexible as possible with your travel plans so that you can take advantage of lower rates. What if you have to leave on a Thursday instead of a Friday or return on a Monday instead of a Sunday? Isn't it worth $100?
- Ask about excursion rates, with minimum and maximum lengths of stay. It may be that by adding or subtracting a few days from your planned trip, you can save yourself a good deal of money.
- Ask the airline whether a standby fare exists on the route you're planning to take. This will make sense in the not-so-popular vacation periods. Standby status is for flexible travelers who will do anything to save a buck.
- Note that special excursion fares can be reserved in the United States, but must be paid for abroad. Travel agents neither promote nor encourage the sale of these tickets because they do not make a commission on them, but ask about them anyway.

Stopover or Extension Privileges

- Flights to and from minor cities within a foreign country may be no more expensive than flights to major ones. You may save yourself the price of train or plane fare to a small town by asking whether your fare would take you there in the first place—at no extra charge!

Off-season Travel

The weather may not be so hot in the off-season (from November to March), but the savings are substantial. By combining the other strategies outlined in this section with travel during this period, you may save hundreds of dollars.

- *Special off-season tip:* The person most willing to lose often wins. Check on charter flight prices each Thursday by calling a local agency known for specializing in low-cost travel to Europe (their ads will appear on Sunday). Prices for tickets often begin to slide down as flight time approaches if all seats are not sold. If you are willing to take the risk, you may be able to purchase a ticket for far less at the last moment by following this strategy. It is critical for you to call before the ad appears. Once prices reach bottom, tickets will sell out immediately.

- Note that you'll also find slightly lower fares in the "shoulder seasons" of spring and fall. Contact the airlines for exact cutoff dates of each season. You might be able to take advantage of lower rates by changing your trip dates by no more than a week or two.

Trouble-savers for Booking your Own Flight

- Call before 7 A.M. or after 7 P.M. to get through to the airline without a long wait.
- Make a point of being very specific. Repeat the day and date several times to avoid mix-ups. Get the name of the person helping you. Mark down the date and time of your call along with the information concerning your flight.
- Early flights are less frequently delayed. The earliest flights rarely suffer from the cumulative effects of mounting earlier delays.
- Try to book nonstop or at least direct flights, so that you won't have to get off the plane.
- If you do have to make connections, try to stay on the same airline to avoid long walks and check-in hassles at the connecting airport. Airlines usually have a block of gates in each terminal; if you fly with one airline, you'll have only a short walk to a connecting flight.
- Airline tickets can be purchased on credit; charges vary depending on the repayment schedule. Compare these charges with rates available from your bank to come up with the best loan terms.

Special Meals

Scheduled airlines often offer special meals to passengers with specific dietary restrictions, either for cultural, religious, or health reasons. Ask about these meals when making a reservation. Specify your needs at that time. Charters may or may not have special meals available. Special meals are rarely available in Eastern Europe or on smaller carriers within Europe. Either carry appropriate food and drink with you, or eat before or after the flight. I recommend carrying some food and water at all times in Eastern Europe.

Picking Up Tickets

- Pay for and pick up tickets in advance to avoid the crush at the airport. It's a good feeling to have the ticket in your pocket, an assurance that now no one will be able to bungle your important reservation.
- When you get your tickets, check the dates, flight times, and flight numbers for accuracy. Read all materials closely so you know your rights.
- Count the flight coupons to make sure the number matches the total number of flights. Otherwise you'll pay twice for the flight.
- Check to see if you've paid for the departure tax in the ticket price. If you're not sure, ask.
- Don't leave the return date blank, even if you are traveling without a set date of return. Have the clerk fill it in with an approximate date of return. For some reason, it is easier to make a new reservation when you have an already-dated, versus an open, ticket. Naturally, cancel the reservation and reschedule the return date in Europe.

Selecting a Seat

- Find out about available aircraft and best seats at the time you pick up your ticket—don't wait until you're in the hurried atmosphere of the departure lounge. Ask to see a seating chart, choose where you'd like to be (mark down some alternates), and reserve a seat right away if you can. If you can't do so, mark down the seat choices on your ticket folder so that you can ask for them when checking in at the gate (see pp. 100–101 for tips on choosing seats).

By Ship

Going to Europe by ship is the old-style, romantic way of getting there. In good weather it's a vacation in itself. Not only can the food and company be great, but such a trip also allows for a gradual adaptation to time changes. If you have lots of time and enough money, going by ship can be a great experience.

But note the disadvantages. Ocean travel is very expensive for most people, costing far more than airfare. It takes time—from 5 to 10 days, depending on the size of the ship. In rough weather, most people do get sick; even if you do not, you'll be stuck on board with people who do.

The tips in this section apply to both transatlantic travel and cruises (such as through the Greek islands).

Booking a Cabin

Travel agents specializing in cruises are your best resource. Booking a cruise is really booking a tour—the very heart of travel agency business. For information on agents specializing in cruises only, send a stamped, self-addressed envelope to the National Association of Cruise Only Agencies. You may request information on agencies in any two states for free:

NACOA
P.O. Box 7209
Freeport, NY 11520
Tel: (516) 378-8006

The Cost

- The cost of a cruise varies dramatically by line, length of the cruise, and choice of cabin.
- If you want to travel alone (single cabin), the cost will be exorbitant.
- The higher up in the ship you get, the higher the cost. Cabins on upper decks are far from engines and noise. They also offer the best views.
- Bigger rooms (or suites) cost more because space is precious. A bath instead of a shower adds to the cost for the same reason.
- Portholes, because they offer a view, add to the cost. This is an outside, versus an inside, cabin.
- If money is really tight, ask if there are any ways to reduce the cost, such as agreeing to standby status.

Extra Costs

- On some cruise ships, tips are not included in the fare. Ask to be sure.
- Any land tours or excursions to the mainland cost extra on almost all cruise ships. These can be quite expensive, especially if they include a guide and transportation.
- Wine, beer, and cocktails all cost extra. On some lines you'll get complimentary wine with your meals.

Length of the Cruise

- Most cruises last 1 or 2 weeks, providing adequate time for rest.
- A few cruises offer 3- and 4-day voyages (the first and last days are often write-offs).

Motion Sickness

- Some people get sick at the sight of sea water (see p. 228 for advice).

Special Cruise Tips

- Get as much information on the ship as possible, including its age (has it been renovated?), its size, and its overall reputation for service and food. Although smaller ships are rougher for those prone to sea sickness, they are much more practical for shore excursions, since fewer people need to be ferried. Larger ships are much better for those interested in meeting people.
- The lowest-priced cabins on most cruises go first.
- Cruises are not geared to getting to know places. Europe will be a backdrop, not the main performance.
- Cruises frequently offer shore excursions during mealtimes—very annoying, but a fact. Ask about the exact schedule when booking a cruise!
- Space is critical, so rooms on luxury liners are tight, and baths minuscule.
- If you drink, bring a bottle of your favorite alcohol on board. This makes you less dependent on overpriced and often undersized (or watered-down) drinks.
- There are so many free snacks and edible extras on board that someone may whimsically remark that you board as a passenger, disembark as cargo.

Tipping on Board

- Ask about the company policy on tipping before you buy a ticket. Tips may be included in the ticket price. If they are, the ticket is really costing you considerably less than a comparable ticket on a line where tips are not included.
- If tips are not included, tip room stewards, waiters, and other service staff for special services. The more service you ask for, the more you should expect to tip. Tips are best given immediately for services such as bringing late-night snacks.
- One very effective way of tipping: hand the room steward or waiter an amount adding up to half the tip you expect to give him altogether. Tell him exactly what you expect, and tell him that you will give him the other half of the tip at the end of the trip (the day before you disembark). This is up-front bargaining for good service. And it works!

Transportation in Europe

Where are you going to go in Europe? How great will the total distance be? Are you on a tight budget? When are you going to go? How much energy do you have? Are you traveling by yourself, as a twosome, or in a group?

Not until you have answered each of these questions should you decide whether travel by plane, train, car, motorcycle, bicycle, or hitchhiking makes sense for you. Each way has its advantages and disadvantages.

Basic Considerations

If you start with a few basic considerations, you will have an easier time choosing the mode of travel that best suits you.

Saving Money

- If you're traveling alone, you'll have to travel by train, motorcycle, bike, or thumb if you want to save money.
- If you're traveling with one or more people, you can bring the cost of car travel down to a more reasonable amount.

Saving Time

- Car travel is fine for short trips (less than 150 miles per day), but not for longer ones. It is just too time-consuming in most European countries.
- Train travel is superb for intercity trips of 300 miles or less. In fact, for short runs, a train will get you there as fast as a plane will.
- Planes are great for trips of 300 miles or longer.
- Hitchhiking and biking are out.

Saving Human Energy

- Plane travel is superb, especially for long trips. (So is going by tour bus.) Train travel is also great if you've got a seat, if the trip lasts no more than 8 hours, and if you have little luggage.
- Driving, biking, and hitching are out. Driving in Europe requires an enormous amount of energy.

Getting Off the Beaten Path

- Car travel, hitching, biking, or motorcycling are often the only ways to have complete mobility and freedom. A car or motorcycle is an absolute necessity in Greece and rural areas. It is also highly recommended in Eastern Europe if the costs are within your budget.
- Train travel is OK, but not great. Trains will get you to most smaller towns, but only after interminable waits and enough transfers to puzzle an electrical engineer.
- Planes? You guessed it. They're useless!

Cost per Mile of Various Modes of Transportation*

Transportation Mode	Cost per Mile
Plane	An average of 28 cents per plane mile per person.
Train	A first-class average of 15 cents per train mile per person.
Car	If you travel more than 1,000 miles per week, it will cost less than 32 cents per car mile. If you travel less than 1,000 miles per week, it will cost you more than 32 cents per mile. To find cost per person, divide cost per mile by number of people in car.
Motorcycle	An average of 4 cents per mile, not including initial purchase price.
Hitchhiking	No charge, unless you agree to split gas costs.
Biking	No charge.

*These costs are more valuable as comparisons rather than actual costs, because fuel prices are in constant flux.

Planes

If you want to travel widely in Europe in a relatively short time and are willing to pay the high cost, take a plane.

Advantages of Plane Travel

- For city-to-city trips of 300 miles or more, plane travel is the fastest way.

- It's the only way to get to some places, including many of the more popular islands.
- For a solo traveler covering great distances in a short time, it can be the most sensible way to see Europe.
- You waste little precious time getting from one place to another.
- It's safe—popular misconceptions aside.

Disadvantages of Plane Travel

- Plane travel can be expensive, especially for shorter city-to-city trips. It's doubly expensive for twosomes and exorbitant for groups.
- Plane trips are oriented to travel between major cities.
- Plane travel can actually be slower than train travel for trips of 300 miles and less.
- You've got to spend money and time on transfers.
- You can be locked in by bad weather.
- You pass over, not through, the countryside.

Plane Travel Strategies

- London is one of the best bases for buying inexpensive tickets. (Ask for "bucket shops.") Note that prices may vary depending on the London airport you fly from.
- Otherwise, try to buy all tickets for inter-European air travel in the United States. You'll save money. For some flights, you'll find that you can reserve seats in the United States, but will still have to pay for them abroad. You can try asking travel agents for help or information on this point, but you may find that some are ignorant of European excursion fares, and some are unwilling to help because they don't make a commission on such sales.
- Have flights and flight times written on the ticket folder. It's also better to reserve a return seat on a tentative basis than to leave the return date open. If you have to change a reservation, just call it in.
- Check into stopover privileges whenever you buy a transatlantic ticket. You might be able to see several cities on route to another one.
- Check into the possibility of adding another leg onto a ticket you've already purchased. It might be less expensive than buying a separate ticket.
- Get free brochures from the airlines that show you the seating arrangements on some of the most popular aircraft.
- Contact the airlines for information about special clubs and waiting rooms available in many airports, including a few in Europe. For a yearly fee, you can take advantage of them. These clubs are most useful for business people and other frequent travelers.

Trains

Train travel is a sensible way to see Europe, especially if you're going from one major city to the next. It's also a low-cost, low-risk mode of transportation—but it has its drawbacks.

Advantages of Train Travel

- You spend less money when you go by train. It is far cheaper than plane or car travel, especially for solo travelers.
- Train travel is not only safe, but also convenient, because it takes you from city center to city center with no transfer fees to pay and no weather delays.
- Train travel is less tiring than car travel.
- Going by train is the fastest way to cover short distances between major European cities, even faster than plane travel for trips less than 300 miles.
- Best of all, you see the land; it can be a visual feast.

Disadvantages of Train Travel

- Each day on a train is wasted—unless trains turn you on.
- Since train travel is oriented to city centers, you may find it confining.
- Trains don't wait for you; you wait for them.
- Over an extended period of time, train travel becomes monotonous.
- Trains are crowded, especially in second class. The low price draws crowds like a bargain basement sale; the corridors are so full of so many people and packs that a trip to the bathroom becomes one long stutter of "Please" and "I'm sorry."

Railway Passes

Some countries offer special passes for unlimited train travel within their own borders. You can buy these for travel in Austria, Belgium, Denmark, Finland, France, Germany, Great Britain, Greece, Ireland, the Netherlands, Norway, Portugal, Scotland, Spain, Sweden, and Switzerland.

- Note that Eastern European countries are now getting into the pass act with individual and combined rail passes.
- Regulations vary, and some of the passes must be purchased in the United States. Check with travel agents or National Tourist Offices (see pp. 247–250) for up-to-date restrictions and fares.
- For information on passes, request a copy of Europe's Rail Passes from:

The European Travel Commission
630 Fifth Avenue, Suite 565
New York, NY 10111
Tel: (212) 307-1200

- The main agency which deals with day-to-day ticketing and has current information:

  Rail Europe, Inc.
  226-230 Westchester Avenue
  White Plains, NY 10604
  Tel: (800) 438-7245 or 848-7245

Eurail and Youthrail Passes

The Eurailpass and the Youthpass are two of the most popular with American and Canadian travelers. They have been available for years from travel agents and can be an excellent choice. Comparable passes are also available for Eastern Europe. Information is available from the organizations mentioned above.
- Many agencies do not like working with rail travel. The following agency does, as long as you have decided exactly where and when you want to travel and on what kind of pass (if any at all). Do your homework ahead of time before calling this agency:

  Accent on Travel
  112 North 5th Street
  Klamath Falls, OR 97601
  Tel: (800) 347-0645
  (503) 885-7330

Advantages of Eurailpasses

The Eurailpass offers you unlimited train travel in the following countries: Austria, Belgium, Denmark, Finland, France, Germany, Greece, Hungary, Ireland, Italy, Luxembourg, the Netherlands, Norway, Portugal, Spain, Sweden, and Switzerland. It covers various lengths of travel time.
- You know your overall travel costs from the start, since you must prepay them in the United States. And you never have to exchange currency for tickets. Furthermore, you can take any train without a surcharge.
- You go first class, which is very comfortable, uncrowded, and clean in most areas. You can bypass boring ticket lines.

- You're free to plan your itinerary by yourself—at whim.
- You won't have to explain things to the conductor in foreign languages.
- You get many free extras. A sample of these includes a free 400-mile voyage on Irish Continental Line from Cherbourg to Rosslare, free trips on Swiss lakes, free boat rides on the Mosel and Rhine, a free ferry from Stockholm to Finland. The trip from Brindisi (Italy) to Greece is free from October to mid-June, and the rate is reduced in the peak season.

Disadvantages of Eurailpasses

- Although you don't have to buy tickets, you do have to make reservations for some of the most popular trains. That can mean long waits in long lines for super trains.
- You must pay a small fee for each reservation.
- The pass is not honored on privately owned railroads, which may link portions of your trip. Ask to see a map showing all available routes to avoid any unpleasant surprises.
- If you lose your pass after it has been validated, you may not get a refund. Contact the nearest Eurail Aid office for advice. Refunds are discretionary.

Where to Buy Eurailpasses

- Technically, you must buy all Eurail and Youthrail passes in the United States. This is the safest and easiest thing to do if you're sure that you'll be using one.
- Some travelers have written to say that they have purchased Eurailpasses abroad from major travel agencies that requested them from the United States. They also claim that you can pick them up from National Tourist Offices abroad.
- The advantage of this is that you can wait and see if you really want a pass.
- The disadvantage is that it can take up to a week or more for the passes to be delivered, and you may have a hard time finding an office willing to do this for you.

When to Buy a Eurailpass

If you intend to travel fast and far, buy one. The longer-term passes are most economical because they cut the cost per mile. Buy one if you intend to travel more than the following:

- 1,900 miles in 15 days
- 2,300 miles in 3 weeks
- 2,800 miles in 1 month
- 4,600 miles in 3 months

When Not to Buy a Eurailpass

- Don't buy one if you'll be visiting a few major cities that are close together. You'll do .much better buying second-class tickets for those few runs.

Getting the Most from a Eurailpass for Extended Trips

- Validate your Eurailpass at the last possible moment. Or combine it with separate, second-class train tickets to cut the overall cost of your trip. Example: you arrive by Icelandic in Luxembourg, pay for a second-class train ticket to Paris, spend 10 days there, and then use a Eurailpass valid for only part of your whole trip.

Youthrail Passes

The Youthrailpass, available to anyone under 26, is a variation of the Eurailpass, offering 1 or 2 months of unlimited, second-class rail travel for a set price that is lower than the Eurailpass.
- No longer do you have to specify the starting date of rail travel. The pass is now validated on the first day you use it.

Doing Without Eurailpasses

- Even if you don't buy a Eurailpass, you can save money by buying rail tickets in the United States.
- You can save more by traveling second class. But go first class in Greece, Italy, Portugal, and Spain if you want to avoid huge crowds and people sitting in the aisles.

Getting Reserved Train Seats

- If you're on a tight schedule and have very little time to waste, try to make seat reservations in the United States. Regulations change frequently. However, a good travel agent can keep you up-to-date.
- Ask ahead of time about any charge for this service. If the cost seems too steep, settle for making reservations abroad.

Cars

Car travel is for independent spirits who are aware that freedom has its price. It's the best way to see Europe if you want to strike out to unusual and offbeat locations. Sightseeing, picnics, charming hotels, unusual restaurants, out-of-the-way spots—all are open to motorists. It is one of the most efficient ways to get around in Eastern Europe.

Advantages of Car Travel

• You don't have to worry about reservations, tickets, and ticket lines.
• You're free to change schedules at whim.
• You're part of the living jigsaw puzzle around you.
• You can go almost anywhere.
• It's economical for a group of three or more.
• It's comfortable, convenient, and fast.

Disadvantages of Car Travel

• A car can be a major hindrance in big cities. If your trip is oriented to major cities, you will do better taking a train or plane.
• Car travel is expensive. Purchasing, renting, and leasing cars are all very costly options, making car travel prohibitive for solo travelers.
• Car travel is much slower than either train or plane travel. In many countries, it can take as much time to drive 1 mile as it would take to drive 5 to 10 miles in the United States.
• Car travel can insulate you from meeting Europeans.
• Finding a parking place in major European cities can give you a migraine headache.

Buying, Leasing, or Renting a Car

• Buying a car in Europe only makes sense if you plan to travel for three months or longer.
• Leasing can be a better option than renting for trips of 5 to 10 weeks. Costs are still very high, so leasing is only worthwhile for groups of three or four people.
• Renting is the best option for people who are traveling for less than a month.

Comparison Shopping for Cars to Buy Abroad

If you do some comparison shopping, you'll shave dollars off the initial cost of a foreign car!

- You can pick up many makes of foreign cars from Ship Side Showroom at Amsterdam Airport. For information, contact Ship Side Tax-Free Cars and Trading Corporation at 600B Lake Street, Suite A, Ramsey, NJ 07446, Tel: (201) 818-0400.
- Europe by Car, Inc., 1 Rockefeller Plaza, New York, NY 10020, Tel: (212) 581-3040, will send you information on buying a car abroad. Write for information on current prices and models.
- Students can sometimes get a special discount on car purchases through the CIEE (see p. 9).
- You can also purchase a car from a dealership in the United States and have it delivered to you in Europe.

Car-buying Guide

- If you're planning to bring the car back to the United States, check with U.S. Customs to make sure the car you're purchasing will pass pollution control standards, which may not be enforced in Europe.
- If you intend to resell the car, ask the dealer about which models, options, and colors sell best. The best names for resale in the United States are BMW, Fiat, Mercedes-Benz, Porsche, Volkswagen, and Volvo.
- Plan ahead, especially for summer delivery. Order your car 3 months or longer in advance.
- Find out the total cost, including all options, taxes, licenses, documents, and miscellaneous charges, and get it in writing. You will not have to pay major foreign taxes unless you keep the car for more than a year in the country where it was manufactured.
- Get the dealer's cost and delivery date confirmed by the manufacturer, in writing.
- Make sure your agreement is for the newest model on the assembly line. If you're buying late in the year, order the next year's model. (Get the year down in writing, too!)

Car Insurance for Buyers

- Most American companies will not write policies covering European travel.
- Car manufacturers do write such policies, but at rip-off prices. Ask the dealer to get you a brochure that outlines the rates before you sign any agreement.
- If the dealer has no idea of the rates, have him wire the manufacturer for them. Insist on knowing what they'll be ahead of time to avoid hidden costs.
- For more information, see p. 172.

Car Accessories

- Ask what the cost of a reflective triangle (danger sign) and first-aid kit will be. European law requires all drivers to have these, and it's often much cheaper to bring your own from the United States.
- Always carry an extra set of car keys. Hide them in a magnetic box that will stick to the underside of your car. You'll never lock yourself out this way.

Taking Delivery on a Car

- Get the delivery date in writing, and have it confirmed in writing by the factory. If a car isn't delivered on that date, you have the right to ask the factory to pay for your room while you wait. They have the right to refuse, but they'll speed up delivery under pressure.
- There's no charge for delivery at the foreign plant.
- Plan to pay for the car with a certified check or traveler's checks. A sale can be completed in about an hour.

European Warranties and Service

European warranties have about the same value as tissue paper. They cover the car for 3 to 6 months and include a series of so-called free service inspections, for which you get a coupon book. But only about half the listed service stations and garages honor the coupons.

- Do some garage hopping to find those that honor the coupons.
- Or be willing to pay for the "free" service for the sake of convenience.

Car Leasing

This is really just long-term car rental with a discount, oriented to two or more people traveling together with the idea of splitting costs.

- Leasing is sensible for trips of a month or longer, but it is still very expensive. You can get information on leasing cars from the same outfits that rent them.

Car Rental

- Reserve a car well in advance of your arrival, especially if you will be abroad between May and September. Get a confirmation number in writing (see p. 173).

Car Insurance for Renters

- Check with your insurance company to see whether you are covered abroad or need to pay extra fees for insurance in Europe.
- Bank of New York (formerly Dreyfus), Chase Manhattan Bank, and American Express offer coverage for specific card holders. Coverage is either primary (valuable) or secondary (not so valuable). Secondary means that your present insurance company really ends up footing much of the bill. Carefully compare this kind of offer on a company-by-company basis.

Base Prices for Car Rental

The following chart shows how base prices vary by company for each country. Though the names have been omitted, companies A, B, and C do exist, and the prices listed were all in effect at one time (prices fluctuate constantly). Note that if you choose a car from a company offering the best rate and can start your trip in a low-rate country, you'll save money.

Country	Cost by Company		
	A	B	C
Austria	200	199	208
Belgium	172	175	190
Denmark	181	207	172
Finland	248	289	254
France	220	248	162
Germany	182	182	201
Great Britain	159	145	123
Greece	151	170	158
Ireland	99	164	126
Italy	221	198	194
Luxembourg	166	257	204
Netherlands	182	200	179
Norway	231	224	235
Portugal	129	123	126
Spain	134	166	103
Sweden	256	217	208
Switzerland	214	288	290

Shopping Around for Rental Rates

- Note that base prices vary not only by company, but also by country, time of year, and changes in the economy, so comparison shop before you rent. Using the toll-free (800) numbers in your telephone book, call major car rental firms, such as Avis, Budget-Auto, Hertz, and National.

- Ask these companies to send you their free worldwide directories listing current car rental rates.
- Contact Europe by Car, Inc., 1 Rockefeller Plaza, New York, NY 10020, Tel: (212) 581-3040, and ask for its rates. This firm also has offices in Chicago, Honolulu, Los Angeles, San Francisco, and Washington, DC.
- Contact Auto Europe, 27 Pearl Street, P.O. Box 7006, Portland, ME 04112, Tel: (800) 223-5555. It deals with rentals in Western Europe and most countries in Eastern Europe.
- Always compare any offer with that of Connex International, 23 North Division Street, Peekskill, NY 10566, Tel: (800) 333-3949 or (914) 739-0066. Connex is a car rental consolidator and often comes up with excellent prices for rental abroad. It covers Western Europe. In Eastern Europe it has rental available in Czechoslovakia and Hungary at the present time.
- Note that airlines offer fly-and-drive tour packages, combining airfare and the cost of car rental in Europe. These are couple-oriented. You can get information on such packages from travel agents and airlines.
- Explore auto club discounts for members.
- Students should check with the CIEE (see p. 9) for rental discount information.

Rental Pitfalls

- Do not plan to rent a car on any *island* where it's impossible to take out full insurance on the car. Instead, avoid potential legal hassles by hiring a taxi daily.
- Never rent a car in *Great Britain* and take it across the channel. To avoid stiff surcharges and premiums on insurance, leave the car in England and rent another car on the Continent.
- Some Eastern European countries have required the purchase of gas coupons in hard currency. These are then exchanged for gas at the stations. This practice is dying out, but ask about it before traveling to a particular area. Countries may also occasionally offer gas coupons through auto clubs to reduce the cost of travel for foreigners. In this case the car must have plates from another country, whether owned or rented. Italy has done this once in awhile, but the coupons are mostly a thing of the past.
- If you plan to pick up your car in one city with the intention of leaving it in another, you usually have to pay an additional fee. Ask about these charges when making a car rental reservation.

Rental Taxes and Additional Fees

The base price is just that. You'll notice how the base price is augmented by taxes at the following rates in Western European countries. The same concept applies in the East. Rates may vary from time to time, but the concept doesn't.

Country	Tax Rate
Austria	20 percent tax plus a 1.2 percent contract fee
Belgium	25 percent tax
Denmark	22 percent tax
Finland	19.05 percent tax
France	33.33 percent tax
Germany	14 percent tax
Great Britain	15 percent tax
Greece	20 percent tax
Ireland	10 percent tax
Italy	18 percent tax plus 12 percent gas tax
Luxembourg	17 percent tax
Netherlands	19 percent tax
Norway	20 percent tax
Portugal	8 percent tax
Spain	5 percent tax
Sweden	23.46 percent tax
Switzerland	no tax

Motorcycles

You can go anywhere on a cycle—up rutted mountain paths or over to an old, abandoned Moorish castle that's stranded miles from a main road. You're always close to the earth, the smell of mimosa trees or manure, the colors of bright-red poppy fields or pastel-pink Portuguese walls, and the sounds of clicking tracks and buzzing mosquitoes or grape flies. It's an exciting sensation.

Advantages of Motorcycle Travel

- You can park a cycle almost anywhere.
- The gas costs are extremely low—you get from 60 to 90 miles to the gallon.
- You can pass long lines of traffic anywhere, in the city or at borders.

- There's no doubt about it—it's an exciting way to travel!

Disadvantages of Motorcycle Travel

- The once-low initial cost of a bike is now very high.
- All parents and lovers are afraid you'll fall. You will. But the odds are 50-50 that you'll survive the scraped knees, twisted feet, and close shaves.
- Motorcycle touring appears glamorous in the movies and on television. In real life, it can be dirty, tiring, cold, annoying, and frustrating. Have you ever changed a bike's tire and taken it off its rim by yourself? If not, you don't understand motorcycles, their absolute unreliability, the exhaustion of riding, and the experiences you're in for.
- That's not all: you're at the mercy of the weather, and a bike is easy to vandalize and easy to steal.

Buying a Motorcycle Abroad

- Buy a prestige bike for high resale value.
- Order the cycle for foreign delivery months in advance, since the supply may not cover the demand.
- Be willing to pick it up at the factory.
- Read the sections on buying and driving cars abroad (see pp. 171–184) for other helpful hints.
- Remember that a cycle takes thousands of miles to break in (something you should point out when you sell it).

Motorcycle Options

- Don't get a tank lock. When you're cold and exhausted, you don't want to have to undo your coat to look for a key. And tank locks rattle.
- Try to replace the side kickstand with any other kind. Side kickstands are useless because they sink in sand and tar. (If you do have a side stand, you'll have to carry a board with you!)
- Equally useless is the average rearview mirror that comes with the bike. If it's the kind that you can loosen with just a quick turn of the hand, have it immediately replaced with a good one—one that won't jiggle loose after 20 miles and then smash as it flies off onto the pavement.
- Although crash bars that protect your legs are sometimes called sissy bars, that's a misnomer. When you dump, you'll know why. Get them!
- The electric starter is worth every extra cent you pay for it. There's

nothing worse than trying to kick-start a bike that is cold, wet, or overheated.
- Pay extra for a luggage rack.

Other Motorcycling Equipment

- Wear a helmet. The law requires it.
- A tinted bubble that covers your whole face is much better than goggles. Dust stings; bumblebees and fat bugs explode when they hit your face; and rain is unbearable at normal driving speeds (60 to 80 miles per hour).
- Always carry spark plugs, because they foul constantly.
- Carry spare light bulbs.
- Use plastic laundry bags to protect the contents of your pack from getting soaked when it pours.
- Bring a pair of sunglasses with hardened lenses for low-speed driving.
- Bring or buy abroad hooked rubber straps to keep your pack from flying around.

Special Clothing for Motorcyclists

- Since bike-riding can be cold even on a summer night, think about bringing a down-filled parka or comparably warm jacket. Note that a leather jacket and leather pants offer the best protection in case you fall.
- Buy the best rain gear available, since you will be miserable if it leaks. It should snap closed around the sleeves and pant cuffs. Rain gear should be brightly colored (yellow or orange) to glow in the dark. It can double as a windbreaker in clear weather.
- Bring heavy, comfortable boots. Combat boots work perfectly.
- Wear leather gloves to protect your hands from the cold and from the blisters you'll get as you work in the clutch and front brakes, which are always stiff on a new bike.

Hitchhiking

Hitchhiking is known as *auto-stop* in Europe. It is accepted in some countries and loathed in others. The accompanying chart will give you a good idea of how successful you should expect to be in each country. (See also pp. 188–190.)

Advantages of Hitchhiking

- Hitchhiking is as cheap as free can be. It offers total freedom—with one hitch: you've got to hitch a ride. So the only thing that can break down is you.
- Hitchhiking is also the best way to meet Europeans because it's a direct and immediate appeal for help.
- Hitchhiking is a sport, and like all sports it reveals inner qualities in its participants. It's also an art, demanding skill, intelligence, and patience.

Disadvantages of Hitchhiking

- Hitchhiking is time-consuming, tiring, and potentially dangerous—especially for women traveling alone.
- Furthermore, it doesn't always work, as hitchhikers soon discover in southern Spain. You've got to be tough, patient, and wily.

Gear for Hitchhikers

- Backpacks with metal frames distribute the weight evenly, are great for walking, have convenient zippered compartments, take a lot of abuse, don't get dirty quickly, and are harder to steal than most other packs.
- Packs made of leather and canvas are good too. They take up less space, rip less often, and never suffer from frame damage (because there is no frame to be damaged).
- Make sure the straps of the pack won't cut into your body or tear off. Check the stitching carefully.
- Bring a large poncho to cover both you and the pack in heavy rain.
- Pack a sleeping bag (down compresses the most, but comparable synthetics stay warmer when wet) and a thin foam pad.
- You'll also need a water container, a flashlight, some insect repellent, a Swiss Army knife, some soap in a plastic container, and matches.
- Carry most of your funds in traveler's checks or plan to use credit cards. Carrying cash is risky.
- You can buy gear abroad. Try Kaufman's (throughout Germany), Black's of Scotland (London), or Galleries Lafayette (Paris).

Prospects for Hitchhiking in European Countries[1]

Country	Prospects
Austria	Good
Belgium	Very good
Denmark	Excellent
France	The worst (especially in the south)
Germany	Excellent
Great Britain	Excellent
Greece	Poor
Ireland	Excellent
Italy	Good (despite hostility)
Liechtenstein	Does it matter? (Famous for stamps and about the same size)
Luxembourg	Very good
Netherlands	Very good
Norway	Tough
Portugal	Fair
Spain	Lousy
Sweden	Good
Switzerland	Good to very good

[1] This chart does not cover Eastern Europe. Traffic is light in several of these countries. As to safety and legality, it will be a few years before reports will come in. Public transportation is reasonably priced, and in these areas you'll often be asked to share for gas costs anyway.

Bicycling

The tremendous popularity of the Tour de France gives you some idea of the reverence for biking in France. Biking is highly recommended in Belgium, Denmark, Germany (the North), parts of Italy, Luxembourg, and the Netherlands. Essentially, it is most practical in relatively flat areas. It is grueling in steep areas.
- Read books on biking through Europe before going abroad.
- Make several long bike trips in the United States to see whether you really will enjoy the experience.
- Buy the best bike you can afford. Check on packing and shipping costs with the airline you'll be using. If these are too steep, buy your bike abroad.
- Remove the tire pump, the water bottle, and the seat from the frame whenever you stop to eat, rest, or sleep. Many cyclists carry

the pump in their gear to avoid being ripped off. Routinely lock the bike.

- Carry a tool kit and material for tire repairs. Reflective striping on you and the bike can help avoid accidents. Bring a flashlight since flats have a way of taking place at dusk.
- Don't overextend yourself. Until you're in shape, you should keep long-distance riding to a minimum.
- Read the section on motorcycles (see p. 65) for hints on recommended gear, including the best rain gear money can buy!
- Note that bikes are allowed on most European trains as freight for a reasonable cost.
- Bikes are available for rent at a number of railway stations. They are also available through the tourist offices in some major cities (Copenhagen and Florence, as examples). Copenhagen offered a fleet of 5,000 bikes free of charge with a deposit to cut traffic. Other cities may follow with similar programs. Write the tourist offices ahead of time to find out about current bike rental programs (see pp. 247–250).
- Note that biking is illegal on some roads. For example, roads with one-digit numbers are off limits in Hungary. Ask about local restrictions in each country. Obey them for safety reasons and to avoid stiff fines.

Lodgings

Choose a place to stay in Europe that matches your personality and pocketbook. Following is an overview of some of the fascinating places to stay in Europe and tips on making reservations whether before or during your trip.

Varieties of Lodgings

A variety of places to stay—that's what Europe has to offer. And that's part of its charm and challenge to Americans not used to such diverse choices.

- *Apartments*. The following is an agency that specializes in getting apartments in Prague. This city has a serious room shortage and inflated prices. For more information contact:

  Uniglobe Cihak Travel Agency
  6302 Cermak Road
  Berwyn, IL 60402
  Tel: (800) 426-8826

- *Bed and breakfast (B & B)*. You'll find these small family hotels and boardinghouses throughout Great Britain. You'll get a comfortable, small room and a good breakfast for a fairly low set price. You can usually get rooms without advance reservations. Look for B & B signs posted out front.
- *Boardinghouses*. Boardinghouses (*pansinyons, panzio, pensions, pensiones*) are in every country in Europe. They come in all categories, from luxurious to dismal. Generally, you rent a room without a bath. You eat in a central dining area. In some cases, you'll be expected to stay at least 3 days or so. The price you pay includes however many meals you agree to eat. Prices range from inexpensive to moderate. You normally don't need to make reservations for these accommodations.
- *Bungalows (cabanas, papas turisticas)*. Small huts or cabins are available in a number of camping areas, especially in Eastern Europe. These are extremely popular and often reserved far in advance by locals. Note that it may still be hard for foreigners to get into campsites in Bulgaria (hopefully, this is changing).
- *Castle hotels*. Many castles in France, Germany, and Great Britain have been converted into unusual hotels that vary from ultradeluxe

to quite uncomfortable. You can get information on castle hotels (*châteaux*) from both the Austrian and French National Tourist Offices (see Appendix B). A brochure is also available from Gast Im Schloss, D3526 Trendelburg 1, Germany. Lufthansa, the German airline, often stocks good brochures on castle hotels. Keep in mind that both cost and comfort vary enormously among castle accommodations (some even serve as youth hostels).

- *Cottages*. These comfortable, little homes are most commonly available in Great Britain and Italy. Contact the National Tourist Offices for information (pp. 247–250).
- *Farmhouses*. Stays on farms have become increasingly popular in recent years, especially for families. Farmhouse programs are strong in Austria, Denmark, Germany, Great Britain, Iceland, and Italy. Contact the National Tourist Offices for information (pp. 247–250).
- *Flats*. For long-term stays, for families, or for larger groups these can make good sense. They are most commonly available in London and Paris. Contact the National Tourist Offices for information (pp. 247–250).
- *Gîtes*. In France, 25,000 privately owned residences are now available for 1-week stays. Lists are posted in county halls (*préfets*). The French Experience, 370 Lexington Ave., New York, NY 10017, Tel: (212) 986-3800/986-1115 arranges for stays on a fee basis.
- *Historic inns*. Great Britain is world famous for its atmospheric inns. Some date back to medieval times. Comfort varies from inn to inn, but rates are uniformly reasonable. For a brochure and map, contact the British Tourist Authority. In Switzerland, you can find many comparable historic inns, and a booklet will be sent to you free upon request from the Swiss National Tourist Office. (See pp. 247–250 for a list of National Tourist Offices.)
- *Home exchange*. To exchange your home with a foreign person, contact:

> Vacation Exchange Club
> P.O. Box 650
> Key West, FL 33041
> Tel: (800) 638-3841

- *Home stays:* To live with foreign families for brief periods of time contact:

Home & Host International
2445 Park Avenue
Minneapolis, MN 55404
Tel: (800) 768-4388
(612) 871-0596

US Servas, Inc.
11 John Street, Room 407
New York, NY 10038
Tel: (212) 267-0252

- *Hotels.* Most tourist offices will send you booklets or pamphlets with addresses and telephone numbers of hotels throughout each country. Note that they will contain no subjective comments, just facts on cost and conveniences. Hotels with kitchens are called residences and are most common in the larger cities of Belgium, Great Britain, Italy (*residenze*), and Sweden. (See also pp. 247–250.)
- *Huts.* In many mountainous areas huts are open to foreign visitors who enjoy hiking (trekking). The most famous huts are in Norway. Charges are reasonable. Getting to these huts is often quite a challenge, but scenery can be breathtaking. For information contact the Norwegian National Tourist Office (p. 250). Mountain huts (*bouda* or *chata*) are common in Czechoslovakia as well (see p. 248).
- *Inns.* Families often run private inns (*gastehaus, gasthaus, gasthof, gosciniec, zajazd*). These inns or guesthouses are often similar to bed and breakfast or boardinghouses, although they are sometimes more formal and don't require meals to be eaten in the inn. They are available in many countries, but most famous in England (See Historic inns, above).
- *Kroer* (singular: *Kro*). These Danish country inns are often filled with the kind of atmosphere worth traveling thousands of miles to enjoy. And the food is often tops. These inns are quite expensive but offer good value. You'll find them throughout the country. For a list of some of the most interesting, contact the Danish Tourist Board (p. 248).
- *Mission hotels.* Throughout Scandinavia, mission hotels offer modest, comfortable rooms at reasonable rates—reasonable for Scandinavia, that is. The only catch: no drinking is allowed. These hotels are very popular, and you'll want to reserve a room well in advance from May through September.
- *Monasteries.* It is possible to stay in a number of monasteries throughout Europe. Women are not allowed in all, so make inquiries ahead of time. The monasteries on Cyprus do accept women for overnight stays. Donations are expected. For information contact the National Tourist Offices (pp. 247–250).
- *Motels.* For someone traveling by car these are convenient and often reasonably priced. They have become more prevalent in recent years, although not nearly as common as in the United States and Canada.
- *Paradores.* The Spanish government has supported the construction and maintenance of inns throughout Spain, some of which are starkly modern, while others are filled to the brim with native ambience. The *paradores* are located in areas of historic or cultural interest, and they offer excellent value, comfortable rooms, and

good regional cooking. Get a list from the National Tourist Office of Spain (see p. 250). Make reservations as far in advance as you can, especially during the peak season.

- *Pousadas.* These are Portugal's version of Spain's *paradores,* and very fine at that. Both countries have regulations on maximum stays, and you should make reservations as far in advance as possible. Even during the off-season, the *pousadas* and *paradores* can be packed!

- *Pubs.* That's right. Throughout Great Britain and Ireland you can find rooms in pubs. Note that these have unusual hours, so that you can be locked out of your room unless you ask about closing times in advance. Fun, good value. Don't try to reserve such rooms in advance.

- *Relais de campagne.* These country inns offer excellent atmosphere, idyllic settings, comfort, and some of the best cooking in Europe. Most of them are located in France, but others are scattered throughout Belgium, Great Britain, Italy, and Sweden. For full information, contact the French National Tourist Office. Note that they are quite expensive, especially when it comes to quality cuisine.

- *Resorts.* These are very common in seaside areas. The ones along the Baltic in Bulgaria will be better known in the future. If you plan to stay in one spot for an extended stay, these make a lot of sense. Contact the appropriate National Tourist Office for more information (pp. 247–250).

- *Romantik hotels.* A group of Austrian, German, and Swiss hotels offer family-owned-and-operated inns to travelers. Each is atmospheric, comfortable, and reliable concerning its kitchen, which usually specializes in regional cooking. Many of these inns are located off the beaten path for a true glimpse of the local culture. Prices range from moderate to expensive, but they are always reasonable. For information contact Lufthansa, the German airline, or the German National Tourist Office. You can also write directly to the central office of the group: Romantik Hotels and Restaurants, 8752 Gross-Weldheim, Germany.

- *Rooms in private homes.* Renting a room in a private home (*prywatny pokoje, szoba, zimmer frei*), can be a fascinating and relatively inexpensive experience. As you would guess, there are so many rooms available all over Europe that it's impossible to give any overall conclusion except this: they usually give you good value, and people respond to you according to your warmth and openness. Note that in Eastern Europe the rental of private rooms forms part of a black market service at present. In theory, you are supposed to register with the police each night. This may change, but be aware that many private parties skip the registration process in order to collect hard currency from foreigners without the government knowing it. Unless you fully understand and are close to public transportation, rent rooms as close to the heart of the city as possible. Note that many travel agencies (especially in Eastern Europe) handle private room accommodations. Some local tourist offices in smaller towns also are helpful in this regard.

- *Rorbu.* Nothing more than fishing shanties, open to foreigners on the coast of Norway throughout the summer season. Cost varies from nothing to next-to-nothing. For the adventuresome. For information, contact the Norwegian National Tourist Office.
- *Spas.* Europe is famous for these. Germany has some of the finest. But Bulgaria and Hungary are also renowned for their spas. They are extremely popular with local residents during the summer, and reservations must be made far in advance for most. Contact the appropriate National Tourist Office for additional information and lists of spas (pp. 247–250).
- *Student hotels.* These are not the same thing as youth hostels. If you're a student or living on a student's budget, get in touch with the CIEE (see p. 9) for details on an assortment of student hotels and dorms.
- *Traditional settlements.* Greece has developed a number of complexes in scenic locations to take advantage of the local culture and natural setting in certain areas. For more information on these contact the Greek National Tourist Organization (p. 248).
- *Villas and apartments.* Many homes, villas, and apartments are available for rental in Europe. Contact tourist offices abroad or the following organizations for information:

At Home Abroad, Inc.
405 East 56th Street, #6H
New York, NY 10022
Tel: (212) 421-9165

Chez Vous
220 Redwood Highway,
    Suite 129
Mill Valley, CA 94941
Tel: (415) 331-2535

Hideaways International
P.O. Box 4433
767 Islington Street
Portsmouth, NH 03802
Tel: (800) 843-4433
(603) 430-4433

In The English Manner
515 South Figueroa Street,
    Suite 1000
Los Angeles, CA 90071
Tel: (800) 422-0799

LaCure
11661 San Vicente Boulevard,
Suite 1010
Los Angeles, CA 90049
Tel: (800) 387-2726

Rent A Vacation Everywhere, Inc.
(R.A.V.E.)
383 Park Avenue
Rochester, NY 14607
Tel: (716) 256-0760

Swiss Touring USA
5537 North Hollywood Avenue
Milwaukee, WI 53217
Tel: (414) 963-2010

Villas International, Ltd.
605 Market Street, Suite 510
San Francisco, CA 94105
Tel: (800) 221-2260

Vacation Exchange Club
P.O. Box 650
Key West, FL 33041
Tel: (800) 638-3841

- *Xenia*. These comfortable government-subsidized hotels are located throughout Greece. For information on these fine hotels, contact the Greek National Tourist Organization (see p. 248).
- *Youth hostels*. Hosteling—simple, modest, dormitory-style living—is one of the least expensive ways to get by in Europe. See Chapter 12 for tips on hosteling and where to write for information.
- *YMCAs and YWCAs*. The Ys in Europe are much better than their counterparts in the United States, and they give you very good value for your travel dollars. For information, call any local branch or contact:

YMCA
101 North Wacker Drive
Chicago, IL 60606
Tel: (312) 977-0031

YWCA
726 Broadway
New York, NY 10003
Tel: (212) 614-2700

Room Reservations

Reservations are not necessarily essential for enjoyable travel, but they certainly can save you a lot of time and hassle, especially if you're on a short trip. A poorly made reservation may be worse than none at all, however. Here are some tips on doing it right.

When Reserving a Room Makes Sense

- Have a reservation for the first night abroad. Since you'll be exhausted when you arrive in Europe, you won't want to look for a room.
- Make reservations if you want rooms of great charm or value, especially during the peak season.
- If you're on a short trip with little time to waste, have reservations for every night abroad. You can't afford the hassle or the time involved in looking for rooms once you're there.

Problems with Reservations

- You may have to pay a fee for room reservations or else foot the cost of cables and phone calls.
- You're usually renting sight-unseen. Unless you have great confidence in your source, you might be disappointed.
- You'll end up paying for higher-priced rooms or paying the highest price for a room. Reservations take away all your bargaining power and make it very difficult for you to shift from one room to another.
- Reservations tie you down. If you're on a short trip, this will make no difference, but when a trip stretches to 3 weeks or longer, a reservation schedule can begin to feel like an ill-fitting shoe on a 10-mile hike.

Avoiding Getting Bumped by Hotels

Many hotels routinely overbook by 10 to 15 percent. Unless you have a confirmation in writing, you could be one of those bumped.

- Make reservations as far in advance as possible. Note that some hotels in major cities fill up six to nine months in advance.
- Get your reservation confirmed in writing. If you know that you'll be arriving at a hotel after 6:00 P.M., make sure that the hotel knows this. And have this late arrival time noted on your room confirmation slip.
- Pay a substantial deposit on the room. With your money in the bank, few hotels will worry about your showing up.
- If you make reservations through a travel agent, choose one with clout—preferably one with many offices abroad, so that you will have someone to call if things go awry.
- If you get delayed unexpectedly, notify the hotel. Few hotels will rent your room if you have contacted them.

Travel Agents' Reservations

- Most agents charge nothing at all for making room reservations, unless doing so involves a special service, such as phoning or cabling (their commission is paid by the hotel). They can often get better rates than individuals.
- Ask the agent whether you'll be charged for cables or phone calls—or for anything, for that matter! Some agencies are beginning to charge for services.
- If the agent insists that there is no charge at all, ask whether a surcharge will be added to your hotel bill abroad.
- If the agent says that no such commission need be paid, ask for a

letter typed on the agency stationery stating this in straightforward terms. If a hotel in Europe then tries to stick you with a surcharge, produce the letter and refuse to pay it.

Airline Reservation Services

- With enough advance notice, airlines will gladly reserve a room for you at any destination or stopover point, both of which are stated clearly on your ticket. They charge no fee for this service.

Credit Card Reservations

- Note that with some credit cards you can get confirmed room reservations in major hotels throughout Europe. Call major credit card companies for current information on making confirmed room reservations.

Making Your Own Reservations

- Larger hotel chains with many branches abroad have toll-free (800) numbers listed in the phone book. All you have to do is dial the number and make a reservation. Be specific about dates and ask them to send you some sort of confirmation in writing. Also ask for a reservation or confirmation number.
- You can write directly to hotels listed in guidebooks. If you use business stationery, request information on business discounts (up to 30 percent).
- Send your letter by airmail, and ask the hotel to reply by airmail. Include international reply coupons (available in main post offices) to cover the cost of the hotel's airmail reply.
- Most hotels will reply with a request for a deposit to show good faith. An international money order will do the trick. Sometimes just a check is good enough.
- Another method which is expensive but effective: Call the foreign hotel during local business hours. Someone at the front desk may be able to speak English. Talk very slowly and clearly. Repeat the dates of your intended stay several times. Ask for written confirmation. Get the name of the person with whom you are talking. Follow up with a deposit and confirmation of your own.
- If cost is your major concern, ask what discounts are available. Rates often vary greatly by room. Rates often drop on weekends, and rates are usually negotiable for stays 3 days or longer. Rates should be the lowest during off-season months, unless the city is hosting a convention or special celebration.

Discounts through Travel Clubs

Recently a number of fee-based clubs have been formed to reduce the overall costs of travel. Many of these offer cards or coupons to reduce hotel costs by 50 percent. Most properties are in the expensive to very expensive range, so that savings are substantial. Fees vary by club. If you want to stay in upper-bracket hotels, these cards make sense. Find out the number and location of hotels in making your choice of club or clubs. Once a member, make reservations as far in advance as possible. Note that in peak holiday periods they may be of little value.

Concierge International
1050 Yuma Street
Denver, CO 80204
Tel: (800) 346-1022
(813) 286-8798

Entertainment Publications
(HalfPrice Europe)
P.O. Box 1014
Trumbull, CT 06611
Tel: (800) 285-5525

INFINET Travel Club
186 Alewife Brook Parkway
P.O. Box 1033
Cambridge, MA 02140
Tel: (800) 966-2582
(617) 661-8900

International Travel Card
6001 North Clark Street
Chicago, IL 60660
Tel: (800) 342-0558
(312) 465-8891

Packing

What should I take? How should I pack it? These are two of travelers' most common questions. Read this chapter to find the answers.

Traveling Light

Traveling light means less hassle and less frustration. But the advantages don't stop there.

Advantages of Traveling Light

- If you travel light, you'll save money on porter or extra taxi charges. You can handle your luggage yourself—easily.
- Traveling without big bags allows you to take inexpensive public transportation. You can hop on buses, trams, and subways to avoid stiff taxi fares.
- If you travel light, you can bargain with clerks in hotels over hotel rates. With several bulky bags you're stuck, no matter what the rates are. With just one piece of luggage you can move on.
- You never miss connections waiting for bags to be spewed out of the belly of a 747. You're the first through customs, the first out—saving hours of frustrating waits in baggage claim areas.
- You never lose anything. You've got your luggage with you, and you're not dependent on anyone else.
- All of this adds up to less stress, less worry, and a sense of freedom—you will feel much happier.

How to Travel Light

- Do it like the pros—flight attendants, travel writers, experienced businesspeople, correspondents—and bring only one piece of hand luggage or a backpack. If you can't carry it on a plane, it's too large. If you can't carry it for a mile without setting it down, it's too heavy.
- It's natural for you to feel somewhat skeptical about traveling with only one piece of carry-on luggage. You are probably wondering if you can really get by with only a few clothes, and if you'll be embarrassed by wearing the same outfits over and over, and whether you can get by in formal places with less-than-formal clothes, and what you will do about climate changes, and what happens if something gets stained.

- If you choose your clothes wisely, you'll have no problem at all. In fact, others will be envious of your freedom and will think you were smart to travel light. As long as you're clean and comfortably dressed, you'll exude an aura of contentment and confidence. Europeans judge you more by this attitude than by your clothes! In fact, Europeans themselves often have limited wardrobes (due to prohibitive prices) and wear the same things over and over.
- Leave electrical items at home. They're heavy, bulky, and can be damaged by varying voltage.
- Pack only items you need to survive—the essentials. I met one person who considered a toothbrush the only item essential for travel!
- Make each item serve as many purposes as possible. A two-piece bathing suit can pass as underwear. Shampoo can wash not only hair, but also the body—think versatility.
- Go for comfort first, style last. The two need not be mutually exclusive.
- Make sure all clothes are light, easy to wash, and quick drying. Test them before you leave. Pick up heavier items for special needs abroad.
- While traveling, wear your heaviest clothes whenever possible.

Use Light Luggage

- Travel with one small carry-on bag or backpack. Either should be able to fit under the seat of a plane or in the overhead bin.
- Try a nylon, canvas, or vinyl bag or a backpack, which will be relatively inexpensive, feather light, and soft-sided—avoid frames of any kind unless you are planning on hitchhiking (see p. 67). You want a bag that is light, pliable, and durable.
- Get a bag with a shoulder strap to make carrying easier. It should also have some small outer compartments for odds and ends, from toilet articles to an umbrella.

Garment Bags

If, no matter how hard you try, you can't get the things you need into one small bag, carry a garment bag onto the plane and hang it in one of the coat compartments.

- You'll pay half the price for the same bag if you buy it in a discount outlet.
- If you're industrious, you can make your own garment bag at home. Patterns appear in magazines and can be found in many fabric shops.

- The bag should have some outer pockets for odds and ends. These should have snap or zipper closings.
- It's much easier to carry the bag if it has a shoulder strap. Most do.
- Airlines sometimes discourage the use of garment bags by stuffing them in compartments in the rear of the plane. As a result, you have to wait for all the passengers to disembark before getting your bag.

When You Can't Travel Light

- Never carry one huge bag. Split the contents into two lighter bags for easier handling.
- Think about using a luggage roller. They stick in cracks, but they make lugging baggage much easier, except on stairs.
- Think about taking a backpack. If you've ever worn one, you know how much easier it is than carrying a suitcase.
- Store your bags in lockers at airports and train stations whenever possible. You'll be free to sightsee without dragging bags around with you.
- Remember that hotels will store bags well past checkout time if your flight or train leaves late at night.
- Don't overpack! You can't collect insurance on baggage damages if your bags are really stuffed.

Dress in Europe

- Dress is casual in most parts of Europe. No one expects you to dress up, except in fancier restaurants, hotels, and night spots.
- Formal dress, black tie or blue suits and comparable dress for women, is extremely rare—suited to business or diplomatic occasions, a few casinos, and "dress-up" nights at deluxe restaurants.
- Generally, even in stuffy places, you can get by with a sports coat and tie and equivalent dress for women. The average tourist can slide by with simple, casual clothes—nothing stylish at all.

Dressing for the Weather

- Worry more about the weather than how you'll look. Try to match your clothes to the altitude (high altitudes are much cooler), the season (Southern Europe sizzles in the summer), and the place (who needs long pants on a beach?).
- The climate chart (Appendix A) tells you the average temperature and rainfall in many areas. Match your clothes to the month you'll be traveling.

Tips for Women

- Keep makeup extremely simple while traveling.
- Leave your valuable jewelry at home. You can buy inexpensive silver- and gold-imitation jewelry in countless stores and street stands. Only experts can tell it from the real thing.
- Remember that strong perfumes and cosmetics can make you sun-sensitive. So can some antibiotics (see p. 229).
- Samples of beauty products are light, small, and easy to carry. Collect them for short trips.
- A denim skirt is more comfortable than jeans. It has all the advantages and more—it doesn't stain easily, doesn't show wrinkles, and it breathes.
- Carry a flat, large purse for all your odds and ends—a folding umbrella, a camera (best kept out of sight), a snack—you name it. Keep your makeup case and your money in a wallet or change purse. These fit nicely into the large purse.
- Keep your shoes comfortable. Forget style. Shoes can be very casual. Many young and old travelers wear nothing but tennis shoes for the whole trip. Visiting ruins, climbing steep stairs, walking on cobblestone streets, strolling along a beach—these are activities that require comfortable, casual shoes. Fashionable shoes are only necessary if you plan to go to nightclubs and elegant restaurants. If necessary, buy a pair in Europe, famous for its fine shoes.

Basics of Packing

Use the rolling technique to keep clothes wrinkle-free and accessible in a small bag.
- Lay slacks or pants out on a flat surface (such as a bed) with the leg seams together. These will serve as a base.
- Fold such things as a T-shirt, sweater, or turtleneck in half lengthwise, with sleeves together. Lay these out evenly on both the top and bottom portion of the slacks.
- Roll the clothes into a loose ball, working from the pants legs up, and slip the ball into a plastic bag.
- Clothes in a plastic bag slip in and out of luggage very easily. The plastic also protects them from dust, dirt, and any liquids that might spill accidentally.
- You just unroll the ball to get to whatever item you need later on.
- Slide each shirt, jacket, or skirt in a separate plastic bag. Lay the clothes flat or folded once into the suitcase. The film of air retained

between the plastic and clothes will keep them wrinkle free. Jackets and coats can be kept on hangers so that you can whip them out of the suitcase in their plastic wrap and hang them immediately in a closet. The plastic bags used by average dry-cleaning establishments are just fine.
- Remember to leave some extra space for the things you may buy while on your trip.

Packing Garment Bags

- Hang a number of clothes on no more than two hangers. If you use too many hangers, the bag will become bulky and hard to handle.
- Light plastic hangers with rounded corners work best. They don't rust or jab you with pointed ends, and they help keep clothes in their original shape.
- You can stuff an incredible number of small items into the bottom of a garment bag. Don't do it. If you do you'll be carrying around a heavy bag!

Packing Toiletries

- Put all liquids in plastic bottles. Place each bottle in a separate, locking plastic bag so that your luggage won't get soaked if it leaks.
- To prevent leaking: gently squeeze the bottle as you put on the top to create suction. Seal the top with tape for full protection (just for plane flights).
- As you use your toothpaste and other creams in tubes, roll tubes up tightly so that they will take up less space. If you'll be traveling extensively, carry two small tubes of such products instead of one large one.
- Keep all toiletries in one place, like in a makeup case, so that you can get to them easily at any time.

Protecting and Carrying Valuables

The best way to protect and carry valuables such as a passport, plane tickets, traveler's checks, and money is to make or buy a secret pocket that slides under your clothes against your hip. It is attached by loops directly to your belt (see p. 137).

Marking Your Bags

- If you have to check your bags, strap them closed. Mark each with bright tape, a decal, or a bumper sticker. This will save you time identifying them at the baggage carousel.

Companies Specializing in Travel Items

You can buy travel odds and ends from the following companies, which specialize in such merchandise:

Pacific Traveler's Supply
529 State Street
Santa Barbara, CA 93101
Tel: (805) 963-4438

Travel Mini Pack
P.O. Box 571
Stony Point, NY 10980
Tel: (914) 429-8281

Traveler's Checklist
335 Cornwall Bridge Road
Sharon, CT 06069
Tel: (203) 364-0144

TravLTips Mart, Ltd.
163-07 Depot Road
Flushing, NY 11358
Tel: (718) 939-2400

Travelers' Checklist

A trip should start off relaxed, so pack well in advance of your departure. If you do, you will have a chance to check and recheck what's packed and to remember things you've overlooked.

Use this checklist to help you pack. It's an exhaustive list—choose those things that will be essential to your enjoyment of a European trip.

☐ *Acidophilus tablets* (see p. 222).
☐ *Adaptor.* Since currents vary from country to country, you'll need an adaptor to use with electrical items. My recommendation: do without all electrical items completely. If you can't, get information and adaptors from the Franzus Company, P.O. Box 142, Murtha Industrial Park, Beacon Falls, CT 06403, Tel: (203) 723-6664.
☐ *Address book.* Don't leave home without a small, light, thin address book to fill with the names of new acquaintances and to refer to if you write home. Absolutely invaluable!
☐ *Alarm clock.* Take one only if you have important meetings abroad and don't want to rely on hotel wakeup services (which is smart). You'll find tiny travel alarm clocks on the market. Some watches also have built-in alarms.
☐ *Alcohol.* If you drink, take a quart of your favorite brand into Scandinavia, where prices are exorbitant. Don't bother when going to other areas, unless you have a penchant for bourbon (a rarity abroad) or if you're taking a cruise and want to save money on alcohol.

- ☐ *Antacid*. Everyone should carry a few tablets. If you've got chronic problems, take all you could possibly need.
- ☐ *Antibiotic ointment*. Get free samples from your doctor.
- ☐ *Aspirin*. A must. Take along one of the small plastic or metal boxes that contains at least a dozen tablets. Or put some into a small, easy-to-carry pillbox.
- ☐ *Bag* (see Fish-net shopping bag).
- ☐ *Band-Aids*. Bring a few. They're light and take up little space.
- ☐ *Bathing suit*. Bathing suits can double for underwear if they're easy to wash, quick drying, light, and comfortable. Fifteen minutes in the sun is all it takes to dry out a suit after swimming or washing. If you're skeptical, test the idea before you start a trip. Pick suits that don't bind or have tight elastic belts.
- ☐ *Bathrobe*. Not essential and easily replaced by an overcoat or trench coat. Leave it at home!
- ☐ *Belt*. Men should bring one reversible or money belt. Women can easily replace belts with scarves, which are far more versatile and lightweight.
- ☐ *Birth certificate*. Essential for long-term study abroad. It must be translated into the foreign language. A notarized copy will be helpful if you lose your passport.
- ☐ *Birth control pills*. Bring extra, just in case you stay longer than you expect.
- ☐ *Black tie*. Only for the casino crowd.
- ☐ *Blazer*. A great idea. It should be made of tightly woven material, stain and wrinkle resistant, and dark colored. Spray it with water repellent to prevent stains.
- ☐ *Blouse*. Take two at most—one light colored, one dark (or print). They should be lightweight and easy to wash.
- ☐ *Boots*. Bring either one pair of boots or one pair of shoes, but not both. They should be broken in and very comfortable. You can always buy beautiful boots and shoes abroad, if you run into a special occasion demanding elegant footwear!
- ☐ *Bottle opener*. One of the most useful and easy-to-forget items! (See Knife.)
- ☐ *Bra*. Bring no more than two. Substitute a bathing suit top if possible.
- ☐ *Bunji cords* (see Rubber baggage tie-down straps).
- ☐ *Business cards*. Saves time. Good leverage for discounts.
- ☐ *Calamine lotion*. Great for relieving the itching of insect bites and bee stings, but rarely needed.
- ☐ *Calculator*. A thin, ultralight model for currency exchange and bargaining.

- ☐ *Camera, film, and spare battery.* Great to have, but a hassle. Bring only if you're serious.
- ☐ *Camping carnet (the camper's "passport").* Essential for campers (see p. 128).
- ☐ *Cane.* Collapsible.
- ☐ *Can opener.* Absolutely essential, if you'll be shopping in grocery stores for picnics. Some Swiss Army knives come with these. Get a good one.
- ☐ *Cards, playing.* Easy to forget, but a wonderful way to while away the hours on planes and trains.
- ☐ *Chapstick.* Essential for outdoor types.
- ☐ *Coats.* Bring one only. (See Raincoat, Trench coat, Overcoat, and Poncho.)
- ☐ *Collapsible cups.* Lightweight, easy to use.
- ☐ *Comb.* Essential.
- ☐ *Compass.* Essential for trekking and hiking. Watches are now made with removable compasses.
- ☐ *Corkscrew.* Get a Swiss Army knife with one of these on it.
- ☐ *Credit cards.* Increasingly helpful, with many travel advantages.
- ☐ *Curling iron.* Can you get by without one? If not, make sure it's the lightweight, flat, plastic kind. (See Adaptor.)
- ☐ *Currency.* Bring $100 in $1 bills to avoid the currency exchange rip-off. For extensive travel in Eastern Europe bring $300 in small bills.
- ☐ *Decongestant.* Prone to earaches on planes? Take a decongestant before flying.
- ☐ *Dental floss.* Easy to forget. An unusual use: it cuts through cheese easily, making perfect thin strips for a picnic! It can also replace thread (very strong, durable).
- ☐ *Deodorant.* Take a small stick—not an aerosol can (they can explode on planes).
- ☐ *Desenex (or Micatin).* Bring one small tube for athlete's foot.
- ☐ *Dinner jacket.* Hardly a necessity for most travelers. A dark sports coat is usually acceptable attire even in stuffy places.
- ☐ *Dress.* Take one at most. It should be wrinkle resistant, easy to wash, and easy to dress up or down. Dresses of T-shirt material are excellent. If the dress gets clingy on the trip, hang it in the bathroom while you take a shower or bath. The steam will be absorbed to prevent static electricity.
- ☐ *Dress shirt.* Rarely needed and easily replaced with a nice white shirt.
- ☐ *Drugs.* Take as many prescription drugs as you'll need for the entire length of the trip, plus enough for a week or two to spare.

Never remove drugs from the original containers. And be sure to learn their generic names in case you lose them. Carry a doctor's prescription for additional medication just in case you do lose any. Note that this may not be honored abroad. You may have to see a local physician.

☐ *Ear plugs.* If you're sensitive to noise, these are great on planes and in noisy hotels. Get the easy-to-mold kind, like Flents. I'd suggest that all travelers carry ear plugs, just in case.

☐ *Electric razor.* No, don't take one. It's nothing but a hassle. If you have to, try the battery-operated models. Small, light travel kits consisting of a compact safety razor and blades make a lot more sense.

☐ *Eurailpass, Youthrailpass.* It's safest and easiest to buy them in the United States before you leave (see p. 55).

☐ *Evening bag.* Not necessary, but nice at times. Maybe you should buy one abroad.

☐ *First-aid kit.* Required for auto travel abroad (see p. 60).

☐ *Fish-net shopping bag or tote bag.* Very smart to have. Light, compact, useful. Highly recommended.

☐ *Flashlight.* All bikers, campers, motorists, and travelers to Eastern Europe, Greece, Ireland, and Portugal should have one. Bring spare batteries.

☐ *Garters.* Only if you can't do without.

☐ *Girdle.* Likewise.

☐ *Glasses.* One spare pair of both sunglasses and prescription glasses or contact lenses.

☐ *Gloves.* Only when necessary, as for off-season travel and when traveling by motorcycle.

☐ *Hairbrush.* Essential.

☐ *Hair dryer.* Another gadget requiring an adaptor. People got by without them for centuries. Can't you? (See Adaptor.)

☐ *Hair conditioner.* If you use it, bring it with you, because it's hard to find in Europe. Make sure it's in a plastic container, tightly sealed, and placed in a plastic bag. Or carry travel packets given away as samples or as bonuses in hotels.

☐ *Hair spray.* Get by without it, if possible. Take a small plastic container with pump, if not.

☐ *Hangers.* Plastic or inflatable hangers work great. Many hotels do not provide them or have the kind that cannot be moved around—useless for washing clothes.

☐ *Hankies.* Use disposable tissues instead. Buy some as necessary in Europe.

☐ *Hat.* Highly recommended is a cloth or khaki fisherman-style hat, deep enough to stay on your head in heavy winds, with a wide brim to protect you from rain or sun. Spray it with water repellent. It may be frumpy looking, but it will do the job!

☐ *Health certificate.* Needed only for extended foreign study. It must be translated into the foreign language.

☐ *Heater, immersible.* A very clever gadget that heats up water quickly. Necessary only for long-term travel. You can usually get water hot enough for tea or hot chocolate by letting the faucet run. (See Adaptor.)

☐ *Helmet.* Required of motorcyclists, who will get fined for dis-obeying the law if they don't wear them. Get a helmet with a bubble to protect your face from rain, sleet, and bugs. Helmets are recommended for bicycle touring as well.

☐ *Hostel card.* All hostelers should have one (see p. 126).

☐ *Imodium.* Excellent for diarrhea. Better for long-term use than Lomotil (see below).

☐ *Insect repellent.* Only necessary for campers and ardent bathers. Get the strongest stuff available, in small plastic containers.

☐ *International driver's license.* Don't leave home without one if you intend to drive in Europe (see p. 7).

☐ *International student identification card.* Every student should take one along (see p. 8).

☐ *Iron.* Don't bring one. Instead, take clothes that are wrinkle resistant or wrinkle-proof.

☐ *Jacket.* Fine for casual travel, but don't bring one if you're taking an overcoat.

☐ *Jeans.* Accepted almost everywhere, even in sophisticated places. Europe has gone casual, imitating the millions of youth-ful American vagabonds. Simple is best, and jeans typify the trend. Jeans make excellent ski pants if you spray them with water repellent.

☐ *Jewelry.* Leave it at home. Or wear simple, all-purpose jewelry that you'll never take off. Scarves are a much better and more versatile way to add variety to your wardrobe.

☐ *Knapsack.* One of the smartest ways of carrying weight, if you can't force yourself to travel light. Also a very good item for trekking. Only in the more expensive hotels would knapsacks be frowned upon. Frankly, do you care?

☐ *Knife.* Essential. Get a good Swiss Army knife with a bottle opener, can opener, corkscrew, scissors, and tweezers. Because of recent airline restrictions, you may have to buy one abroad if you travel light (knives are sometimes not allowed in carry-on luggage).

☐ *Laces.* Change the laces on your shoes or boots before going to Europe. This way you won't have to take along a spare set.

- [ ] *Laundry soap.* Get a few travel packets.
- [ ] *Lighter.* Take one if needed. Or take several. Lighters make great gifts, especially in Eastern Europe and Portugal.
- [ ] *Lomotil.* A very strong medicine that works wonders for diarrhea and requires a prescription from your doctor. Get some and bring it!
- [ ] *Magic marker.* Ideal for making signs if you'll be hitchhiking. It should be permanent ink, which won't run in the rain.
- [ ] *Maps.* Get the best available, in a light and easy-to-handle form. Free maps are sent out by tourist offices. If you're a member of travel or auto clubs, they'll often provide maps free of charge. Highly detailed maps are available in bookstores abroad.
- [ ] *Mirror.* A tiny one.
- [ ] *Money clip.* Not necessary and a come-on to crooks.
- [ ] *Moleskin.* Dr. Scholl's adhesive felt—better for blisters than Band-Aids.
- [ ] *Nail clippers.* Easy to carry and worth bringing.
- [ ] *Nail file.* The same.
- [ ] *Nail polish and remover.* Can you get by without it? If not, put polish in a plastic bag. It's simply disastrous when polish leaks on your clothes. Note that remover comes in tiny travel packets—easy to use and carry.
- [ ] *Nasal spray.* Great for hay fever victims. Also good if you're prone to earaches on planes.
- [ ] *Needle and thread.* Bring one needle and a little thread (off the spool). If you have trouble threading the needle, dip the thread in nail polish. To shield the point during your trip, poke the needle into half a dozen twist ties.
- [ ] *Nightgown.* Almost all women travelers replace a nightgown with a T-shirt.
- [ ] *Nylons.* Bring no more than two pairs of nylons or knee-highs per travel week. If nylons get baggy, just dip your hands in warm water and rub them from the ankles up. To stop a run: use a dab of nail polish. In desperation: if the opposite legs of two pairs of panty hose have been damaged, cut them off. Then wear both as if they were one pair.
- [ ] *Overcoat.* If you take an overcoat, get one made of tightly woven material that doesn't pick up lint, doesn't stain easily, and doesn't wrinkle. Take one coat that best matches your style of travel. Spray the coat with water repellent so that it can double as a raincoat; it can also be used as a bathrobe when you trip down the hall to take a bath. It makes a good blanket in a freezing train compartment: wrap it loosely around yourself like a straitjacket to trap your body heat and keep you warm. You may

want to have a button-down flap or zipper sewn on the inside pocket. This will protect anything placed there from pickpockets and keep things from falling out accidentally. You may also want to sew in extra pockets—a very simple technique to increase what you can carry on your body.

☐ *Pajamas*. Totally unnecessary. It's this kind of thing that's got to go if you're going to travel light.

☐ *Panties*. You can substitute a bathing suit for one pair. Since they're so light, you can bring several pairs—all nylon for fast drying.

☐ *Pants*. Don't carry more than two pairs, one of which should be jeans. The other pair should be easy to wash and dark-colored to hide stains.

☐ *Paper clips*. Bring a few. If you have a visa, place a clip on that page of your passport to make it easy to find.

☐ *Passport*. If you forget this, forget the trip. Carry your passport with you at all times and guard it with everything but your life! You'll need it when crossing national borders, exchanging currency, cashing traveler's checks, picking up mail at *poste restante* (General Delivery) or at American Express, signing in at the hotel, and whenever the police ask to see it. If you're involved in a traffic accident abroad and are not carrying your passport, you may end up in the clink.

☐ *Passport wallet*. A good way to carry a passport, currency, credit cards, papers, etc.

☐ *Pen*. One of the most useful items abroad. Bring one or two.

☐ *Petroleum jelly*. Excellent for outdoor types. Special use: cover ticks with it, and they will let go of your skin to get oxygen. This avoids having to pull on them and possibly contaminating your body with disease organisms (see sections on encephalitis, p. 224, and Lyme disease, p. 227).

☐ *Photos*. Photo booth photos can be used in a number of ways— for an international driver's license, for study abroad (identification papers), ski-lift passes, etc. It's a good idea to carry a few extras.

☐ *Plastic bags*. Bring along bags that lock shut and are durable. Possible uses: to hold bottles containing liquids, to carry soiled or damp clothes (such as a swimsuit), to protect clothes from the rain (as in backpacking), to sit on at picnics or spectator sports, to hold food while in a car (plastic keeps banana and cheese odors contained).

☐ *Plastic flask*. A gem, to be filled with water, alcohol, fruit juice, or whatever. Great for long plane rides when you don't want to rely on the whim of a flight attendant, and especially good for car and train travel. Also a good way to avoid the high liquor prices in hotels. Don't leave home without one or two flasks! You may prefer metal to plastic. Metal stands up to abuse and doesn't absorb odors.

☐ *Poncho*. Although this is a good replacement for an overcoat, the latter will prove more versatile, except for hitchhikers.

☐ *Purse*. Don't be timid! Carry a huge purse with room to spare. Forget about style. It should have tight-fitting clasps to prevent spills and thwart thieves. Within a larger purse you can put smaller cosmetic cases for odds and ends. These keep things from getting jumbled together in one large mess.

☐ *Radio*. Leave it at home. If that's not possible, bring a portable radio/cassette player and a few spare batteries. Great for plane trips and listening to foreign music.

☐ *Raincoat*. Replace this with a trench coat or overcoat, both of which can be sprayed with water repellent.

☐ *Rain gear*. Essential for backpackers, bikers, hitchhikers, and motorcyclists. Get the best money can buy with rugged seams, snap-tight cuffs, and a durable hood.

☐ *Razor*. Take one with a few extra blades. Minuscule travel kits are on the market.

☐ *Rollers*. Can you make it without them? Can you change your hairstyle to make them unnecessary? If your hair gets a little messy, pull it up or back or cover it with a scarf. If you do bring rollers, here's a tip for a quick set: roll dry hair, cover with damp towel for five minutes, remove it, and let hair dry. You can get free or inexpensive washes and sets in many foreign beauty schools. Ask the concierge to look them up in the foreign telephone book.

☐ *Rubber baggage tie-down straps*. The best way to hold gear on a motorcycle.

☐ *Rubber bands*. Place around wallet to thwart pickpockets. Use to hold bills after exchanging money.

☐ *Rubber or nylon braided clothesline*. Inexpensive, light, and useful. Great for hanging up wet clothes in limited spaces. Never let foreign room attendants see them, however, or they'll take them from you. Technically, you're not supposed to do laundry in hotel rooms (but everyone does).

☐ *Safety pins*. Bring a few. Use them to keep your pockets closed to protect your wallet.

☐ *Sandals*. Buy an inexpensive pair abroad if needed. Tennis shoes are much more versatile.

☐ *Sanitary products*. Take tampons and a few minipads. These are often available in Western pharmacies, but are not easy to find in Eastern Europe. When they are available there, they are of very poor quality.

☐ *Scarves.* Just like gold to women travelers, because they're stylish, lightweight, compact, and versatile (they can be used as belts, skirts, and even shawls). Scarves replace jewelry, transforming one outfit into many.

☐ *School transcript.* Students who wish to study abroad must have a school transcript with a seal imprinted on it. It must be translated into the foreign language.

☐ *Scissors.* The small travel scissors prove useful, but are not indispensable. Better to bring a Swiss Army knife that includes scissors.

☐ *Seeds.* You may think this item's for the birds, but packaged flower or vegetable seeds make a great gift, a wonderful way to say thanks to a foreign host. Since they're lightweight and easy to carry, think about bringing a number of packets, especially into Eastern Europe.

☐ *Shampoo.* Bring as little as you can get by with in a plastic container. Little packets from beauty shops and hotels are ideal for travel.

☐ *Shirt.* Two at most. They should be easy to wash and dry. Dark colors are best.

☐ *Shoes (men).* Take one pair of your most comfortable walking shoes. Don't bring shoes that need polishing. You don't want to worry constantly about how they look, and you want to avoid the hassle of having shoeshine boys tagging along behind you. You can replace shoes with boots, but don't take both. Make sure they're comfortable.

☐ *Shoes (women).* They should be comfortable and durable. Do not worry about how they look. When you travel, you can overlook style. If you need an elegant pair of shoes for a special occasion, buy a pair in Europe. Do not wear high heels. Much of the enjoyment of travel comes from walking ancient streets and visiting hard-to-reach sights. High, thin heels are forbidden in many museums and castles, because they damage the floors!

☐ *Shoe polish.* If you follow the advice under Shoes, shoe polish is an unnecessary item.

☐ *Shorts.* Replace with a bathing suit in resort areas. Elsewhere, put on pants, skirt, or dress. In Europe, shorts are for tennis courts only.

☐ *Shower cap.* If needed, get the light plastic kind found in hotel rooms. It scrunches down to nothing. On the other hand, you can wrap your head in a towel like a turban and do without a cap.

☐ *Ski jacket.* A good replacement for an overcoat if you'll be hitchhiking, skiing, or cycling. Make sure it's down-filled or made with top-quality down substitute (like Polargard).

☐ *Skirt.* Bring one at the most. It must be easy to wash, dark colored to hide stains, and wrinkle-resistant.

☐ *Slacks.* You need no more than one pair. Some come with elastic—very useful for fluctuating weight!

☐ *Sleeping bag.* If you'll be camping out, get the best and most compact you can afford. A bulky item that should be carried only if necessary.

☐ *Sleeping pills.* Get a few from your doctor to help you with jet lag.

☐ *Sleeping sheet.* Required in hostels. You can make or buy one (see p. 126).

☐ *Slippers.* Unnecessary. If you disagree, get the fabric kind that fold into a tiny package.

☐ *Slip.* No more than one.

☐ *Soap.* Take small, individually wrapped bars—the kind you find in hotels. Tuck them into a plastic locking bag. Some hotels offer soap, some don't. Liquid soap may be more manageable than bars and can be found in plastic containers. In a pinch, use shampoo or shaving cream for soap: both work well. Empty film containers with rubber tops make excellent containers for powdered soap and detergent.

☐ *Socks.* One pair to wear and one for a spare—of synthetic material. Both wool and cotton hold up well, but are difficult to wash and take a long time to dry. Many hotels do not have stoppers in the sink. A sock works well as a replacement. To wash socks quickly, put them on your hands like surgeon's gloves and scrub them with a bar of soap.

☐ *Spare keys.* One for the house. For car purchased or rented abroad, place spare keys in a small magnetic box that can be hidden anywhere on the car.

☐ *Sports coat.* Only necessary if you plan to dress up occasionally—that is, if you'll be staying in nicer hotels and going to fancier restaurants. Take one that's lightweight, but not a wash-and-wear jacket, which will end up looking like a used handkerchief after two days. Tweed is one of the better materials, because it's tough and rarely looks like it needs cleaning, even if it really does. Corduroys are OK. So are some double knits.

Choose a dark color to hide stains. Spray the coat with water repellent. You'll get rained on for sure, and the repellent will fend off dirt as well.

The inside pocket should have a button-down flap or a zipper to lock in its contents. You can add this yourself at home or have it done inexpensively at a dry cleaner that specializes in simple garment repairs and alterations. If you forget to have this done, use a safety pin to fasten the top of the pocket.

☐ *Spot remover*. This should be unnecessary if you travel with easy-to-wash clothes. But if you must, Goddard's is one of the best.

☐ *Stamps*. Colorful American stamps—the lightest, least expensive, most appreciated, simplest gift to carry for foreigners you meet.

☐ *Suit*. Unnecessary, except when on business trips. An attractive sports coat can replace a suit almost everywhere.

☐ *Suntan lotion*. If needed, bring one small plastic bottle or buy some in Europe.

☐ *Sweater*. One at most, none if possible. If you take one, wear it to save precious packing space.

☐ *Tape*. Occasionally helpful, but not indispensable.

☐ *Tennis shoes*. These are accepted just about everywhere now. Only a few stuffy restaurants might not let you in.

☐ *Tent*. If you'll be camping out, bring a light one. And be sure to try it out before taking it to Europe.

☐ *Tickets*. Easy to forget, but don't!

☐ *Tie*. One at most. Spray it with water repellent. This will make it easy to remove any stains!

☐ *Toilet paper*. Tuck a small wad into your purse or wallet. Take a whole roll off the cardboard support for travel to Eastern Europe. This may seem comical—it isn't, as you will find out.

☐ *Toothbrush and toothpaste*. Bring a small tube and replenish as needed.

☐ *Towel*. A real hassle to carry, but many European hotels give you miniature versions of the real thing, and sometimes you have to pay extra for them. In Eastern Europe they may not be available at all in some areas.

☐ *Tranquilizers*. Get a few from your doctor, just in case.

☐ *Traveler's checks*. Most money should be carried in this form (see p. 9).

☐ *Trench coat*. Take either one trench coat or one overcoat—but don't take both. Trench coats should have removable linings. These linings make good pillows. If your coat has a flimsy pocket, replace it with a deep and solid one. This will give you added space and protection. The pocket should have a button-down flap or a zipper. Add extra pockets, if you have the time. They'll come in handy. And be sure to spray the coat with water repellent, which will protect it from stains and rain.

☐ *Triangle danger sign*. Required by law for motorists in Europe (see p. 60).

☐ *T-shirt*. You'll probably live in it. You can also sleep in it.

☐ *Tucks*. Available at drugstores, Tucks will be of interest to hemorrhoid sufferers.

☐ *Turtlenecks*. Not recommended, because they're hard to wash and they dry slowly. However, they do not wrinkle and are warm.

☐ *Tweezers*. A handy item that takes up very little space. Some Swiss Army knives have tweezers on them.

☐ *Umbrella*. Bring one that folds down to less than 14 inches long. If you shop around, you can find them really cheap. Put the umbrella in one of the outside pockets of your carry-on bag.

☐ *Underwear*. Bring synthetic-fiber underwear: it's easy to wash and quick drying. Underwear can easily be replaced by bathing suits.

☐ *Velcro*. Replaces buttons nicely.

☐ *Visas*. Necessary for long-term study abroad and for travel in some Eastern European countries (see pp. ix and p. 6).

☐ *Washcloths*. Do they exist in Europe? If you must have one, bring it along!

☐ *Watch*. Toothpaste will help clean a fuzzy crystal.

☐ *Wet Ones*. These premoistened cloths, available in drugstores, are not necessary but are nice, especially if you're traveling with children.

☐ *Windbreaker*. Good in the Mediterranean areas and anywhere along the Atlantic. Can be used in place of a shirt. Or simply buy what's known as a wind shirt.

☐ *Windshield scraper*. For obvious application and easy to forget. Get the small, stiff, slightly curved kind. They take up little space and work best. Credit cards work on thin ice in a pinch.

☐ *Woolite*. Bring a few travel packets if you have any woolen items along.

☐ *Work papers* (see p. 218).

Final Steps

Taking the few steps discussed below will ensure a smooth departure and will bring you peace of mind while away from your home or apartment.

Plant Care While You're Gone

No one wants to spend weeks, months, or years growing beautiful house plants, only to return to a withered mass of brown mold or leafy splinters. To avoid these losses, use a plant-sitter, especially if you'll be gone 3 weeks or longer.

Using a Plant-Sitter

- Give the sitter a key and basic instructions on care.
- Put an identifying mark or a reminder note on each plant needing special care (misting, infrequent watering, etc.).

Doing Without a Plant-Sitter

If you'll be gone less than 3 weeks, you can get by without a plant-sitter.
- Remove all dead leaves, flowers, and buds.
- Place a plastic bag on the bottom of your tub and cover it with several layers of newspaper.
- Spray the paper with water until it's thoroughly moist.
- Cover the paper with another sheet of plastic and sprinkle it with water as well.
- Soak plants thoroughly, allowing excess water to drain completely before setting them on the plastic.
- When all your plants are in the tub, cover them with a clear plastic sheet and tape it in place. Poke some holes in it to let air circulate.
- Leave the bathroom shades up (or turn on the light if there are no windows).
- If you have more or bigger plants than your tub holds, group them away from direct sunlight and follow the same general procedure to trap humidity after a thorough soaking and draining. Poke holes in your plastic coverings to ventilate plants.

Home Security

With more than 2 million burglaries a year in the United States, it's reasonable to be concerned about home security. If you take the following precautions, you'll feel much more relaxed during your vacation.

Home Security Checklist

- ☐ Cover or screen garage windows so that a potential burglar will not know if your cars are gone. Bring tools inside from the garage.
- ☐ Set timers to turn your lights on and off at varying intervals.
- ☐ Put valuables and important documents in a safety deposit box.
- ☐ Never talk about upcoming trips with strangers.
- ☐ Get an engraving pen and ID number from the local police and mark your valuables. Put "Operation Identification" stickers on doors and windows.
- ☐ Make sure basement windows are locked or protected with grilles.
- ☐ Place removable drop bars on sliding glass doors.
- ☐ Never leave spare keys in their "secret" hiding place while you're gone.
- ☐ If you leave your car at an airport parking lot while you're away, don't leave a house key on your car key chain.
- ☐ Leave window shades and blinds in different positions, the way you would if you were at home.
- ☐ Stop mail and newspaper delivery a week before you leave so that you can be sure the service has actually stopped as you've directed. Pick up the mail directly at the post office for that short time.
- ☐ Ask a neighbor to pick up any letters, packages, or papers that may get through.
- ☐ Have a gardener continue to keep up your garden and lawn.
- ☐ Ask your neighbor to park in your driveway occasionally.
- ☐ Have a neighbor fill up a garbage can or two from time to time.
- ☐ Unplug your telephones or set the bells at their lowest ring so that any potential burglar will not hear the phone go unanswered from outside the house or apartment. If you have an answering machine, set it to answer after only one or two rings.
- ☐ If your trip has been announced in a local paper for any reason, hire a house-sitter. Burglars use these announcements as one of their main sources of information.
- ☐ Never leave notes outside the house.

☐ Steal the most valuable items from a potential thief by carting TVs, radios, stereos, guns, and so on, to the house of a neighbor or friend.
☐ Make sure your insurance policy is paid for and up-to-date.

The Last Few Days

Sensible handling of last-minute travel details can help avert all sorts of problems.

Three Days Before Your Flight

- Reconfirm your flight reservation, according to the procedure outlined on your ticket.
- Get the name of the person you are speaking to and note the day and time you call.
- This procedure drastically lowers the odds of your being bumped; but if you should get bumped from your flight, you will have grounds for legal action.
- Reconfirm your order for a special meal if already requested.

The Day Before Your Flight

- Check to make sure no mail or papers are delivered.
- Take pets to the place where they'll be staying.
- Check through the things you'll be taking (see pp. 83–94).
- Place a label with your name and address on the inside of each bag. Make a list of what's in each bag. If a bag gets lost, you'll be able to identify its contents exactly. When the bag is opened after 3 days (airlines wait this long before opening any misdirected baggage), you and it will be reunited quickly.

The Day of Your Flight

- Call the airport to ask whether your flight will be leaving on time. If you are a member of a tour, you'll usually be informed about any delays, but if you are an individual traveler, this would be rare indeed.
- Turn down the heat in your house (if it's possible).
- Water the plants for the last time.
- Make sure the house is secure and that all windows and doors are locked.

Getting to the Airport

- Figure out how long it takes to get to the airport. Then allow an extra 45 minutes for delays and traffic jams.
- Add another 30 minutes for Friday and Sunday nights or for either Los Angeles International or New York's JFK.
- Now add another hour if you intend to register items with customs (see p. 99).

Parking at the Airport

Airport parking can be a problem. Often there are lots in isolated areas at more reasonable prices than those located close to the airport itself. Ask travel agents about these. Many agencies have coupons for discounts for parking in such lots, which offer a shuttle service to the airport as part of their parking fee. This can save you a great deal of money.

At the Airport

All you want to do is get to the airport, check your luggage, walk through the security check, and board the plane with a minimum of delay and hassle. Today, that's asking quite a lot.

Checking Bags

Over a million bags are lost per year. The best way not to lose luggage is to travel so lightly that you never have to check anything!

- Check in with time to spare. Most luggage that's lost is checked in less than 30 minutes before flight time. Never use curbside baggage-check service if you're running late.
- Put your name, address, and phone number on a sticker inside the luggage. Lost bags are opened after 3 days if they haven't been claimed. The sticker on the inside will get your bag back to you, particularly if you include a note with a dated itinerary.
- Remove tags and stickers from past trips. They make handling difficult and may send bags in the wrong direction.
- At check-in, watch to make sure that each bag is tagged and placed on the conveyor belt. Never assume that either step has happened.
- Keep your claim check in a safe place—or have it stapled to your ticket folder. You'll need to show it to claim your baggage.

Protecting your Belongings

- Lock and strap every bag. Straps keep bags from popping open even under grueling conditions, and they discourage pilfering, an increasing problem.
- Never pack cash, documents, fragile items, furs, jewelry, medicine—anything valuable or hard to replace—in your checked baggage. These should always be carried onto the plane. Baggage containing expensive items is sometimes "lost" on purpose. Furthermore, the airline will not reimburse you for such things.
- Baggage insurance, available at a set price per $100 of declared value, can be purchased to cover more expensive items. Note that it rarely pays off at full face value. Leave expensive things at home!
- Never leave bags unattended anywhere for any reason. Ask someone you trust to watch them or take them with you—even to the bathroom.
- Airport security is increasingly stringent. If you accidentally leave a bag unattended, it may be removed and immediately destroyed.

Registering Valuables

It's best to register valuable items before you get to the airport, but if you forget, do it there. Otherwise, when you come back to the United States, you may have to pay duty on items that you did not actually purchase in Europe.

- You'll find registration booths in international airports as a part of the Customs Department.
- You'll be asked to fill out a small white form with pertinent information, including a description of the article and serial numbers when applicable. You must have the items with you in order to register them! The official will check over the information, verify it, stamp the form, and give it to you as proof that you had these items before going abroad. The slip is valid for all future trips, so don't throw it away.
- If you have items to register, allow yourself an extra hour for the process. Occasionally, the booths are closed—inexcusable, but true.
- Never carry gifts to and from any foreign country for another person. The unwary sometimes end up transporting narcotics in this way. If you are caught, you will have a nearly impossible time proving your innocence.

Boarding a Plane

It all used to be so simple. All you had to do was tie a string on your finger and point yourself toward the plane. It's not quite so easy nowadays. To get on a plane, you need a ticket, a boarding pass, and in most cases a seat-selection card.

- If you don't have your ticket yet, you'll wait in line.
- If you have to check baggage, you'll wait in line.
- However, with a ticket in hand and bags either with you or checked, you can proceed straight to the boarding gate. If you arrive too late, you may lose your seat.

Security and Customs

To get to the gate, you'll have to pass through a security check. In a crowded airport, this can take 45 minutes or longer.

- If it's obvious that you're in danger of missing your plane, go right to the front of the line and calmly explain your predicament to security personnel.
- Under no circumstances should you make joking remarks about hijackings, bombs, or drugs!
- If you get hassled for carrying a Swiss Army knife, have them put it in a package to be given to a flight attendant on your flight. If they refuse this courtesy, have them put it in an envelope to be sent to your home. You'll have to pay the postage. Or, you can ask for it to be held in the security office until your return.
- On some international flights, you'll pass through a customs inspection, which may add another 30 minutes' delay. Start for the gate as soon as possible.

At the Boarding Area

- Unless you already have a seat assignment and boarding pass, you'll wait in line at the boarding area counter. You'll be given both at this time.
- Until you have a boarding pass in your hand, you essentially have nothing—except a contract that gives you specific legal rights. In short, you can still be bumped.
- When the plane is ready for boarding, the flight will be announced. If you don't board the plane when you're supposed to, your seat can be given to a standby.

Seat Assignments

Match the seat you select to your needs.

- For leg room, ask for an aisle seat.
- For sleep, get a window seat.

- If you're traveling with children, ask for a partition or bulkhead seat.
- For quiet, avoid partition seats and seats near the galley or toilet.
- For getting off quickly, ask which exit will be used and ask for a seat close to it (it may be different from the door used to get on).

Seating Strategies

- If you are traveling with one other person, reserve the window and aisle seats in a three-seat section. Few people select middle seats unless a plane is fully booked. If someone should sit down there, just switch seats so that you and your friend can sit together. If no one shows up, it will be easy for one of you to find a single seat while the other person sleeps. This way you can guarantee yourself at least a few hours of slumber.
- Find out whether any infants are traveling on your flights. Flight attendants like to seat parents with young children in the first row of seats behind the partition nearest the galley; so if you relish peace and quiet on a long flight, choose a seat far enough away from that first row.
- If you're traveling alone, be the last person to board. Look for a block of three unoccupied seats. If you board late enough, most flight attendants will allow you to sit anywhere, possibly even in first class (if you're dressed well).
- If they go by the book and force you to take an assigned seat, agree. You can move as soon as the cabin door is locked.

Problems with Flights

This section gives you information about problems that you may run into when flying and strategies to help you cope with them.

Lost Airline Tickets

- Whenever you buy an airline ticket, write down the ticket number, date and place of purchase, and method of payment. Carry this information separately from your ticket—perhaps on the same piece of paper as your list of traveler's check numbers.
- If you lose a ticket or have one stolen, immediately go to or call the refund department of the airline from which you bought the ticket. You'll be asked to fill out a refund application.
- If you want to replace the ticket, you'll have to buy a new one, using the original form of payment. (If you paid for the original

ticket with a credit card, your account can be credited immediately for the lost or stolen ticket. If you paid with cash or by check, you will be reimbursed only after a 120-day waiting period. This is one big advantage of using credit cards!)
- You're liable for the loss should the ticket be used illegally during the 120-day waiting period.
- You may be given a card to send in for a refund after the waiting period is over. If you don't send it in, you will not get the refund.
- In short, treat airline tickets like cash and expect nothing but grief if you lose one!

Getting Bumped by Airlines

Your plane ticket is a legal contract with an airline. It guarantees your right to the flight, under specific conditions.
- An international ticket is valid only if you reconfirm your flight within 72 hours of departure. Always get the agent's name when you reconfirm a flight.
- You must arrive at the airport within the time limit specified on your ticket. If you do not confirm your flight or if you arrive late, the airline can sell your seat to another person (bump you from the flight)—legally! If you do reconfirm your flight and arrive on time, the airline cannot legally sell your seat. However, airlines do so—about 150,000 times a year.

Voluntary and Involuntary Bumping

Nowadays, airlines ask for volunteers to be bumped for a free round-trip ticket or a sum of money that varies with each airline and situation. If there are not enough volunteers, then some people will be bumped involuntarily. This could include you.
- If this happens to you, ask for a written statement outlining compensation for being denied boarding. Depending on the value of your ticket, you'll be paid a minimum to a maximum amount as denied boarding compensation (DBC). This money is yours for the inconvenience caused you by having been bumped.
- Note that DBC is only paid to passengers bumped from flights that actually take place (not canceled or delayed flights). It's meant only to discourage overbooking, which airlines do to survive.
- If an airline cannot get you to your original destination within 2 hours of the original scheduled arrival time for a domestic flight, or within 4 hours for an international flight, the DBC must be doubled, and the airline still must get you to your destination.
- Naturally, it's to your advantage to work out all problems with the airline on a fair, even-handed basis.

Taking it to Court

You are under no obligation to accept DBC, since you can take the matter to civil court. The odds are against you there, however. And it's an unbelievable hassle.

- Don't accept DBC if you plan to take your case to court. Once you accept the compensation, the affair is closed. You have no further legal redress.
- Be sure you have a case before you act. The airline does not have to pay DBC if the government takes over a plane (very rare), if a smaller plane is substituted for the original aircraft (occasionally happens), if you have not reconfirmed your flight, or if you check in later than the time specified on your ticket.

Flight Cancellation

If your flight is canceled, the airline should get you on the next available flight. It will do little good to complain about the cancellation.

- Note that each country has its own way of dealing with this situation. As long as you're being treated the same as other passengers, don't make a scene.

Change of Fares

Once you have paid for and received a ticket, you cannot be charged more money to board a plane within the United States. However, in Europe you may be forced to pay whatever fare is applicable on that day.

- Ask the airline about its policy when purchasing a ticket for international flights.

Flight Delays

- When a flight is delayed after initial boarding has started, the airline is obligated to provide meals, lodging, transportation, and a free phone call to each passenger.
- If you have not started to board a plane and a delay is announced, you have no legal right to demand compensation of any kind. Nevertheless, most airlines will provide necessary amenities to stranded passengers.
- You will usually be given a voucher for a set-price meal and, in extreme cases, even a free hotel room.
- If the airline does not volunteer such things, don't hesitate to ask— and be polite, firm, and fair in your request.

Changing Travel Dates

Most discounted tickets require passengers to fly within specific time periods, with no changes allowed. If you try to make a change, the airline may ask you to pay full fare. This rule can be overridden for humanitarian reasons, and it's up to the airline to decide what that means in any given case.

- Note that you can take out special insurance to cover changes in travel plans caused by illness or death in the family.

In-Flight Precautions

- Never leave money, valuable papers, or your passport unattended at any moment on a plane. They should be carried on your person at all times—even when you go to the bathroom! This advice is doubly important for when you get off the plane during a stopover.
- Get up and stretch occasionally; it will keep your body relaxed and your blood circulating.
- Water and juice served on board will not be enough fluid to prevent dehydration, which is one of the factors leading to jet lag. Bring a flask or bottle of cold water or juice to drink on the flight. (The water on board is usually lukewarm.) Avoid alcohol altogether on international flights. It will just add to dehydration.

Disinfecting Aircraft

- If you're allergic to ragweed, you can get very sick from the pyrethrin insecticide sprays that are occasionally used in planes during a flight.
- If spraying is announced, warn the flight attendant of your allergy, which will give you time to cover your nose with a wet cloth.

Jet Lag

When people cross a number of time zones, they experience something known as jet lag. The condition, a foul-up of the natural body rhythms, varies from mild to dangerous, depending on the person and his or her physical condition. People with strong internal clocks (who wake up each morning at exactly the same time without an alarm) tend to have marked jet lag.

- Any person 50 or older who has diabetes, high blood pressure, or pulmonary or arterial problems should consult a doctor before crossing many time zones. Jet lag has recently been linked to heart attacks.

* Jet lag symptoms: fatigue, irritability, anxiety, headache, insomnia, and hunger in the middle of the night.

Avoiding Jet Lag

Today there are several theories about how to avoid jet lag.

The light theory. Use light to control your body clock. Beginning on the first day of your trip and for 3 days afterward, avoid light until 10:00 A.M., while exposing yourself to as much light as possible from 1:00 to 5:00 P.M. On your return follow the same procedure. Use dark glasses to stop light exposure if necessary.

The diet theory. The Argonne National Laboratory claims that a special three-day diet will help your body quickly adjust to a new time zone. For a free copy send a self-addressed, stamped envelope to Argonne National Laboratory, 9700 South Cass Avenue, Argonne, IL 60439.

The Whitman theory. Here's my remedy:

* Don't make a marathon of any trip. Break long trips into smaller segments, taking advantage of stopover opportunities.
* Drink lots of nonalcoholic fluids to reduce the effects of jet lag. If you have to fly at night, sleep through the entire trip. If you have to take a sleeping pill, do it. Don't drink—alcohol poisoning combined with jet lag can be lethal (almost).
* Use pillows and blankets (in the compartment above your seat) to get comfortable and warm. Get them down early in the flight.
* Take off your shoes and loosen all tight-fitting clothing.
* Use ear plugs and eye masks. (Who cares what you look like? They work!)
* Draw the shades and tell the flight attendants not to bother you, not even for snacks and meals.
* Relax the first day abroad.
* Take a sleeping pill for 1 or 2 more nights to stop yourself from waking.

Part II
The Trip

Arriving in Europe

Getting from the airport to the hotel is a fairly straightforward process, but things can and do go wrong. The hints in this section deal with customs, obtaining foreign currency, handling luggage, and finding a way to your hotel.

Foreign Customs and Currency Exchanges

Most people are a little bit nervous going through customs, and that's natural. However, people who seem overly nervous or who make jokes may find themselves going through a customs check.

In some airports you'll find two gates set aside for incoming passengers. One is marked "Nothing to declare." Naturally, if you have nothing to declare, you simply walk through the gate and out to the real world. Of course, you can still be stopped for a spot check. But normally a person carrying very little baggage sails through customs!

Common Customs Questions

- Never volunteer information while going through customs! You'll seem suspicious if you do.
- Customs officials can ask you to tell them the exact amount of money you're bringing in and in what form you have it. If you're low on money, tell them you plan to stay only a week or so in the country, and that you plan to stay with a friend (have a name and address ready). But only say these things if they ask.
- Always tell officials that your reason for travel is pleasure.
- Say that all belongings are for your personal use, unless it's obvious that you're bringing in a gift.
- Never go through customs with illegal drugs, not even a small amount of marijuana. Do not carry more than a quart of liquor or a carton of cigarettes.
- Remove all film from its boxes to show that you have no intention of reselling it. You can usually avoid paying duties on large quantities of film for your personal use in this way.

Getting Foreign Currency

- The rate of exchange is usually poor at airports and other locations where travelers are most dependent on the service.

- Exchange only enough to cover costs from the airport to your hotel ($40 is usually sufficient).

Luggage Handling

Your luggage—especially if it's heavy—can cause all sorts of trouble. Of course, the lighter you travel, the less the likelihood of snags—but here are a few hints at how to avoid them.

Getting a Porter

Once you're through customs you can hire a porter (though porters are a vanishing breed). Most travelers nowadays can get by without them, though.

- In order to assure a fair price, ask the charge per bag before the porter picks any of them up.
- If you're disabled or have any serious medical problems, ask the airline for help in getting from the airplane, through customs, and on your way to your hotel.

Losing Luggage

It's frustrating to lose luggage. If you follow the advice in Chapter 8 and don't pack irreplaceable items in bags you check on to the plane, however, you'll be relatively calm in your dealings with the airline. And that's the best way to be.

- Report the loss to the airline representative immediately. Be polite but vocal about the loss, and note the representative's name.
- If the airline can't find your bags after checking the plane and baggage area, file a written claim notice immediately. Give a detailed list of the contents of the lost luggage.
- Make sure you get a copy of the claim and do not surrender your claim checks, the only proof you have that the airline has indeed lost your bags. If the airline insists on keeping a claim check, get a written receipt for it, and get the name of the person who takes it from you.

Making do when your Luggage is Lost

- Ask the airline representative for an overnight kit and emergency funds to purchase essential clothes and toiletries. Even if the luggage is found, you can keep the kit and anything you've purchased with the money (but be fair in your demands).

- Ask the airline to deliver your bags to your hotel in town if they are recovered shortly.
- If the airline loses your luggage permanently, you'll be paid a set amount per pound by the airline, usually no more than $700 altogether. The exact reimbursement plan is on your ticket.
- You'll be paid more than that if you've taken out extra luggage insurance (see p. 12).

Dealing with Damaged Luggage

- If there is any sign of damage to your bag, check the contents immediately.
- If you find damaged goods, immediately file a claim with an airline representative. Make sure you get a copy of the claim form. You'll be reimbursed for damage done to the bag or its contents.
- Any bag that is overpacked will disqualify a claim.

Getting from Airports to Hotels

You can almost always find relatively inexpensive local transportation to take you from an airport to the center of a town or city.

Finding Cheap Transportation

- Go to the airline counter, the information booth, or the local tourist office, and ask for the most economical way to get into town.
- Sometimes several people can split the cost of a taxi and come out ahead. But most of the time local buses will offer the best value.
- If you want to take a taxi, ask the airline or information clerk for the approximate cost of the trip and about tipping practices and percentages.
- When you enter the bus or taxi, show the driver the name and address of your hotel, and be sure he or she can take you to your destination.
- If you take a taxi, ask what the price will be before you begin your journey. If it varies from the information given inside the airport, find a different driver who quotes a fair rate. Taxis are notorious for overcharging in all countries. If there is a language barrier, hand the driver a pen and paper. Have him write down the cost.

Hotel Strategies

In this chapter, you'll find helpful tips on everything from getting settled in a hotel to staying in boardinghouses and youth hostels. The information should help make your stay in Europe an experience truly worth remembering.

Arriving at a Hotel

Although sometimes getting settled in a European hotel is easy, many things can go awry. Here's how to avoid problems.

Bringing Bags into a Hotel

Whether you use public transportation or a taxi, you'll eventually arrive at the steps of your hotel. Taxi drivers normally do little more than remove the bags from the car and set them on the curb.
- If the driver carries your bags into the hotel, you should tip him or her as you would a hotel porter. Normally, whoever is behind the desk will see you struggling and come to your aid if the cabby doesn't.
- Do not leave bags unattended on the curb while you search for someone to bring them into the hotel.

Checking into a Hotel

At the front desk, give the clerk your name and the dates of your reservations. You will then be asked to fill out a police form. If you've memorized the number, date, and place of issue of your passport, filling out this form will be easy.
- If the clerk asks for your passport in order to fill out the form for you, say you'd rather do it yourself.
- If the clerk insists, ask for it back in half an hour (a little longer in Portugal, where the local police may need to see it). Under no circumstances should you surrender your passport for any longer—it's your document, and you need it!
- While you're checking in, ask the clerk for stationery or matches—something with the hotel's name and address on it. It may sound ridiculous, but almost everyone forgets the name and address of a hotel at some time during a trip, especially on an extended one.

112

Hotel Costs and Services

Check-in is the time to get everything straight on costs and services. Avoid conflicts by asking questions right away.

- Is the cost of breakfast or any other meal included with the room price?
- Will there be any additional service charges?
- What's the tax on rooms and services?
- Are there any additional charges for laundry, local calls, television, etc.?
- How much does a bath cost?
- Does the hotel supply towels with the bath?

Inspecting Your Room

If the porter shows you to your room, tip according to the amount of luggage. If there's anything wrong or you want to change rooms, let the desk clerk know right away!

- Check the room for noise. A room near a subway or railroad, over-looking a main boulevard, next to the elevator, or by a bathroom is hard to sleep in.
- Check the smell. Does the room smell fresh and clean?
- Check the posted price on the wall or on the back of the door. Does it match the one quoted to you in the lobby?
- Check for hot water. It can be a luxury in a small hotel. Do the faucets drip?
- Check the heat. If you'll need it, make sure the system is working. This can be difficult, because some hotels shut off heat during the day. Ask whether a space heater is available.
- Check the bathroom (or shower) and the toilet (WC). Many superb small hotels don't have baths or showers in individual rooms. Accept this and the subsequent savings!
- Check the bedding. If you must have an American-style pillow, make sure one is available (they're often stuffed in closets or bureaus). Ask about extra blankets if you'll need them.

Getting Bumped Despite Written Confirmation

Many hotels overbook by 10 to 15 percent to make up for no-shows and then they bump the overflow. Unfortunately, if you don't have a written confirmation of reservations, you have no legitimate grounds for complaints. But if you do have such confirmation, you have some recourse.

- Insist that the hotel come up with a room. Also insist that they pay your cab fare from the hotel to a new hotel if you must move.
- If the management refuses to do anything, create a small scene. No hotel likes a scene in its front lobby! The very least the hotel should do is pay your way to the local room-finding service (see below).

Getting Bumped Without Written Confirmation

If you don't have a written confirmation, expect no sympathy. A telephone conversation or a voucher may be helpful, but neither has the clout of a written confirmation.
- Stay calm and polite. Ask the clerk to help you find a room. Clerks will often make many phone calls to help a stranded tourist.
- Failing that, get directions to a room-finding service (see below).

Reservation Services

The big advantage of traveling without reservations is the freedom you will have. Many people prefer to travel in this fashion. When you arrive in a city without a reserved room, you can almost always get one from a reservation service. Eastern Europe is an exception. Rooms should be booked far in advance during the peak season, especially in Prague, Czechoslovakia. Reservation services are available in Eastern Europe, and the availability of rooms is improving rapidly. However, room shortage remains a critical problem for the time being.

Tourist Information Offices

When you arrive in a new city without a room reservation, go directly to the nearest tourist information office. These are located in railway stations, airports, docks, and city and town centers. If you don't know where the tourist office is, the clerk at the nearest hotel can tell you.
- Many of these offices have a room-finding service or can direct you to one. They are generally open from 9:00 or 10:00 A.M. to 10:00 or 11:00 P.M., though they might close on holidays and Sundays.
- You're always served on a first-come, first-served basis. Time will pass more quickly if you bring a snack and something to read while you wait.
- When it's your turn, tell the clerk what price range you want. Note that the cheapest rooms fill up fast in peak seasons and may not

be available. It will take anywhere from 10 minutes to 2 hours to book a room.

- Ask about the fee structure for booking and determine how much it will cost before you book a room.
- When a room is found and booked, ask the clerk to mark its location on a free map from the tourist office. Write down its full name and address as well—partial information or unknown locations spell trouble.
- For members of racial minorities: discrimination is less likely to occur when you use room-booking services.

Other Booking Services

- *American Express*. Check with American Express and other large travel agencies in Europe for help in finding and booking available rooms. Note that there is usually a charge for this service and that these agencies deal in higher-priced rooms.
- In Eastern Europe many travel agencies handle both expensive and inexpensive accommodations. Go to several if necessary to find the kind of price range which fits your budget. Note that many of them are an excellent source for private rooms as well.
- *Airline offices*. Ask airlines for help in locating available rooms. Some keep books listing moderate-to-expensive rooms. Agents will often make a call and book a room without any fee if you have a ticket with that airline.
- *Student offices*. Head immediately to local student offices abroad for help in locating less expensive rooms, especially during peak season. Get lists of foreign student offices from the CIEE (see p. 9).
- *Youth hostel organizations*. Go to youth hostel offices abroad for help in locating inexpensive rooms. Hostels often fill up in peak seasons, but people there can steer you to good alternatives. They can also book rooms in advance in other locations (see pp. 126–127).
- *YWCA/YMCAs*. Try European branches of the YWCA or YMCA for less expensive rooms. If these are booked, the locals can often help you find comparably priced rooms. This informal networking often works miracles in a crowded city (see p. 127).

Finding Your Own Room

The obvious alternative to having an agent or a tourist office clerk book a room for you is to book one yourself! The big advantage of this approach is that you get to see the room (and the hotel) before you rent. That advantage pales in extremely crowded cities during the peak season, but you can often find the best deals when you do the searching yourself. It's quite easy and can save you a bundle if you know a few basic principles and techniques.

Hotel Rates

- In general, the larger the hotel, the higher the rates. "Name-brand" hotels are especially expensive.
- Almost all hotels in Europe have a wide variety of rooms that vary from abysmal to great. Even large and overly expensive hotels sometimes have bargains.
- The more Americans in a hotel, the higher the rates. Americans are just not bargain-hunters when it comes to lodgings. The British, Scandinavians, and Germans tend to be more skillful travelers—the smaller hotels they choose often offer more for your money.
- Hotels grow progressively more expensive as they get close to the heart of the city. Near the airport, railway station, or docks of main cities, you'll also find inflated rates.
- During festivals, pilgrimages, sporting events, fairs, and conventions all rooms are overpriced—if you can find any at all—even on the outskirts of town.

Hotels in Nearby Cities

More and more travelers are using this strategy. Instead of staying in major cities where prices are high, they get a room in a minor city nearby. If the city is on a rail line, the commute in may be quite inexpensive. This is especially effective if you have a rail pass. In this case, you trade inconvenience and time for money.

Hotels in Outlying Areas

On the fringes of larger cities, you'll find small hotels that will make a trip to Europe memorable. True, you will have to commute to city centers for sightseeing, but it will be worth your while to check out these hotels for several reasons.

- Hotel rates in outlying areas are low!
- These hotels are not what every American has seen or visited; and they are more typical of the area you are in.
- You may have to forgo television or a private bath, but you'll meet Europeans more readily.
- Hotels in outlying areas tend to be far from bright lights and traffic, so you'll sleep better.

Using a Travel Guide to Find Lodging

- Use travel guides to help you find lodging. Travel guides are most useful for the off-season, from late September through April.
- Buy a guide that lists telephone numbers along with the hotel descriptions.
- If you want to avoid the expense of making many calls, go to an area that's thick with listings. Then check that area out on foot. Often this will lead you to a gem that's not even listed.
- To get a room in a crowded city, your timing must be right: the earlier in the day you try, the better the odds are.

Room-Hunting Preliminaries

- Never judge a hotel by its exterior or lobby. Smaller, less expensive hotels may not put money into appearances but may still offer comfortable, charming, clean accommodations.
- Go into the hotel and ask the person at the front desk if a room is available. (See p. 118 for ways to get past a "No Vacancy" sign.) Ask for room rates. If one's open in your range, ask to see it. If none is open, ask the clerk to recommend a nearby hotel that might have rooms and rates that suit you.
- If there's a room open in your price range, look at it before renting it (see pp. 113–115). Then you can begin to bargain.

Bargaining on Room Rates

Once you find a room you like, you'll want to come up with the best price possible. Although it goes against the American grain, bargaining is acceptable throughout much of Europe. Naturally, it's only effective in an area with many open rooms, and for that reason it's done more successfully in the off-season.

- Remember that you can play a big part in determining the price of the room.
- Begin by being flexible. Tell the clerk that the room is great, but that it's too expensive for you. This will often bring the price down.
- Or be blunt: tell the clerk that you like the room and will pay such and such an amount—a lower, but still fair, price. This often works, but you have to have the right temperament to try it.
- Or be hesitant: clerks can sense this. They'll often respond by showing you a room that's just as nice but costs less.
- If you find a hotel you like in which the cheaper rooms are filled, ask whether you can rent a more expensive room for one night

and then move to a cheaper one the next day. This puts the clerk in the position of weighing cost reduction against the bother and cost of cleaning an extra set of sheets. Sometimes a clerk will agree to give you the more expensive room at a lower rate to avoid moving you at all.

Room-Rate Discounts

- You should get a room-rate discount in most countries during the off-season. Rates posted in a room vary from a minimum (off-season) to a maximum (peak season). Insist on the lower rate in the off-season!
- You should not have to pay as much for a double bed as for two twins in comparable rooms, because the hotel saves money on the number of sheets it has to wash.
- Always ask about discounts for prolonged stays (usually 3 days or longer). If none exists, the hotel will tell you so. You can then either accept the standard rate or shop around.
- Ask for weekend discounts, especially at hotels in larger cities appealing to business people.
- In hotels serving continental breakfasts only, rent a room without breakfast included, because continental breakfasts cost far more than they are worth. During the peak season many hotels refuse to do this, but in the off-season most of them give in. In areas where breakfasts are substantial, pay the extra price for the morning meal. You can often make sandwiches for lunch from these, getting two meals for the price of one. Always ask about breakfast before choosing a hotel. A large, hearty breakfast can add lots of value to a room price, especially in parts of Eastern Europe where food may be hard to come by.

Beating the "No Vacancy" Sign

It can be frustrating at times, this process of finding a room on your own. It's particularly frustrating when you see "No Vacancy" on every door (*Complet, Besetz, Occupato*—dirty words when you're looking for a room). When things look very bleak, try some of the following techniques.

- Tell the people at the front desk that you stayed in this hotel once before and want very badly to stay here again. When they try to remember your face, tell them how much you like the hotel and the town. They may sense that you're lying, but they will probably smile and try to find you a room in the hotel or call friends in a hotel down the street.
- When you walk up to the clerk and the first thing you hear is,

"How long do you intend to stay?" you've got to answer, "A week," even if you intend to stay only a day or two, or there may suddenly be no vacancies. Short stays cost hotels more in overhead.

- At about 11:00 P.M., walk into the lobby of a small hotel, hand the clerk a piece of paper with the hotel's name scribbled on it, tell the clerk that Andre Papillon (make up any name) recommended the place to you, and ask if there might be a room available. At this point the clerk may take the gamble of giving you a room reserved for someone else. The hotel collects double, and you have a room.
- In desperation, try a taxi driver. The word *hotel* is an international one. The driver may just steer you to a nearby spot. More than likely he'll take you for a ride, but the ride as a bribe sometimes pays off.
- The coupon or voucher system may still exist in certain Eastern European countries. These coupons give you a discount on room prices. When you first arrive at a hotel, ask whether rooms are available before discussing coupons. If a room is available, then produce your coupon. If the hotel tells you that no rooms are available, produce your coupon and state that you were told that hotels keep rooms open for coupon holders. In essence, so-called "full" hotels really aren't. They do hold rooms open for tourists with vouchers. For more information on coupons or vouchers contact the individual Eastern European tourist offices (pp. 247–250) to see whether they are still required or offered.

Miscellaneous Charges

- Watch for miscellaneous charges. Unless you understand them in advance, you'll end up paying far more than you planned.
- Prices for hotel rooms are sometimes quoted on a per person basis, especially in Italy and Spain. Get the price straight to start with: "Is that per person or the total price of the room?"
- Avoid having the hotel set up tours or arrange for nights on the town. Naturally, this is a legitimate part of their business, but you'll save money if you use them only when you really can't get tickets or tour seats yourself.
- If you make long-distance phone calls from a hotel room, you can legally be socked with a surcharge that may be as much as 40 percent on any bill. Therefore, before making such calls, find out about possible surcharges. If they seem steep, make your call from the central post office (see pp. 199–201) or nearest telephone booth. Frankly, some hotels lie about surcharges, and I no longer make calls from them for this reason. These surcharges are often hidden in the bill sent to you by your long-distance company even when you make collect calls or use a calling card. In fact, this is

one of the most common rip-offs worldwide in the travel industry.
- If there's a charge for hotel parking, just leave your car in the street under a light. Remove all your belongings from the car, leave the glove compartment open to show there's nothing in it, and lock the car. If you have a bike, moped, or motorcycle, pay a charge to have it locked in a secure place. They are commonly vandalized or stolen.

Room and Board

The term *full room and board (pension complet)* means that you're staying in a hotel and eating all meals there. *Half room and board (demi pension)* indicates that you're skipping either lunch or dinner at the hotel. Most European hotels offer good rates for both full and half room-and-board arrangements.
- If you're eating meals at your hotel, find out whether there is a discount for full or half room and board. Make sure any discounts you opt for show up on your final bill.
- Some hotels won't rent you a room unless you agree to have meals there. In the peak season you may have to submit to this racket, which is intended to jack up the price of government-controlled room rates.
- Many hotels will not offer room-and-board discounts unless you stay for a minimum of 3 days. But they won't tell you this in advance, so ask about it.
- If you do stay on a room-and-board basis, find out whether there is an extra charge for anything, such as wine, dessert, or coffee.
- As unbelievable as it may sound, you must pay an extra charge in some hotels for not eating breakfast. This forces you to get up early so that the room can be made.
- In resort areas, many luxury hotels have agreements for reciprocal lunches and dinners for guests staying on room-and-board terms. Ask the clerk at the front desk for information on such arrangements.

Idiosyncrasies of European Hotels

Half the pleasure of travel comes from discovering the difference between "them" and "us." However, some differences come as a shock. Here are some bridges for cultural gaps in hotels.

The Front Desk

- Get the clerk's name when you check in. Ask for all prices to be written down on a slip of paper to avoid confusion about rates at checkout time.

- Don't assume that your name is easy to spell or read. Write it down for the clerk.
- Ask as late in the day as possible for a morning wake-up call. With luck you'll be leaving it with the person responsible for calling you in the morning, and your message won't go astray.

Elevators

- The elevators in most hotels do not work like Swiss watches. The clunk when you push the call button means it's heard you. The whine means it's on its way. The second clunk means someone has intercepted it on the third floor, and it will now head in the opposite direction.
- Once you've cornered the elevator, you must shut the outer gate tightly before closing the inner door and pushing the floor button. If the gate isn't closed, the elevator won't work—no matter how much you swear.

Bathrooms and Showers

Although more and more European hotels have American-style rooms that include a tub or shower, many still have detached rooms for bathing. The room with the shower or bath is always separate from the toilet. Both may be at the end of the hall, but they could also be four floors up, tucked under the slanted roof where only cats and bats can live. You often have to get a key for the bathroom or shower from the clerk at the front desk. The clerk will ask a room attendant to bring you a towel.

- Ask the owner about the best time to take a bath. Some hotels arrange hours for their guests so as not to disturb sleep.
- You pay extra per shower or bath unless you've agreed that it's included in the price of the room.
- There are public baths in most cities. You'll also find them in many train stations.

Hot and Cold Water

- In small hotels with a central water heating system you may be out of luck (and hot water) if you don't time your bath or shower properly.
- The red spot on a faucet means hot, the blue means cold. After five minutes of running the red spot without getting warm water, assume the plumber was color-blind, or more likely, the hotel is out of hot water.
- Quite a few hotels have individual gas water-heating units for the

shower or bath. When you turn on the hot water faucet, the unit will burst into flame, heating only the water you'll need.
- The water will be scalding. To get the right temperature turn the hot water on full and turn the cold water on gently, or you'll end up with a cold stream shooting at you. Cold water has priority over hot.
- One out of 10 small European hotels has broken pipes.

Toilets

- Toilets are generally labeled WC (water closet) and are intended for both sexes unless they're designated otherwise. Watch out for *signori* (men) and *signore* (women) in Italy.
- Many toilets do not have a light switch. As soon as you lock the door, the light will go on.
- If the light doesn't go on, the switch may be outside the door.
- Light a match or two in smelly toilets. You won't notice the smell.
- Most toilets have some form of toilet paper: real stuff, pieces of newspaper, a kind of dark crepe paper, or magazine pages. Some don't have any—a good reason to carry some tissue in your purse or wallet.
- In some parts of Europe, toilets are no more than holes in the floor with two tile steps to squat on. You'll feel like an experienced traveler after you've visited your first *steppe*.

Bidets

You'll find bidets in many European hotel rooms and WCs. If you care to experiment with these toilet-shaped porcelain fixtures for your personal hygiene, do so. (Europeans can't believe that Americans do without them in their bathrooms!)
- In a pinch, use them for sponge baths, for hair washing, or for hand-washing clothes.

Mattresses and Bedding

- If you're the kind of person who can sink a basket without jumping, ask to see the bed in a room before renting it. You may have to settle for a double bed on which you can lie diagonally.
- You'll find a mattress every now and then that gives you a spinal tap for no extra charge. Just toss it on the floor and sleep there.
- In some countries, you'll find pillows that look like short, rolled-up rugs. If you don't like them, check in the closet or bureau drawers for American-style pillows *(oreillers)*. If you can't find any, ask the front desk for some. If they don't have any, you're stuck.
- Many European hotels substitute wedge-shaped bolsters under the

mattress for pillows. If you don't like these, just pull them out and look or ask for American-style pillows.
- Pat the feathers in the down quilts you'll find in Germany, Austria, Italy, and Scandinavia until they spread out evenly under the thick white cover. Then toss the comforter up and down a few times. This fluffs up the feathers.
- If you want to slide two beds together to make one, place the box springs side by side, but always place the mattresses across them. If you don't, someone will disappear during the night.

Lights

The lights in the hall can be a problem in some hotels, because they'll stay on for only a minute after you push a button on the wall. This conserves electricity but forces you to grope for that button if you don't want to trip and fall down the stairs.
- You may want to beat the system by carrying a small flashlight.
- Turn off the lights in your room when you leave, or Frau Weber, with characteristic wit, will say, "So, you think this is Christmas?"
- If you want strong lights for reading, you may have to carry a high-wattage bulb with you. This is a real pain, but may turn into a necessity in parts of Eastern Europe where bulbs may not turn on at all in a number of hotels.

Guests

Hotels are strict about letting you invite guests to your room. The landlady will look at you and your new friend heading up the stairs and say, "Excuse me. You paid for one person, not two."
- If you are expecting, or hope to find, a partner, pay for two from the start.
- In most countries it is illegal for unmarried people to share a room. The restriction is almost universally ignored, however, as long as the bill has been properly paid.

Room Attendants

Room attendants will do everything possible to wake you up. If your door isn't locked, they'll open it, say the equivalent of "oops!" and then slam it closed. You can avoid this by locking the door when you go to bed and placing a "Do Not Disturb" sign (if there is one) on the outside knob. Some experienced travelers carry such a sign with them just in case. But this won't stop the hotel help from jabbering with other help in the hall, coughing, laughing, singing, telling jokes, and making other room attendant sounds—which are not very subtle ways

of letting you know that it's time for them to make your bed.
- Unless you put small things in a drawer or in your luggage, they may disappear. Usually they're not being stolen, they're being thrown away.

Laundry

Placards in most hotel rooms say that it's illegal to do laundry in your room; virtually every traveler ignores this warning, once burned by outrageous laundry service prices. Hand-washing your clothes saves time as well. (Hotel laundries take 3 days!) Besides, today's fabrics are practically maintenance-free.

Washing Clothes in Your Room

- Roll clothes in a towel to collect excess moisture and speed drying before you hang them. (But don't wring out drip-dry clothes.)
- Bring a braided rubber clothesline on which you can hang your wash.

Hanging Clothes to Dry

- Never hang your laundry out a window to dry. That will cause an international incident, either with the room attendant or with the management itself.
- Don't lay wet clothes on a stained wood surface; they'll bleach the wood and end up stained themselves.
- Try not to flood a room with dripping water. Place plastic over a newspaper in any area prone to water damage.
- Separate the back portion of any wet clothing from the front.
- Smooth to eliminate wrinkling.
- Button the two top buttons of a shirt and set the collar in the correct position.

Wrinkles, Lint, and Stains

- To get rid of wrinkles in shirts, slacks, or dresses after they are dry, hang them in a steamy bathroom.
- Run any moist item over a hot light bulb—it acts like an iron.
- Use any kind of tape to pick up lint off clothes.
- To remove blood stains, soak them in cold water.
- Sprinkle salt or soda on wine stains and talcum powder on grease stains to help absorb and remove them before washing.

Alternatives to Hotels

Europe has a wide variety of accommodations. If you're on a budget or if you prefer a more intimate experience than hotels can offer, boardinghouses, youth hostels, other youth-oriented accommodations, and camping (or simply sleeping out) are some of the options you can consider.

Boardinghouses

Boardinghouses *(pensions)* are as common as hotels in Europe. They offer most of the advantages of hotels and the added element of personal attention. They provide rooms and meals at reasonable prices.
The rate in a pension varies according to the room-and-board plan being offered. The full pension *(pension complet)* arrangement includes all meals plus a room, while half pension *(demi pension)* covers the room, breakfast, and either lunch or supper.

Boardinghouse Rates

- Note that the basic room rate generally includes the cost of breakfast and the price of a bath; but you'll have to work this out in advance.
- Have the price of the room written down on a slip of paper and hang on to it. Or pay ahead of time. This way any misunderstandings, hidden service charges, and surprise taxes will surface before you move in.
- If you plan to stay in a boardinghouse for more than 3 days, ask about long-term rates. The difference may really surprise you.

Food at Boardinghouses

Meals are generally served at a common table where you'll get to know the other boarders.
- You are not expected to tip the cook or waiters, although a token tip would be in order when you leave.
- If you want to affect the quality of the cooking, honestly tell the cook what you think of different dishes, either verbally or in sign language.

• Never start off with a full pension *(pension complet)* agreement. You want to be able to eat out at local restaurants as well. If a boardinghouse insists that you eat all meals there, look somewhere else for a room.

Youth Hostels and
Youth Accommodations

Europe has more than 2,000 hostels, including camps, castles, lodges, huts, villas, ships, and schools. Often the adventurous people who stay in them make them interesting.

The American Youth Hostels (AYH) association issues youth hostel cards, which you must have if you're planning to hostel your way around Europe. Costs vary according to your age. You can get information from any local branch or the central office:

American Youth Hostels
1108 K Street.NW
Washington, DC 20005
Tel: (202) 783-4943

All mail should be directed to:

AYH
P.O. Box 28607
Central Station
Washington, DC 20038

Technically, as an American you can't get a youth hostel card abroad, but many Americans get around this by giving a foreign address.

Basics of Hostels

• Check ahead if you're 25 or older; some hostels impose age limits to keep rooms available for youths.
• Sleeping arrangements are mostly dormitory-style setups on simple cots. Some hostels insist that you have a sleeping sack (two sheets sewn together to form a sack) of your own. Others provide them or let the rules slide. Still others insist you rent one even when you have one of your own. Either make a sack yourself or buy one from:

New York International AYH
891 Amsterdam Avenue
New York, NY 10025
Tel: (212) 932-2300

- Save money by trying out the communal dining rooms. The meals are filling and sometimes quite good.
- If you find that a certain hostel restricts its space to foot travelers, park your car around the corner and hike in.

Ground Rules for Hostels

- You help with the cleaning.
- Neither smoking nor radios are permitted in the sleeping area.
- Alcohol is allowed only with meals in France, Italy, Portugal, and Spain.
- There's a 3-day limit on stays (unless there's lots of room).
- Lights go out by 10:00 P.M., and you get up by 7:00 A.M.
- Hostels often close from late morning to late afternoon—so get there early to register for the coming night!
- Many hostels will take reservations for the next day. All it costs is the price of a phone call.
- If you want to reserve a room in advance, write to the hostel requesting a reservation. Enclose one night's fee and enough international reply coupons to cover an airmail reply.

Inexpensive, Youth-Oriented Rooms

- If you're young and on a budget, take advantage of the many youth-oriented facilities available, which include student hotels, dormitories, and the many YMCA/YWCAs throughout Europe.
- Get information on these facilities as far in advance as possible; make reservations by mail in time to beat the summer rush!
- For information on facilities abroad, contact your local Y or one of the following:

YMCA
101 North Wacker Drive
Chicago, IL 60606
Tel: (312) 977-0031

YWCA
726 Broadway
New York, NY 10003
Tel: (212) 614-2700

- For information on student hotels and dormitories, contact the CIEE (see p. 9).
- Note that facilities in Europe tend to be better than those in the United States.
- Note, too, that you will find better facilities in Central and Northern Europe than in the South.

Camping

Camping is for people who have a loose, free-flowing style of travel, and not for those with limited time. If you've got the time, however, you'll find that European campgrounds are well organized and often offer facilities such as showers and grocery stores. You'll find them everywhere, even in major European cities.

International Camping Carnet

- Get an international camping carnet, the passport to camping abroad, that entitles you to small reductions in fees. Contact the National Campers and Hikers Association, 4804 Transit Road, Building 2, Depew, NY 14043, Tel: (716) 668-6242.
- If you forget to pick one up in the United States, ask for one at an automobile association abroad.

Camping Equipment

- Know your outfit before traveling abroad, which means trying it out in the United States before you leave. Nothing's worse than a so-called waterproof tent that lets the rain in or a mosquito net that's worn through. If you camp out before going to Europe, you'll find out quickly what gear you're missing (or what needs replacing).
- Bring the minimum gear: sleeping bag (down or comparable synthetic), plastic sheet, tent, warm clothes, bug spray, and flask.
- Bring a good knife with a corkscrew and bottle opener. A Swiss Army knife is excellent. If you're traveling with carry-on luggage, knives may not be allowed on a plane. So it may be best to buy the knife in Europe.
- Plan to use a butane stove and a large refillable cylinder of gas. Buy these abroad.
- Travel by car, not by truck or trailer. Can you imagine taking a trip to a fjord in a car pulling a trailer?

Camping Etiquette

- Always ask permission to camp on someone's property.
- Avoid building fires; they are illegal in almost all areas.
- Leave the campsite spotless.
- Note that saying thank you and goodbye to your European host, with a handshake, is minimal good manners.

Sleeping Out and Other Tactics

Thousands of young people travel throughout Europe each year without spending a cent for a hotel room. While this practice is officially discouraged by most police departments, it's nevertheless tolerated in most countries. Be cautious in Eastern Europe, though.

Sleeping Out

Sleeping out is a cinch in most rural areas. It has some advantages over sleeping in campgrounds, where you have to pay an entrance fee for the privilege of being surrounded by a milling crowd. You become a part of the spot you've chosen: the farmer waking you up could either ask you to leave or invite you to have breakfast with him!

* Try to find as isolated and protected a spot as possible.
* Be prepared to end up with two cat's eyes peering down at you over a flashlight in the middle of the night. Be polite, show your visitor your passport, offer him or her a cigarette.
* If you try sacking out on a beach, be as inconspicuous as possible. They're often patrolled. However, there are soft-water showers in many beach areas where you can wash off a week's grime for nothing.
* If you don't mind noise, ask permission from gas station attendants to sleep on any available grass. Most stations sell snacks, and you can use the washroom.
* If you sleep out, put all your valuables down in the bottom of your sleeping bag, not in your knapsack.
* Consider paying the small entrance fee for a campground when you are in a city. It's harder to sleep out in urban areas, although wily vagabonds often do, mainly in parks and church grounds (including cemeteries). However, these days the low cost of campgrounds in these areas are worth it for safety reasons alone.

Alternatives to Sleeping Out

* Try the train station: it's the warmest, safest place to sleep for free in Western European cities. The police will wake you up if you're lying down; but if you can sleep sitting up, you've got it made.
* In major Eastern European cities in mid-summer this may be your only practical choice if you haven't booked a room in advance. You should have a train ticket of some kind to prove that you are "waiting" for a train. The advantage here is that they will often let people lie down until early morning. Check your bags to avoid theft while you sleep.

- Don't count on getting the police to put you up in a cell for the night if you can't find a room in a crowded town. Usually, the police will not want you around, because many unpleasant things can happen in jails.
- If you have a Eurailpass, try sleeping on trains. This is less comfortable than some know-it-all travel writers insist (they've never done it). If you try it, pull out the leg support (if there is one) from underneath your seat. Always take your shoes off if you put your feet on a train seat.
- If you have friends in the army, try to stay in the barracks with them. Although this is quite illegal, it will save you a wad. Someone always pulls night duty, which will leave a bunk open for you.
- In a pinch, try restaurants, bars, or even rooftops of small hotels (great idea in Greece). The cost is usually just a token charge.

Staying with Europeans for Free

If you get along well with a European, it's possible that you'll be invited to stay in his or her home. Bring a small token gift (a bouquet, American stamps or books, special coins) when you arrive. And remember the saying, "Fish and visitors stink after three days."

- Keep addresses of people you meet during your travels. You'll enjoy an area much more if you have a contact there. You'll often be asked to stay for a night or two as a courtesy.
- Keep your needs to a minimum. In some areas the heat will be lower than you're used to. Simply put on a sweater.
- Hot water is expensive to heat. Many Europeans consider a daily bath both unnecessary and bad for your health (many doctors agree). So follow the bathing patterns of your host.

Money Matters and Safety

Foreign Currency

One of the realities of foreign travel is the necessity to exchange American money for foreign currency. You'll need your passport for each exchange. Money-changers charge a fee for their service. *Each time you exchange money, you lose money.* The more exchanges, the greater the loss.

Rates of exchange are posted at banks, in American Express and other travel offices, and at money-changers' offices. Rates fluctuate daily.

Exchanging Currency

- Before going abroad study currency exchange rates for 2 weeks in business papers. This way you'll know whether the dollar is getting weaker or stronger. The trend will tell you whether to exchange a small or larger amount of money on the first day abroad.
- In all transactions, whether at a bank or getting change in a restaurant or shop, count the change. This may seem overly obvious, but short-changing is a common practice. Italians are notorious for it. But it happens in other areas as well.
- Study foreign currency and coins until you are familiar with all the denominations you'll be dealing with. Just as in the United States, size and value may not be related—small coins may be worth more than larger ones.
- If the foreign country's monetary system is not clear to you, have someone explain it. This will save you money in the long run!
- Find out the banking hours and dates of bank holidays of the place you're visiting.
- Don't make fun of foreign currency in public, even if some of the coins will float on water or the paper money would pass as newspaper.
- Never ask how much a foreign currency is worth in *real* money. It's just as real as American currency.

Getting the Best Deal on Currency Exchanges

- Most banks in the United States offer a very poor rate of exchange on all foreign currency transactions.
- Avoid exchanging money in airports, train stations, and hotels. Wherever exchange is most convenient, it's most costly.
- For the same reason, never exchange money at the border between two countries.
- Exchange only about $40—enough to get you to your hotel—when first arriving abroad.
- Know the current rate of exchange before you go shopping. Some shops always give a better rate of exchange than banks as a way of encouraging shoppers to return (a kind of built-in discount). Others try to rip you off.

Where to Exchange Money Daily

- Exchange your money in reputable banks or in traveler's check offices.
- Exchange traveler's checks at their own name-brand offices in order to get the most favorable rates.
- Don't deal with money-changers. Although their rates vary from favorable to unfavorable, they offer a less favorable rate of exchange in most instances. However, in Eastern European countries you may get a better rate by exchanging with individuals than at banks. Know the local currency well before doing this. If you don't, you may get stuck with obsolete and worthless bills. If the practice is illegal, don't do it. Rules are changing. Ask if you are unsure.
- If saving money is more important to you than saving time, check several banks before you exchange currency. Rates sometimes vary from one bank to another, and the right choice can save you 2 to 4 percent.

How Much to Exchange

- Most banks and traveler's check companies charge a set service fee per transaction. Thus, the person who exchanges small amounts frequently gets burned. Always exchange the most you can afford to lose.
- You'll sometimes get better rates of exchange for amounts over $100.
- Unless you intend to return to a country, never carry coins across a border, since most banks won't exchange them. Note that you can exchange coins in either the Amsterdam or Munich train stations (if you forget). A number of Swiss banks are now exchanging coins.

However, you get a poor rate of exchange for coins compared to paper currency.

Traveler's Checks

Everyone knows that it's foolish to travel abroad carrying only cash. If you carry traveler's checks, there are only two possible problems: you can't cash them, or you lose them. Fortunately, there are solutions to both problems.

Getting Traveler's Checks Accepted

You'll sometimes run into a place that won't take your traveler's check. If this happens, you can try two things before going elsewhere.
- Ask the person in charge to call the nearest bank to verify the authenticity of your checks. Try not to create a scene, but be polite and firm.
- Volunteer to go over to the bank and cash your check there.

Losing Traveler's Checks

Keep a record of your checks—both cashed and uncashed—separate from the checks themselves. Don't carry them both in your wallet. If you lose your checks, do the following.
- Go to the branch office of the company that issued the checks and report the loss there.
- Bring your passport as identification.
- Whenever you purchase traveler's checks, ask the clerk where you can cash them on holidays and weekends, when foreign offices may be closed. If they don't know, ask them to call the central office for information before purchasing them. Policies have changed frequently in this regard depending upon the company issuing the checks. Knowing this ahead of time is extremely helpful in emergency situations.

Credit Cards and Money

Many travelers enjoy the convenience of credit cards while they're in Europe. If you use yours, be careful to protect them.

Protecting Credit Cards

- Take along only credit cards you'll need; leave all others at home in a safe-deposit box. Protect credit cards as you would cash or your passport.
- Photocopy all of your credit cards before you leave on your trip. Give one copy to a friend and take another with you. This will be very useful if you lose a card while traveling.
- Note how many cards you're carrying and count them periodically. Many thieves are smart enough to take only one or two cards from a wallet, making the theft less noticeable.
- When you charge something, verify the total amount charged to you, sign the charge slip, and keep the customer copy. Unfortunately, a growing number of establishments alter charge slips in an effort to defraud customers. An extra digit on the charge slip can cause the bill to soar by $100 or more. Never throw your slips away until the charges have been billed and paid!
- If a shop, restaurant, or hotel offers you an excellent exchange rate, have them convert the total charges into dollars and have them record that amount on the charge slip. If the rate of exchange is poor, leave the charge in local currency. Most credit card companies will give you about a 6 percent edge on transactions. Note though that all transactions are exchanged on the date of posting, not on the date of purchasing. Extremely knowledgeable travelers are aware of the trend in the dollar's overall value. If it is getting weaker, they leave the charge in local currency. If the reverse is true, they have the amount converted on the charge.
- If you buy a ticket with a credit card and then have to cancel or change your travel plans, ask for a *refund receipt* when you return the ticket for credit. Note the ticket number and the date and place you bought it, so that you can contact the credit card company if the credit does not show up on your bill.

Using Credit Cards to Get Cash

- You can easily get cash abroad with most credit cards. You'll need both your card and your passport for these transactions.
- Check with credit card companies for current policies and locations of automatic teller machines, now proliferating throughout Europe.

When the Money Runs Out

- You can wire home and ask someone to send you an international money order.

- The American consulate can help in emergencies, but you'll have to repay money loaned to you before you will be allowed to travel abroad again.
- If you don't have enough money to pay duty on your return to the United States, customs will take a personal check with two forms of identification.

Tipping

About the only European country where tips are generally frowned upon is Iceland, so tipping is simple there. Tipping policies are very complex in all other countries. The smartest thing you can do is to ask travel agents, airline personnel, and those who give you service about the tipping policy in each area.

Confusion about tipping can add 10 to 20 percent to the total cost of a trip. Here are some basics for you to follow so that your tipping will be proper but not extravagant.

When Tips are Included

- Although tour packages generally include all gratuities for services included in the tour contract, ask about the policy on tipping before signing a contract.
- Ocean liner ticket prices may or may not cover tips, so you should check into the tipping policy upon boarding. Airline personnel do not expect tips.
- At most European restaurants and hotels, a tip will automatically be added to your bill in the form of a service charge of 10 to 20 percent of the total bill. If you pay this charge, you're not expected to add an additional tip.

Separate Tips

- You should always tip a maitre d', waiter, wine steward, porter, bartender, concierge, room attendant, or service person for any unusual or extraordinarily fine service.
- You should tip cabdrivers, provided that a service charge has not been included in the fare on the meter. Service charges are often included on meters in Belgium, Denmark, and the Netherlands. Ask if you're not sure.
- You should tip washroom attendants if you use their services. Give them as little as you can get away with.
- You should tip theater and movie ushers who guide you to your seat—again, a very small amount will do.

Handling Beggars

Beggars are most common in France, Italy, Portugal, and Spain, although you'll run into a few panhandlers in the central and northern countries as well.

- Sometimes begging borders on extortion. For instance, if you leave your car to do some sightseeing, you'd do well to give a few small coins to the leader of the group crowding around you. He then becomes the car's protector. Surprisingly, you rarely get ripped off if you pay this small fee. (Not surprisingly, if you don't pay, you may find that minor "accidents" occur in your absence.)
- Say "no" to most other requests and keep moving.
- If you are approached by a woman with a baby over her shoulder and an outstretched palm, or by a young woman asking you for money because she hasn't eaten in a week, offer her something to eat. She'll usually turn it down. If not, feed her.

Protecting Yourself and Your Belongings

Suspicion and wariness require energy and are not very pleasant sensations, but they do prevent trouble, which would be even more unpleasant.

Protecting your Belongings

- Leave all expensive jewelry at home. You can pick up all sorts of gold and silver imitations for a song—that's what the Europeans do! Follow their lead.
- Never carry all of your valuables in one place. Split up your documents and money. If you put your passport, tickets, money, traveler's checks, and credit cards in one place, they can all be taken in one shot. *This is basic street sense.*
- Keep anything valuable out of sight and in inconspicuous containers. If you have to leave something valuable in a car (not a good idea), put it in the trunk, but don't do it when anyone is watching. Stow your cameras in an inexpensive carrying bag—one that looks as if it could just as easily be carrying groceries.
- If you do leave something in the trunk of your car, never leave it overnight. Don't leave anything in a trunk in isolated areas either.
- Don't set anything valuable near an open window or on a curbside table (as when dining *al fresco*).
- Never take public transportation, especially buses or trams, after cashing a large amount of money at the bank. Get the money back

to your hotel safe and take just what you need for the day.

- *Just what you need for the day* is the key phrase. You don't need to carry a passport, three credit cards, all your traveler's checks, most of your money, and your airline tickets—leave them in the hotel safe. Take just enough to get you by—one credit card will often do the trick, except in Eastern Europe.
- If a hotel safe is unavailable, you're stuck with carrying everything valuable with you. Again, split up all valuables into different areas on your body.

Pickpocket-Proofing: How to Carry Valuables When You Must

There are times when everything you own is either on your body or in your bags. Violent crime is not common in Europe, but rip-offs of bags and pickpocketing are, especially by Gypsy children in Western Europe and by organized bands of pickpockets in Eastern Europe (where you have no choice but to carry lots of hard currency). Here are some tips:

- A small, durable traveler's pouch that can be attached to a belt and worn under your pants or skirt is the best place to carry valuable documents and money. Anyone with a basic knowledge of sewing can make one of these bags and equip it with a good zipper. You can also buy them. Get one!
- Second best but good is the inside pocket of a coat or jacket that has been modified with a zipper. You can alter these pockets so that they're twice as deep and twice as hard to pick. The zipper is crucial. No zipper? Use a safety pin as a deterrent to nimble fingers.
- Never carry your wallet in a rear pocket! A pickpocket can rip it off in a second. A side pants pocket is only a little better. If that's all you've got, buy a nappy-surfaced wallet or put a rubber band around it—this can make it harder for pickpockets to grab it.
- If you're carrying a purse, put it in front of you with your arms crossed over it. Your wallet should be at the bottom. If your purse is at your side or behind you, a thief will slash it open with a razor blade and be gone in seconds.
- Don't carry cameras hanging from your neck. Thieves just pull them off—hurting your neck in the process!

Situations Pickpockets Like

- Pickpocketing is most common in crowded areas such as markets, buses in rush hour, subways, and beaches.
- Pickpockets prey on careless and drunk tourists—in that order. If

you want to tie one on, carry only what you can afford to lose.

- Be wary of minor accidents: being bumped, having your foot stepped upon, being shoved. If your mind is not on your money, you will be vulnerable to pickpockets.
- Avoid commotions of all kinds. Pickpockets love to create them. Move away from any commotion as quickly and unobtrusively as possible.
- Pickpockets often pose as drunks. If someone wraps his arms around you, watch your wallet—he's probably feeling for it.
- If you're being pushed around in a crowd, drop your arms and turn around to face the person bumping you. A thief will tend to turn his or her head and move away quickly.
- Watch out for Gypsies, especially in crowded, noisy areas. Little children will come up to you on crowded streets and hold a piece of cardboard at waist level, confusing you. Meanwhile, another child ducks underneath the cardboard and grabs your wallet. Be alert and bat away any pieces of cardboard immediately.

Protecting Valuables in Stations

- Safety lockers, if available, provide a good way to store excess baggage or valuables. Ask at information booths for the location of storage facilities.
- Never ask for help when placing bags in storage lockers. Thieves will switch keys on you.
- Many cities have storage facilities for baggage. Some require you to declare the value. When you return to pick up the bags, you'll often be asked to pay a 1 percent insurance fee. Another of countless reasons to travel light.
- Stay with your bags—assume that if they're left unattended for a second, they'll be ripped off. Chances are good that they will be.
- Travel light so you can carry your bags with you onto planes, trains, and buses. The minute your bags are out of sight, you have no way to keep track of them.

Protecting Valuables in Cars

- Try not to leave anything valuable in a car. A good thief can get into a car or trunk in a few seconds.
- If you have to leave things in a car, open the glove compartment to show a potential thief that it's empty. Put your gear in the trunk. Don't leave it too long, and absolutely never leave baggage in a car overnight.
- If you travel in your own car or RV, consider a built-in safe—somewhere underneath the car—it doesn't have to be large. Many expe-

rienced travelers use this "hidden compartment" for valuables and documents—it's unlikely that someone will find it.

- Note that thieves are attracted to cars with plates from other countries. So if you're in Germany with French license plates, you're tipping your hand.

Protecting Valuables in a Hotel

- Many hotels have safe-deposit boxes at the front desk. Take advantage of them. There's usually no charge, unless you lose the key, and then the charge for a replacement will be stiff.
- When getting valuables out of a safe, be attentive. This is one time when thieves will try to distract you.
- If you're in a budget hotel, don't leave valuables unattended. Carry them into the shower or bathroom if you have to. If you're in a communal area, place valuables in a ziplock bag. Hold the bag in your teeth while taking a shower (sounds comical, but it works).
- Note that almost all hotel rooms have doors with locks and bolts. Use them. If the door doesn't close tightly or if the locks seem flimsy, jam a chair underneath the knob to make the door difficult to open.

Protecting Valuables at the Beach

- Leave as much as you can at your hotel, preferably in a safe-deposit box.
- Pin your money to a towel or piece of clothing that no one would suspect as a hiding place. Leave nothing of great value in your purse or bag, which will be the first thing stolen. The purse becomes a decoy.

Preventing Muggings

- During the day, walk close to walls. Do the opposite at night: walk far away from walls. Never, ever walk down a lonely, deserted street at night. Be wary of such places even during the day.
- Never completely turn your back to the sidewalk when looking for a house number or unlocking a door.
- If you've just been to the bank and are carrying quite a bit of cash, walk against the flow of traffic. This makes it easy to spot anyone following you.
- Be wary of approaching motorbikes.
- Finally, if you do get robbed, don't resist. Thieves are usually scared to death; they just want to get the money and run. Give it to them. Say absolutely nothing. If you don't move, resist, or talk,

your chance of bodily injury is minimal—that's what the experts say!

Losing Things

It is very easy to lose things while traveling because you're constantly disoriented, frequently tired and fuzzy, and often moving at such a quick pace that it's hard to keep track of where you are or what you've got.

- Consider a special bag for things that are really important to you. Carry everything in that one bag except money and valuables. You'll be less likely to forget the bag than an individual item, like a pair of sunglasses or a small camera or a favorite pen or a lighter.
- The quickest way to lose something is to set it down. You may put a camera on the seat next to you, and the next minute, you're four blocks away and realize that the camera didn't come with you. What a sinking feeling and a mad dash to claim it—if it's still there!
- Try to establish a place for everything so you'll know where things are at all times. This routine has a calming effect and helps cut down on the loss of items through carelessness, fatigue, or simple oversight.

Hotel Fires

Here are a few basic tips to follow in case of a hotel fire:
- Rent rooms no higher than the seventh floor in any high-rise hotel. Most countries have firefighting equipment that can reach this height.
- Note fire exits. Use these, not elevators, in an emergency.
- Fire alarm? Check your door to see whether it's hot before going into the hall. Take your key with you.
- Escape down if possible. If not, go to the roof.
- If you can't leave your room, call the front desk or fire department. Soak towels and place them under the door. Cover vents. Saturate everything with cold water, especially the doorway.
- Smoke is more often a threat than fire. Stay low to the floor. Breathe through a damp towel. Open windows only to clear your room of smoke. Otherwise, keep them closed.

Earthquakes

Earthquakes are most common in Southern Europe. Here are some tips just in case:
- Many larger buildings have been constructed to sway (but not give way) during major quakes. Do not be alarmed by this motion.

- Get away from walls and windows and take cover, preferably under a table, desk, or bed.
- Stand in a doorway if you're in a small building or a structure that might collapse.
- Never use elevators during a quake and avoid stairways as well. You're better off staying put in a room!
- If you're out on the street, go to the center of the road if possible—watch out for panicky drivers. The facades of buildings tend to crack and fall away in earthquakes, so try to keep clear of them.
- If you're driving, come slowly to a stop and simply sit out the quake in your car.

Safety for Women

Attitudes toward women vary from country to country. Women who travel in Europe—especially those who travel alone—should take note of the following precautions.

Personal Safety for Women

- Do not hitchhike. Although many women encounter no problems hitchhiking in Europe, the police files are filled with exceptions to prove the rule: hitchhiking is more dangerous for women than for men, especially for women traveling alone.
- Make use of inexpensive public transportation instead. Second-class trains don't break the bank and can be combined with travel on buses, trams, subways, and trolleys to get you just about anywhere. You'll meet many fascinating people traveling on public transportation—the low-risk, low-cost way to travel.
- When using any form of private transportation, never travel alone—not even in taxis. Robbery—and rape—in taxis is common enough to be frightening.
- Schedule most of your long-distance travel for the day. Try to avoid travel at night when you're more vulnerable.
- Travel light. Remember that the weight of your luggage will affect both your attitude and your vulnerability.
- Try to get by with a single piece of luggage, one no larger than a carry-on bag for a plane. This gives you freedom and mobility in every situation, from boarding public transportation to checking into a hotel.
- Women should avoid rooms with easy access to the outside, especially rooms on the first floor or with sliding glass doors.

- Never give out your room number in a hotel. Always meet new acquaintances in the lobby.
- When driving anywhere, keep all doors locked.
- Two women traveling together are much better off than a single woman, but you should still be wary and avoid provocative situations.
- In a hotel, have your key in your hand as you make your way to the room. You'll avoid fumbling through your purse outside the door.
- If it's possible, always let someone know where you're going and when you intend to be back. This could be a friend or just someone at the front desk of a hotel.

Problems for Women in Southern Europe

Women do not go out at night alone in Southern Europe—with the exception of prostitutes and foreigners who don't know better. Find an escort for evening entertainment or go with a tour. If you travel alone in Italy and Spain, you must cope with the aggressive behavior of men. In these countries, men will stare, make lewd comments, or pinch women's rear ends—hard. Three suggestions:

- Ignore stares, comments, or gestures. Do not look at hecklers, keep moving.
- Have someone you trust walk directly behind you in a crowd. And place your back against a wall when riding in an elevator.
- Walk against, not with, the main flow of pedestrian traffic when you can.
- If you know who's doing the pinching (it can be hard as hell to figure out!), turn and face him. Say *Basta!* in a firm, no-nonsense tone of voice. This means *enough*—and that's usually enough.

Problems for Women in Eastern Europe

Use common sense as you would in other areas. The following are two important tips:

- Dress conservatively. If you have long hair, tie and cover it up with a scarf. Avoid makeup. Leave your expensive jewelry and watch at home. Be as inconspicuous as possible. One woman I know had stones thrown at her when she got off a train in a rural area. She believes that it was because she was wearing lipstick. When she changed her style, she no longer had problems.
- Women are often hassled when they eat in inexpensive places. Drunkenness in Eastern Europe is a real problem. While the rooms in first-class or luxurious hotels are much more expensive for for-

eigners than for locals, the meals are the same price for everyone. So eat in better restaurants to avoid being hassled by drunk locals.

Up-to-date Information on Personal Safety

- Updates regarding travel safety are available from the U.S. Department of State, Citizens' Emergency Center at (202) 647-5225.
- Updates are available in Canada from the Department of External Affairs in Ottawa at (613) 992-3705.

Eating and Drinking

Crusty and warm French bread fresh from the oven ... moist filets of herring smothered in bits of onion on a piece of rich rye bread ... succulent snails simmering in sizzling garlic butter ... Spanish *paella*—chunks of chicken, meat, and seafood served on a hot bed of saffron-soaked rice ... fettucine, lasagne, rigatoni—pasta in every imaginable form ... pastries from tarts to *petits fours:* just a few of the taste treats that are in store for you in Europe.

Europe is filled with special drinks too, from *schnapps* and *slivovitz* to *genever* and *grappa.* Start off with a few drinks of *aquavit,* chilled in the snow until it's so cold it slides down your throat like a chip of ice; or sip the licorice-tasting *pastis,* which turns cloudy with a splash of water or piece of ice; or try chugging *aguardente,* a favorite of Portuguese fishermen, while you watch it burn holes in the deck where you spilled it.

Ordering Food

There are two basic ways to order food and drink in European restaurants: *à la carte* or *table d'hôte. À la carte* means that you order and pay for each item separately. *Table d'hôte* means that you order an entire meal, from soup to nuts, for a set price.

- A set-price meal is usually a better deal than an *à la carte* meal. Most set-price meals include the cover and service charge, as well as the cost of either a beer or a carafe of wine.
- Synonyms for *table d'hôte,* which includes the concept of a daily special, are *dagens rätt, dagens rett, menu, menù del dia, menu turistico, menu touristique, plat du jour, prezzo fisso, prix fixe, set-price meal, sumarrettir, tagesgericht, tagesteller,* or *tourist menu.* If you want a daily special or a set-price meal, ask the waiter to point them out on the menu.

Fashionable Restaurants

In Great Britain, better restaurants have been given star ratings by Egon Ronay (a travel writer) and the automobile clubs. On the Continent, the most reliable ratings have been done by Michelin. Restaurants are proud of these ratings and display them at the front entrance for all to see.

Reservations

- If you absolutely must eat at a certain fine restaurant, you can make reservations from the States by writing the management and including a deposit. Better restaurants usually require reservations, although this is not a universal law.
- Or, if you are staying at a nearby hotel, ask the concierge there to contact the restaurant on your behalf, particularly if there's a language barrier. (This is a service that you should reward with a tip.)
- Or call the restaurant yourself as soon as you arrive in Europe.
- Restaurant reservations are very important in Eastern Europe. Go to the better hotels or restaurants and make reservations in person for a meal later in the day. In some areas lunch is the big meal. Without reservations in some areas you may not get a meal. Tour operators sometimes book all available tables, so take reservations seriously. Note that prices in first-class hotels are often quite reasonable by Western standards. Only in a few luxury hotels or stuffy restaurants will prices be high. Better restaurants are particularly recommended for women traveling alone, since they will rarely be bothered there by locals.

Best Times for Best Meals

Better restaurants tend to be more crowded in the evening than at lunch, so be flexible if you have your heart set on eating in a certain place.
- Note that in some Western European countries Sunday lunches are crowded in the better restaurants. Also, in parts of Eastern Europe lunch may be the hardest time to get into good restaurants.

Dress Requirements

- Ask whether there are any dress requirements when making reservations to avoid being turned away at the door. Very few restaurants have stringent dress codes these days.
- A dark sports coat with tie for a man and comparable dress for a woman are suitable in most restaurants at noon and night. How-

ever, some places insist on more formal evening attire on certain nights.

Drinking With Meals

In Europe, it's considered gauche to have an American-style cocktail before dinner. Alcohol dulls taste buds and makes it more difficult to appreciate good food.

- Replace cocktails with a glass of sherry, white port, or similar light aperitif.
- Order water after ordering wine or skip water altogether, if it's not important to you. In more sophisticated restaurants, it's considered gauche to order water with your meal.
- Don't feel that you have to splurge on a high-priced wine, which will double the price of your meal. Do what most sensible and experienced gourmets advise: settle for a good, medium-priced wine that goes well with the meal.
- Order wine by the glass if you prefer, just as you would in less fancy places. This is highly recommended for people who drink lightly.

Ordering Wine

- If you know which wine you want, order it.
- If the wine list does not give enough information to let you make an intelligent choice, ask the waiter to bring several possible choices to the table. Don't hesitate to ask for advice.
- You should be shown the bottle before it's opened. If a bottle arrives already opened, send it back. No European would allow such a thing to pass.
- If the waiter tells you that they don't have the bottle of wine you ordered, but they do have one just like it, ask the price. This will avoid angry confrontations at bill time.

Wine Etiquette

- If you choose a red wine, ask the waiter to open it immediately to let it breathe. If it's the only wine you'll be having with your meal, ask the waiter to pour it right away.
- Note that white wine and some Portuguese red wines should be chilled. The long-necked bottles of German and Alsatian white wines make this difficult, unless they're turned upside down in an ice bucket. A good waiter will do this without being told. Don't let the wine get too cold or it will lose some of its taste and bouquet.
- After opening a bottle, the waiter should hand you the cork.

Wines For a Splurge

Red Wines

Country	Region	Best Labels
France	Bordeaux (5-year-old)	Lafite
		Latour
		Haut-Brion
	Burgundy (3-year-old)	Romanée-Conti
		Le Musigny
		Le Chambertin
		Clos de Fèves
		Le Corton
	Beaujolais (1- to 3-year-old)	Brouilly
		Chénas
		Chiroubles
		Côte de Brouilly
		Fleurie
		Juliénas
		Morgon
		Moulin-à-Vent
		Saint-Amour
	Rhône	Châteauneuf-du-Pape
		Côte Rôie
		Hermitage
Italy	Chianti (Classico)	
	Bardolino	
	Barolo	
	Valpolicella	
	Barbaresco	
	Gattinara (Monsecco)	
Spain	Rioja	

White Wines

Country	Region	Best Labels
France	Bordeaux	Sauternes
		Graves
	Burgundy	Chablis
		Pouilly-Fuissé
		Saint-Véran
		Pinot-Chardonnay Mâcon
Germany	Mosels*	
	Rheins	
Italy	Soave	
	Verdicchio	
	Orvieto	

* Look at label: *Qualitätswein* is good; *Qualitätswein mit Prädikat,* better.

Squeeze the cork to make sure it's solid, then give it a quick sniff to check for any rancid odor. Set it on the table. The waiter will then pour some of the wine into your glass.

- Watch out for a foul taste from the cork or an acid (vinegar) bite. You will eventually get a bad bottle of wine, and it is not bad manners to send it back. However, bad bottles are very rare.
- If you think the wine is borderline, let someone else taste it for a final decision—even the waiter. This may not be perfect etiquette, but your enjoyment should come first.
- Large wine glasses and water goblets are best for drinking wine. If you think the glasses are too small, ask for larger ones.

European Table Manners

- It's not unusual for lunch or dinner to last two or three hours.
- You can put your forearms (not your elbows) on the table, and you will fit right in.
- When you eat with Europeans, always wish them "good appetite." If you can't say it in the native language, say it in English.
- In many countries, foods will not be served simultaneously or on the same plate, but as a succession of dishes.
- Europeans eat with their forks in their left hands so that they don't have to shift them back and forth when they use their knives. (It makes sense.)
- Many restaurants use the same knife and fork for all courses. You're expected to wipe them off with a piece of your bread.
- You can also use bread to wipe the plate clean. Or put bread on a fork to mop up sauces.
- Europeans often skin fruit with a knife and fork.
- Americans will spit seeds and pits into an open hand before placing them on a plate. Europeans will spit them into a hand cupped as if it were holding the bottom of a glass, then they will put the pits on the plate.
- Americans place their knife and fork side-by-side on the plate to signal that they are done with a meal, while Europeans often cross them.
- When toasting someone in Europe, don't clink the glasses together. Do look the other person squarely in the eye.
- Note that most Europeans do not order coffee with the meal, but drink it afterward. Coffee tends to be very strong.

The Cloak Room

Leaving an umbrella and overcoat in the cloak room can be taken very seriously in some restaurants, even smaller ones. If someone comes over and practically yanks your coat away from you, you have inadvertently committed a faux pas, namely not leaving your coat where it belongs.

Good (but Less Fashionable) Restaurants

You really don't have to splurge to eat well in Europe. After all, most Europeans don't eat in the fancier places, but they still demand quality for their money. And they get it.

Signs of a Good Restaurant

To determine whether a restaurant is going to be a good risk, look for the following things:

- A menu (in the native language) posted outside near the entrance. This will make it easy for you to judge both the food and the price range before going in. Places with charm and good food often have menus written out in longhand. Specialties change daily, and this is the easiest way for the restaurant to keep up with them.
- A series of set-price meals on the menu. In Europe, it's common to see four or five set-price meals. Each should include an hors d'oeuvre, a main dish (or two), vegetable, salad, dessert, bread, and so on. You won't pay for these items separately, or *à la carte*.
- A well-dressed clientele with a sprinkling of businesspeople.
- A well-lit, cozy, and cheerful interior.
- Lots of people during the main meal hours.
- Only one or two waiters working, because the restaurant is small and intimate.
- Good, moderately priced wines.
- Cloth napkins.
- Flowers simply arranged in inexpensive vases.

Saving on Tips

In most European restaurants, a service charge is added to the bill, so check to see if it's there before leaving an additional tip.

- If you see something like *service compris* or *servizio compreso* written on the menu itself, the tip is included in the prices listed, and the waiter should not add any further charges to the bill. Check it, however, since many waiters make conscious efforts to dupe American tourists.
- If you see *service non compris, service en sus,* or *service net* on the menus, service is not included.

- If you're not sure whether the service charge is included in the listed prices, just ask—preferably before ordering.

Cover Charges

In many restaurants, you pay what is known as a cover charge. Sometimes it's included in the listed prices, sometimes it's not.

- Look for *couvert, coperto,* or *cubeirto* noted somewhere on the menu.
- Even if you don't find these words, ask the waiter whether there is any cover charge.

Cutting the Cost of Meals

- Eat in places offering simple, filling meals, such as in self-service cafeterias (*buffet express* in Eastern Europe), in local beerhalls and pubs, or at milk or wine bars. In some of these places set-price meals often include either a glass of beer or wine.
- If prices are not posted, have a pen and paper handy for the clerk to write down the price.
- Never place money on a counter until you have the full amount. While you're looking for the rest, the money may be taken or exchanged for a smaller amount. Carry small denomination bills so that you can pay nearly the exact amount for any food purchase.
- Eat your main meal at lunch. You'll enjoy the same food at a fraction of the price you'd pay in the evening.
- When a menu lists several separate but similar dishes, order the least expensive dish. The more expensive dishes are usually a snare for tourists and snobs.
- Share a meal with a friend if you're really strapped. Just ask for another plate. You'll be charged a small extra fee for this service.
- Ask the waiter whether the restaurant serves half portions. If it does, you'll cut the cost of the meal considerably.
- Don't order the same dish as someone else at your table if you're both hearty eaters. If you both order crab, they'll often split the crab in two. If only one of you orders crab, they'll give that person the whole thing.
- Follow the drinking habits of the area in which you're traveling. Replace cocktails with a local drink.
- In modest restaurants, ask for a house, ordinary, open, local, table, or regional wine. These terms refer to wine served in carafes (pitchers). Carafes come in one-quarter, one-half, and one-liter sizes. You may have to use sign language to indicate what size you want.
- Avoid ordering a rosé for "split parties." Order a bottle of red and

bottle of white. Those who want rosé can blend the two in a glass—that's how it's done. Avoid sparkling wines (*Schaumwein, spumant, spumante*); most are inferior and overpriced.

- Skip soft drinks, butter, and ice. Most Europeans go without these "luxury" items. When you see the prices, so will you!
- Skip coffee at the end of a meal, if you can, because it's very expensive.

Watching out for Con Games

Most restaurants are reputable businesses. But a lot of money can be made by fleecing unsuspecting tourists—so beware.

- Avoid places with tour buses waiting outside, or any establishment that hires a food pimp to stand in the doorway and usher you in! Good places don't have to be sold.
- Always ask to see a menu. It should be the same one posted outside. Every dish or set-price meal should have a price clearly indicated next to it.
- If a waiter tells you that there are no set-price meals today, despite what the menu out front says, get up and leave the restaurant. That menu is a trap for tourists, since *à la carte* prices will be higher.

  The exception to this is in Eastern Europe, where it is common for items listed on a menu to be unavailable. You may be limited to just a few choices. This is not a con; it's reality.

  However, always insist on seeing the price of any item in writing, either on a written menu or on a piece of paper handed to the waiter. If you can't get anything in writing, go to another restaurant.

- Menus in Eastern Europe often do not list drink prices. Always ask the price of any drink before ordering. Specify local drinks to save money, since imports are often extremely expensive.
- Bait-and-switch techniques are common worldwide. One of the most common: "We don't have the dish you ordered, but we do have one just like it." Ask for the cost of the new dish!
- If a waiter places unsolicited gifts on the table, such as butter or unordered hors d'oeuvres, ask how much they cost. If the cost seems unreasonable, send them back.
- Some waiters write the bill on the tablecloth (really made of paper) or blurt out a figure after mental gyrations lasting a minute or more. To avoid being overcharged, add the bill up yourself. You might make a mental note of the approximate cost while ordering.
- If you think someone has overcharged you, say, "The last time I was here, the wine (or whatever item) was less expensive." If they've made an error, they'll excuse themselves and change the price.

Picnicking

A long-time favorite form of entertainment, picnicking is one of the best ways to keep food costs down in Europe. Europeans avoid the high cost of dining-car food by doing this on trains—so why not give it a try? Naturally, if you picnic on the roadside, get well off the shoulder to avoid possible accidents and a fine.

Shopping for Supplies

You'll find most kinds of food in supermarkets, although in smaller towns you will probably have to go to several shops to get what you need. Each shop will specialize in one product: baked goods, meats, cheeses, produce, wine, and so on. Foods will be sold in metric measures: a kilo, made up of 1,000 grams, is equivalent to 2.2 pounds; a liter is about a quart.

- Never buy picnic food in train stations. Go to a nearby market, where prices will be lower and the quality will be higher.
- Carry a fish-net or plastic bag with you, since many smaller stores won't provide bags.

Buying Bread

- Try to buy bread early in the morning when it is warm and fresh. Since these breads go stale quickly, buy only the amount you'll need.
- Ask to have a larger loaf cut in two if you won't need it all. You'll pay for the half loaf only.
- To prevent bread from going stale, wrap it loosely in a moist towel.

Buying Meat and Cheese

- Meat will often be sliced to your specification. You can specify either a certain number of slices or an exact total weight.
- Whenever you buy meat in a shop, ask for a little less than you think you'll need. Butchers always cut extra, knowing that no one will refuse meat that's already been cut.
- As with fresh bread, you may have trouble with cheese drying out. Wrap it loosely in a towel lightly moistened with vinegar.
- Some cheeses, like Camembert and Brie, taste best *au point,* a French expression meaning creamy in the center. However, these cheeses should be stored in a plastic bag, or the aroma will overpower you as they ripen.

Buying Produce

- Don't be intimidated into buying poor produce just because the owner decides to stuff bruised apples in your bag—but don't offend the owner by fingering too much of the stock.

Buying Unbottled Wine

In some shops, you'll find huge casks from which you can buy wine in varying degrees (*degrés*) of quality. The better the wine, the more expensive it is. Although the French can distinguish them, you probably won't be able to tell the difference yourself, except between the worst and the best wine.

- Always ask to taste these wines. Some of them may have gone bad. Do the same when buying large flasks of wine (as in Italy).
- Supply your own bottle if you can. If you don't have one, they'll give you one at a small charge.
- Never discard bottles; you'll get a refund for turning them back in. And never cross a border without returning bottles; they may not be accepted in another country.

Opening Bottles

- If you forget to bring a bottle opener, don't despair or use your teeth. Just twist a key or small coin under the metal folds of the cap until they start to bend out. Keep moving the key around the base of the cap until it pops off. It takes a little time, but it works.
- If you forget to bring a corkscrew, push two nails or sharp objects into the cork. Place any long metal object between them and twist. This device will work, though not as well as a corkscrew.

Soft and Cold Drinks

- Cold milk is a common drink in Holland, Scandinavia, northern Germany, and Great Britain. Skip it in other areas (or buy it in grocery stores). Beer could really be considered a soft drink in parts of Scandinavia, because the alcohol content is minimal.
- The inflated price of soft drinks in restaurants eventually discourages most Americans from drinking them abroad. However, bottled soft drinks, sold by the liter in grocery stores, are quite reasonable.
- As with wines, return bottles for refunds before crossing borders. Better yet, return them before leaving town if possible, since bottles sometimes vary by region.

Basics on Water

- The water in the bathroom of a train is not drinkable. Follow the Europeans' example, and bring your own in a flask—the cost of bottled water on trains is unbelievably high.
- You'll find faucets for drinking water in train stations and nearby parks. If you've forgotten to bring a flask, buy water or juice by the bottle in stores near the station. The price will be reasonable.
- In some restaurants you'll find carafes of tap water on the table, for which there is no charge. Do what the locals do and drink it— unless you espy unusual forms of aquatic life in the bottle.
- If there is no water on the table, you'll have to ask for it. Ask for tap water to avoid the charges for bottled mineral water. Here's tap water in five languages: *l'eau du robinet* (French), *Leitungswasser* (German), *l'acqua del rubinetto* (Italian), *a agua a torneira* (Portuguese), *el agua del grifo* (Spanish). There is, however, some chance of getting diarrhea. If this is a concern, order bottled mineral water.
- In Eastern Europe much of the water is polluted. The locals often avoid tap water. Follow their lead to be safe and pay extra for bottled (sealed) mineral water. Some of it has a disagreeable taste but is perfectly safe.
- If you order mineral water, waiters will ask you whether you want mineral water with or without *gaz,* or carbonation. If you don't want fizzy water, shake your head and say *no gaz.* This pidgin talk will get the message across.
- If a waiter brings an open bottle of mineral water to your table, send it back. European custom demands that the bottle be opened at the table. Otherwise, it may just be tap water in a mineral water bottle.
- See the section on diarrhea (p. 223) for information on water safety.

National Specialties and Customs

Every country has its characteristic way with food. During your travels, don't miss opportunities to taste special dishes! The following list is by no means exhaustive. *Bon appétit!*

Austria

- Look for taverns (*Beisl*) for inexpensive meals. Try the local *Konditorei* as well.

- Savor the local custom of *Jause,* a midafternoon snack, at a coffee-house. Coffeehouses have become an Austrian institution, a kind of social and intellectual meeting place, where you can sample a dozen varieties of coffee, including Turkish, which is "hot as hell, sweet as love, and twice as black as night."
- Relatively inexpensive and delicious are local sausages, schnitzels, and fried chicken (*wiener backhandl*).
- Austrians are world-famous for their pastries and desserts. Sample a slice of *Sachertorte* in the Hotel Sacher in Vienna—and you'll soon see why.
- Try the young *Heurige* wines in early May. Places serving these wines hang a sprig of evergreen from the eaves.

Belgium

Over a hundred Michelin rating stars have gone to Belgian restaurants, including one of the rare three-star places outside France (the Villa Lorraine in Brussels). Here you can eat game and seafood to your heart's content.

- Try *moules,* steamed mussels prepared in a variety of ways. Use one of the shells as a pincer to pull the meat out from the other shells—a European custom that works perfectly.
- Try some of the Ardennes ham, if you get a chance.
- Chocolates make a great gift, if you can stop yourself from eating them.
- Eat at a country inn. Many rural inns boast kitchens that would do France justice. Some of them are in the *relais de campagne* chain. Write to the French Government Tourist Office (see p. 248) for a pamphlet that includes simple maps and up-to-date prices.
- Belgian breweries make some of the best beer in Europe, a fact unknown to most travelers. Over 300 varieties of beer are available locally.

Bulgaria

Bulgaria is a poor country, but it is known for its wonderful gardens. Fresh produce is excellent during the summer. Bulgarian cuisine combines Greek and Turkish influences.

- Lunch is the main meal of the day. Hotel restaurants are often your best bet for a good meal. Make reservations in advance. Also good are local taverns (*mehanas*), if you would like to try regional specialties in a casual setting.
- Soups and egg dishes are common and often one of the best values.
- Meat is often served grilled or as a kebab.

- Stuffed cabbage and casseroles in many styles are commonly available.
- Most meals are served with freshly baked rolls. When available, these are excellent.
- During the peak season, salads are a good buy, filling, and usually well-prepared.
- Fresh fruits are an excellent choice in season. Strawberries are very fine.
- Yogurt is popular, reasonably priced, and often served with every meal.
- Baklava is popular and very good where available. Bulgarians make good pastries.
- Local wines are quite good. Plum brandy is excellent with dessert. Rose liqueur is a local delicacy.
- Fruit juices are widely available and delicious. They are exported throughout Eastern Europe.

Crete

Many of the dishes found on mainland Greece apply to Crete as well. Look for certain things in season: artichokes (March), cherries (June), olives (January to February), and oranges (winter).

Cyprus

The local *meze* consists of many dishes. Sample some of each for a taste treat. Specialties include traditional Greek fare—roasted lamb, eggplant-based dishes (*moussaka*), and desserts drenched in honey. Local wines are reasonably priced and reasonably good.

Czechoslovakia

- Breakfasts vary greatly by area and hotel. Some serve extremely large breakfasts, which can be the best meal of the day, others offer skimpy fare. Always ask about breakfast when deciding on a room. A large breakfast can add lots of value to your choice.
- Smaller hotels often have good, reasonably-priced food. Make reservations in advance. Note that in some areas finding a place to eat can be difficult.
- Where available try wine bars (*vinárna*) and pubs (*pivnice*) for regional food. Local wines are excellent, and the beer is as good as it comes. Some beer halls offer as good food as you'll find in the country (as hard as it may be to believe). Note, however, that patrons of some beer halls are hostile to women. Their absence is the only clue you need not to go in.

- Self-service restaurants (*samoobsluha*) are common and reasonably priced.
- Cafes and cafeterias are also springing up, and may offer a less expensive alternative for budget-minded travelers.
- Soups are common and filling. They are an excellent choice for travelers on a tight budget.
- Bread is heavy and good throughout the country where and when available. Go to a local bakery (*pečivo*) early in the day to buy it fresh and to increase your odds of getting some in the first place.
- As in Hungary, goulash is one of the most common and popular dishes. So are dumplings. Potatoes and sauerkraut are common, but other vegetables are quite scarce.
- Where available, pork, goose, and duck are generally excellent choices. Prague ham has an excellent reputation. Smoked fish is also good.
- Many areas serve mushrooms in season. These are a delicacy.
- When apple strudel is on the menu, give it a try. It can be delicious.
- Other delicious pastries and fresh-brewed coffee are served in shops (*cukrárna, cukráreň,* or *kávarna*). If you have a sweet tooth, ask about these locally.
- Plum brandy (*slivovice*) is a good choice with dessert.
- **Warning:** Avoid milk. Recent reports indicate that much of it has been contaminated from environmental pollution.

Denmark

Don't leave Denmark without trying a smorgasbord. The Danish smorgasbord, a cold table of Danish specialties with such delicacies as fresh herring and local cheese, is well worth a splurge. It is generally served at lunch and follows the specific pattern described below, which you should observe. A smorgasbord can fill an afternoon and even the largest empty stomach.

- When your waiter comes to your table, give your order for *schnapps* for the first course and beer thereafter. You can substitute apple juice or soft drinks for both, if you prefer nonalcoholic drinks. Etiquette demands that you have something to drink with the meal, even though it jacks up the bill.
- Gulp, do not sip, the chilled liquor. If you let it warm up, you'll taste it (and you don't want to).
- Take your plate to the buffet and serve yourself any amount of herring and fish you want—but only these, nothing else. Then return to your table and enjoy them. When you're done with the fish, leave your plate on the table and get a new one from the buf-

fet table. You can return as often as you like within any course, but you can't circle back to a previous one.

- Now serve yourself salads and cold meats—as little or as much as you'd like. When you've eaten them, leave your plate behind once again and try the hot dishes on a new, clean plate.
- Follow the same procedure for the finale, the cheese and fruit. When you've finished this dessert, the waiter will appear to take your order for coffee. (Note that the waiter has been around all along, removing dirty plates from the table.)
- Other treats: *smørrebrød* (open-faced sandwiches), and *wienerbrød* (pastries). Also good are draft beer (*fadøl*) and milk (served nice and cold).
- Note that imported wines and liquors are exorbitant throughout Scandinavia. And some of the beers are nearly nonalcoholic. Ask for export beer if you want higher amounts of alcohol.
- Don't confuse *kr* ("kroner"—Danish money) for *kl* ("hour") when you read Danish menus posted outside restaurants.
- Stop at one of the country inns known as *kroer* (*kro* is singular). You'll sample typical Danish fare, from freshly sliced smoked salmon to just-caught shrimp.

England

- English breakfasts are usually filling, with everything from porridge to eggs and bacon. The bacon is usually served on the under-cooked side. If you want it crisp, ask for burnt bacon or bacon American style.
- Don't think that pubs offer only beer. Many of them serve snacks and full meals as well—at reasonable prices. Steak-and-kidney pie is a staple, usually filling and nicely prepared at the right price. Note that beer (ale) is served warm—you get used to it.
- Splurge in London by trying one of the East Indian spots that offer spicy cooking—a real change of pace that will curl your hair.
- Join the British for tea from 3:45 to 5:45 P.M. daily. Dress up and do it right at the following London hotels: Brown's, the Connaught, the Dorchester, the Hyde Park, the Ritz, the Royal Lancaster, or the Savoy. Harrod's, the famous department store, is good too. Do not ask for iced tea, even if it is 90 degrees outside!
- The term *rare* for meat translates to mean slightly pink at best or, more often, well-done. Ask for your meat *bloody,* a term that will pale many an intrepid waiter's face.
- Note that quiche is often served cold. You can ask for it warmed up, but you may get an incredulous look.
- One of the best English desserts is *trifle,* a sponge cake soaked in

sherry and covered with jam and custard. The local cheeses, such as Gloucester or Stilton, are also excellent.

- Ask for a *serviette* when you want a napkin; otherwise, you will have ordered a diaper. Remember—they invented the language, we just perfected it.
- Order a double (for which you will pay double) if you want to end up with something similar to a shot of booze. Eschew minuscule drinks served between acts at London theaters, and pop around the corner to a local pub for a real drink instead.

Finland

- Sample game (reindeer) and seafood, fresh mushrooms in season (spring to late summer), and crayfish (from mid-July to September). Herring is popular year-round.
- The local equivalent to a Danish smorgasbord is the *volleipapoyta*.
- In Helsinki you'll find a number of interesting restaurants specializing in Russian food.
- Try cloudberry and brambleberry liqueurs, which are interesting drinks made from local berries.
- In many areas the best restaurant is in the local hotel.

France

- Sunday lunch in France is similar in popularity to our Sunday night dinners out. Without a reservation you'll have a tough time getting into a restaurant. The French dress up for this special occasion. You should too.
- When driving into the countryside, carry a list of the *relais de campagne*. These little inns are noted for superb food and service. Get the brochure by writing the French Government Tourist Office (see p. 248). It gives full information, including simple maps.
- Bread and *croissants* are equally delicious when newly baked. You'll get them with your continental breakfast.
- In France you'll discover over 500 varieties of cheese. Note that when you're served cheese on a platter, you should always leave the cheese in the same shape that it was in when it came to you (triangles should still be triangles). It is considered very poor manners to do otherwise!
- Always feel free to sample a number of varieties of cheese when in a restaurant. Ask for a small piece (*un petit morceau*) of three or four. There's no extra charge.
- Try soup, omelets, *steak frites* (steak with French fries), *yaourt* (yogurt)—these cost *very* little in most French restaurants and are excellent!

- In small French restaurants, you mix your own dressing from ingredients provided on the table. Pour several spoonfuls of oil on a dish, mix in a little vinegar and a bit of mustard. Sprinkle with salt and pepper. Now mix thoroughly and pour over the salad.
- When eating fondue in France, the custom is to kiss the person next to you if you drop bread or meat into the pot. (Men and women sit alternately around the table.) You also buy a bottle of wine for the group.
- The famous fish soup *bouillabaisse* is made only for two or more people. You'll find that it's fantastic in Marseilles.
- French fries are rarely served with catsup. You'll be offered mustard, vinegar, or fresh mayonnaise in most instances. Again, *vive la différence!*
- Popcorn, only recently popular, comes sugared unless you ask for salt (*du sel*).
- An exception to the rule that lunch is a bargain: meals are more expensive at noon in Nice.
- Many French foods are seasoned with garlic. To cut the aftertaste and reduce bad breath, eat cheese and a couple of sugar cubes drenched in crème de menthe at the end of the meal.
- Few French drink cocktails, considered much too hard a drink to begin a meal. If you order a martini, you'll be served vermouth with a Martini label. Don't make a scene. It's delicious.
- Avoid ordering individual drinks if you're in a group at a night club. Ask for an inexpensive bottle of wine, to be shared by all at the table.
- To sample champagne, try the *caves* (cellars) of Épernay and Reims.
- Throughout France, you can sample wines for free wherever you see the sign *Dégustation gratuite*. It is hard to drive through any wine region without seeing several of these signs.
- *Pastis* is an extremely popular drink, vaguely similar to the now-outlawed absinthe, believed to have driven many an artist insane. Try it in almost any cafe.
- *Cognac,* distilled wine or "the heart of wine," is one of the most delicious drinks in the world. The French serve it in snifters so that you can appreciate its delicate aroma by swirling it in the glass.
- Tap beer in France is called *bière à pression*. In France if you ask for a *demi* (half), you'll usually be served a glass of beer.

Germany

- German breakfasts are usually large and filling, often including slices of meat, hearty breads, and a soft-boiled egg.

- Expect excellent cooking in any of the Romantik hotels and restaurants. These charming inns offer regional cooking at its best (see p. 72). The same is true for the castle hotels, combining Old World atmosphere with outstanding local cuisine (see p. 69).
- In most towns you'll find restaurants that offer peasant fare: rough bread (just baked), sausages, sauerkraut, schnitzel, and home brew. Very reasonably priced.
- Note that sandwiches are often made to order in butcher shops.
- Stand-up stalls often serve good sausages with mugs of beer at reasonable prices, if you're on a truly tight budget.
- You'll find that the food in most German railroad stations is surprisingly good.
- For good value eat in an informal restaurant (*Gaststätte*), beer cellar (*Bierkeller*), wine cellar (*Weinkeller*), or in the townhall restaurant (*Ratskeller*).
- Look for self-service cafeterias for even less costly meals. Note that in some of these you may pay a deposit (*Pfand*) for mugs and cutlery. Get your money back!
- For a real treat, eat at one of the many *Konditorei* for coffee and cake.
- When you're offered a large radish in a beer hall, try it. You pay for the radish and cover it with salt. When the water pours out, you eat it.
- Germany produces extremely fine white wines—and many unique ones at that. It produces some reds as well, but they are not as popular. The local wines are judged. Superior wines are marked *Qualitätswein* on the label. Even better wines are labeled *Qualitätswein mit Prädikat*.
- Sample inexpensive wines at any of the wine festivals, justly famous for raucous and wild times.
- The Oktoberfest (starts in late September) takes place in Munich (*München*) and may well be the most famous beer bash in the world. It goes on for days and nights on end.
- If you order *Bier* in Germany, you will usually get a tap beer (technically *Bier fom Fass*), rather than bottled beer. Each community has a brewery, and these freshly made beers are superb. Order by the size of glass. Point if you can't make yourself understood (only a problem in smaller communities).
- Cold milk is popular only in northern Germany.

Greece

- Search out small tavernas serving national specialties from fresh squid to grape leaves with a rice stuffing (*dolmades*).

- Everyone admits that there is a language barrier in rural areas, so don't be surprised when you're asked to pick out your lunch or dinner; without putting your finger in the pot, point out the dish you'd like to eat.
- Meal hours are late by American standards. Lunch begins at 1:00 P.M. and goes to 4:00 P.M. Dinner begins about 10:00 P.M. and stretches to midnight (more or less).
- Take an afternoon snack at cafes, as many Greeks do, to hold you over until dinner. Dawdle all you want; you don't have to eat and run at these places. Try some of the sweets.
- In Athens, you can get something close to an American coffee by asking for *Nescafé*.
- Don't expect to leave large tips in Greece, but do leave token tips. The tip for the waiter goes directly on the plate, while the busperson's gratuity should be left on the table.
- If you don't like the resin in Greek wines, ask for *aretsinoto krasi,* unresinated wine.

Hungary

Hungary is the Eastern European country the most prepared for foreign visitors at the present. Food is generally available and good.

- Breakfasts in some hotels are hearty and filling. Ask about a typical breakfast when checking into a hotel. A good breakfast adds lots of value to the room price.
- The main meal of the day is lunch, with a wider assortment of dishes and generally of higher quality than dinner. Fill up at this time.
- For good value try restaurants in small hotels, regional restaurants (*csárdas*), beer halls (*söröző*), or wine bars (*bórozó*). Cafes (*kavárna* or *cukrázda*) are famous for pastries.
- Inexpensive meals are served at self-service (*ökiszolgáló*) or at stand-up counters (*büfé*).
- You can also find good dishes at delicatassens (*csemege*).
- Goulash, really more like a soup, is one of the most popular and common dishes. Pork stew is equally good and readily available. Meats are often flavored with paprika.
- The most common meat is chicken. It is usually an excellent buy and nicely prepared.
- Try many of the regional specialties, such as local fish where available or stuffed peppers.
- Local wines are very good and reasonably priced. Savor the liqueur-like Tokaji Aszú yellowish wine. Try apricot brandy as well.
- Yes, musicians do expect tips in local restaurants with live music.

Iceland

- Sample fresh salmon if you have the chance.
- Local drinks pack a wallop, and late-night drinking gets rowdy, especially on Friday and Saturday nights. You may find yourself locked into a local bar if it gets overly crowded. This is as close to the Wild West as you'll get.

Ireland

No one goes to Ireland for its cuisine. The food's just as good and just as bad as English food, so the same advice applies.

- Eat a big breakfast in the morning—porridge, eggs, bacon, sausage, soda bread, tea. It may be the best meal you'll get all day.
- Head for the nearest pub and have a sandwich or some oxtail soup for lunch. If you want a big meal, have it at noon, because Irish restaurants serve only light dinners in the evening. If you do go to a fancy restaurant for dinner, be sure to try the salmon.
- Guinness Stout is, of course, the national drink. It's rich, dark, foamy, and somewhat bitter, and in Ireland it's served at room temperature. Give it a chance.
- You'll never drink alone in an Irish pub. Someone will soon join you and buy you a drink. In fact, it's an Irish custom to buy drinks for everyone in the group, and you'll be expected to do likewise. By the end of the evening (pubs close at 11:30 P.M.), you're likely to have a line of drinks waiting for your attention.

Italy

- Coffee shops, wine bars, and *trattorias* are often less expensive than restaurants (*ristorantes*).
- Meal hours are late, as in Greece and Spain.
- In most restaurants, you can pick the table that suits you and sit down. Then look at the closest waiter for a nonverbal sign of approval. If the table is reserved (which is rare), you'll be directed to another one nearby.
- You are not expected to order a full meal right from the start, although you can if you prefer. Italians frequently order only one dish at a time, *à la carte*.
- You'll often find displays of food at the entrance to a restaurant. If you don't understand the menu, you can always point to things you'd like.
- You can expect a surcharge for the music of a local band at a restaurant or cafe.

- Make a meal of spaghetti, which Italians consider to be no more than an antipasto or warm-up dish. Italians eat less sauce on their spaghetti than Americans do. If you want more, ask for it (*"Più di salsa, per favore"*). Meatballs aren't served with spaghetti in Italy.
- *Al pomodoro* means "with tomato"; *alla Bolognese,* "with meat"; *al vongole,* "with clams." *Scallopine* refers to slices of veal, *salsa* or *sugo* is "sauce," and *al dente* pasta is "slightly chewy."
- Italian pizza disappoints many Americans, because it's crusty and served cool (almost cold). In many pizza spots (*pizzerias*), you can buy it by the slice. You pay by weight.
- Italy is one place in Europe where you can get excellent ice cream—and plenty of it!
- If you're near Verona, head to the Bolla Vineyards to sample wines for free.
- Wines are popular throughout Italy and vary from inexpensive table wines to quite expensive bottled varieties. Reds are generally a better buy in most regions.
- In Sicily, the bottled wines are good and cheap (Corvo Malvasia, Marsala, Segesta).
- Tap beer (*birra del barril*) is not particularly popular.

Luxembourg

- This tiny country offers some of the finest dining in the world. Its tradition is French, and it prepares dishes of game, fish, and fresh vegetables as the French would. Don't miss dining in one of the country inns. Sample some Moselle wines.

Malta

- Start the day off with a typical English breakfast, a real surprise in this part of the world. Fresh fruits and equally fresh fish are your best bets for lunch and dinner. *Lampuka* is a fish unique to the area. Rabbit stew is another favorite.

Netherlands

- If you're trying to keep costs down, look for an emblem with a fork on it in restaurant windows. This is a symbol for a restaurant serving tourist menus. Holland has about 600 such restaurants.
- Don't leave the Netherlands without trying one of the world's greatest culinary adventures: the Indonesian *rijsttafel* (rice table), which consists of a dozen or more dishes. It's a symphony of food, very expensive, but worth every florin.

- Seafood tends to be vastly overpriced. Herring's the exception. When the herring comes in, the Dutch go wild, chomping it down right in the streets along with bits of onion spread on rough bread.
- *Genever,* a Dutch liquor, comes in two strong forms: *oud* (old) and *jong* (young). Both of them could peel varnish off a table.
- Sample beer on a tour of the Heineken brewery in Amsterdam.
- Cold milk is common in Holland.

Norway

- Simple continental breakfasts are often included in room prices. Some hotels serve larger, more typical Norwegian fare that may include a morning *smorgåsbord* with everything from sliced tomatoes and cucumbers to pickled herring and sardines. *Rømmeggrøt,* a filling, fattening porridge, may be difficult to enjoy, though it's authentic.
- Breakfast may include many varieties of milk, some of which are similar to sour cream or buttermilk. For "normal" milk simply ask for *melk.* When in doubt, sample a small amount first. But remember that many Norwegians prefer buttermilk on their cereal!
- Norwegians tend to eat a light snack for lunch. A heavier, more satisfying meal is served in the late afternoon or early evening from 4:00 to 6:00 P.M. It's a better buy than lunch in most restaurants.
- For a coffee break try *vaffler,* traditional waffles that are served cold.
- You'll find excellent peasant food in *caffestova,* coffee rooms featuring hearty cuts of meat, fresh potatoes, and vegetables—all served in simple surroundings at reasonable prices. Such places are not oriented to tourists; that's why they're such an exceptional value. They're often tucked away on second floors with only a simple sign on a first floor door or side of a building. Ask for the nearest *caffestova* if you're having trouble locating one.
- Don't leave without trying *smørrebrød,* extremely popular and very tasty open-faced sandwiches that are served in both simple cafes and fancy restaurants.
- Some other specialties most Americans enjoy: fresh trout or salmon (expensive but excellent); shrimp and crayfish, popular along the coast and in southern Norway; any of the preserves that taste almost like fresh fruit; goat cheese; and multer berries, beige mountain berries, as expensive as they are distinctive in taste.

Poland

Most hotels and boardinghouses will serve a large and filling breakfast. Ask about this when choosing a room. The size of the breakfast may add considerable value to your room choice.

- Lunch, however, is considered the main meal of the day. Finding good food late at night is difficult to impossible.
- Hotels are a good choice for main meals. It's best to make reservations in person in advance. Prices tend to be reasonable. Unfortunately, most hotel restaurants only have a few items listed on the menu.
- Budget travelers will try self-service cafeterias (*samoobsluga*), milk bars (*bar mbeczny*), wine bars (*winiaria*), and desserts at local cafes (*kawiarnia*).
- Soup is one of the most common dishes, quite inexpensive, and filling. In some areas, it may be the only choice available.
- Sauerkraut and stuffed dumplings (*pierogi*) are national specialties.
- Meat, unfortunately, is hard to find in many restaurants. When available, it is best avoided since it's extremely high-priced and may have been sitting around for a long time, since the locals can't afford it. Only eat meat in the finest restaurants. Fish is available in limited areas.
- Mushrooms (*grzby*) are popular in season.
- Fresh fruit is also excellent during the peak summer months.
- The Poles make good local beers. These will be served at room temperature, as in England, unless you ask for them chilled (roughly pronounced "jimney pivoy"). Some say their vodka is as good as Russian, reputed to be the finest in the world. Always avoid imported liquor, since prices are exorbitant.
- Currant juice is an excellent and widely available nonalcoholic drink.

Portugal

- The government supports a network of country inns (*pousadas*) throughout the country. Rooms in these inns are a great value, and so are meals. Country inns offer regional specialties and drinks at bargain prices. You do not have to stay in a *pousada* to eat there, but you should call ahead for a reservation.
- As in Spain, search out typical restaurants (*tascas*) which serve regional recipes at reasonable prices.
- In Lisbon and nearby tourist resorts, you'll be pushed into hearing *fado,* wailing love songs sung by black-shawled women in nightclubs. Wherever you hear *fado,* you'll pay a social security tax on the total amount of the bill. Keep it small.
- Chicken and seafood are the staples, along with potatoes and rice. The latter are served with everything, so ask for green vegetables or salad to break up the monotony.

- Try the chicken *piri-piri,* spicy and delicious.
- Also sample the seafood and beer combination offered in *cerve-jarias.* Noisy, informal, jammed—but great. Draft beer (*cerveja a late* or *cerveja a giraffa*) is cheap, but the shellfish isn't.
- Try the *cataplana* if you get to the southern region known as the Algarve—an excellent stew. Also good is fish stew (*caldeirada*).
- Savor the almond sweets, too. This area is one of the main almond-producing regions in the world.
- Port wine, made in the north, comes in many fascinating varieties that you can sample in the *entrepôts* in Villa Nova de Gaia, the town across the river from Oporto. You'll be able to try everything from the newly fashionable white ports to 30-year-old tawnies.
- Not quite free, but very inexpensive, are the port wines served at the Vinho do Porto do Solar, Rue São Pedro Alcantara 42, Lisbon. Ask the concierge for a map showing its exact location in the center of town.
- Port wine is always passed to the left (port vs. starboard?), even if the person who wants it is sitting to your immediate right.
- Try *vinho verde,* which is consumed young and cool. This wine comes from the northern part of the country and is often over-looked by travelers.

Romania

Finding food in Romania can be a problem. Always carry a fish-net shopping bag with you to stock up on food whenever you see it.

- Food is most readily available in hotels. However, tables are often booked in advance by tours.
- As in rural Greece, there can be a language barrier or lack of any written menu. Simply go into the kitchen and point to what you want. Carry a pen and paper. Have them write down the price of the dish.
- Always pay for food in local currency, even if a waiter insists that it must be paid for in hard currency. This is a con.
- Breakfasts are often included in the price of a room. Ask to be sure. They may be the best meal of the day.
- Soup is usually available for other meals. It can be substantial and reasonably priced.
- When available, meat is often served grilled.
- Ground corn commonly replaces rice or potatoes as a side dish.
- Bread is poor by Western standards. Biscuits (*pogăcsa*) are some-what better.
- When available, cakes or puddings are the preferred desserts.
- Local beer, wines, and plum brandy are all good. Order wine by the bottle for best value. Local products are all reasonably priced.

- If you must have coffee or tea while traveling in Romania, bring them with you. They are often hard or impossible to find.

Scotland

- A well-marked, 62-mile trail winds its way through Scotland from one distillery to another for those who would like to sample some of the world's great Scotches.

Spain

- Throughout Spain, you'll find *paradores,* inns that offer both rooms and meals at reasonable prices. You can get a list of these inns from the National Tourist Office of Spain (see p. 250) or from Iberia Airlines.
- Meal hours in Spain are late. Lunch from 2:00 to 3:00 P.M., dinner from 10:00 P.M. to midnight (an hour or so earlier in the winter). If you want to rub elbows with the Spanish, you must change your eating habits.
- If you want to try typical or regional cooking, ask for a nearby *tasca* or *restaurante tipico.* You may experience a language problem once inside, but the food will be worth the effort—both interesting and reasonably priced.
- Join the locals in sampling *tapas,* snacks found on the counters of bars and small restaurants. Order a glass of wine, which is generally delivered with something to nibble on. If you're with a group of hungry people and want a larger order of any particular item, ask for *una racion.* Don't be afraid to use sign language; just point to whatever food you want!
- Note that some restaurants have two prices. A lower price if you're served at the bar (*barra*), a higher one for the tables (*mesas*).
- Fish is one of the most reliable dishes throughout most of Spain, particularly along the coast. Obviously, it's best if it's *pescada fresco* or fresh fish. Ask if in doubt!
- Don't bother ordering beef. It won't measure up to your expectations.
- Sweets, liqueurs, and cheese will cut through the odor and aftertaste of garlic.
- The safest choice for dessert: fresh fruit, usually ripe and juicy. Peel it. *Flan,* a custard with caramel sauce, can be a good choice in more expensive restaurants but something to avoid in lesser places. Note that pastries in Spain are not as sweet as you're used to, but you should try them anyway.
- For an inexpensive breakfast or late afternoon snack from 6:00 to 7:00 P.M., try *churros,* thin, round doughnuts, or *porra,* thick,

straight doughnuts. Neither are as sweet as our version. You dunk them in coffee and milk (*café con leche*) or hot chocolate (*chocolate*), the latter very thick and creamy. You find these in bars and small cafes.

- *Paella,* bits of fish and meat smothered in saffron rice, should be on your must-try list. It takes 40,000 blossoms of an autumn crocus to make 1 pound of saffron—which explains why it is so expensive.
- *Arroz,* rice, is a staple.
- Stick to red wines throughout much of Spain, but give the white ones a chance in Barcelona.
- Beer halls are known as *cervecerias* and serve good draft beer (*cerveza de barril*) at a fair price.
- To sample Spanish sherries, try the *bodegas* (Gonzales, Byass and Company, Ltd.) near Cadiz.
- *Sangria,* a fruit-filled punch made of different wines, is sweetened with sugar or honey and served in an ice-filled pitcher.
- In the northwestern region around Oviedo, try the local apple cider, *cidra,* somewhat similar to champagne and poured with a flourish from a bottle held high above the glass—a real show.
- In Galicia, north of Portugal, don't miss the *ribeiro* wine; it's sour with lots of body.
- If you prefer drinks with a mild alcoholic content, ask for wine or beer *con gaseosa*. The drink will come mixed with charged water similar to 7-Up.
- A special treat: If you're in Madrid during the summer, try a *leche merengada,* frozen milk and egg whites sprinkled with cinnamon. If you would like it flavored with coffee, ask for a *blanco y negro.*
- *Horchata* is another cold summer drink, but with an unusual flavor similar to that of coconut. It originates in the area around Valencia but can also be found elsewhere.

Sweden

- Although not as well-promoted as the smorgasbord in Denmark, Sweden has its own version. Ask where you can try it. Worth sampling: herring, meatballs, thick pea soups, fresh fish (try crayfish during the summer season), and preserves made from wild lingonberries.

Switzerland

- Varied regional specialties make this a gourmet's paradise. The cultures that make up Switzerland (mainly French, German, and Italian) all have touched the local cuisine. Sample each restaurant's specialty.

- *Fondue,* cheese melted in a pot with white wine and a sprinkling of kirsch, is the most famous national dish. Keep adding wine if the cheese gets too thick. If you're in a ski resort, ask about special fondue nights—it will be the highlight of your trip (lots of laughter, dancing, and possibly a torchlight trip down the hill at night).

Turkey

- Meats are generally served grilled or as kebabs.
- Lamb stuffed with rice (*kuzu dolmasi*) is one of the country's most popular dishes.
- Seafood is excellent in waterfront locations.
- Eggplant is used in many ways for regional dishes.
- Yogurt is widely available, reasonably priced, and very good.
- Local wines go well with the regional dishes. A local drink worth trying is *raki,* flavored with anise, which tastes like licorice.

Wales

- At pubs, order food at the bar and carry it self-serve to your table. Lamb and mutton dishes are a treat. The local beer (*ale*) is excellent. If you want familiar beer, ask for a lager.

Getting Around

Inter-European travel can be quite complex. It's a good idea to read about the modes of transportation you've chosen before you go abroad. Then refresh your memory by reading the appropriate parts of this chapter one more time at the beginning of your trip.

Flying

Read the section on planes (Chapter 6, pp. 52–53) for ways to make the most of inter-European plane travel. Below are a couple more helpful hints.

Paying Departure Taxes

- In some countries, you'll have to pay a departure tax at the airport when you check in. This is a good use for spare change. However, it can be extremely frustrating if you have to cash a traveler's check (and lose on the exchange) just to pay this tax.
- Ask the airline ahead of time whether you'll be subject to such a tax on departure.

Arranging for Cars

Having your own car will offer you great flexibility. Avoid trouble when picking one up in Europe by keeping in mind the following suggestions.

Picking up a New Car at the Factory

- In addition to the basic documents, get the *Green Card* for insurance, the *registration* card as proof of ownership, a nationality sticker (needed to cross borders), and the *list of service stations* that provide maintenance repairs.
- Tell the clerk that you have a first-aid kit and a triangular "Danger" sign, even if you don't, because prices are inflated for these items at the factory.
- Check the car from top to bottom. Make sure everything works: horn, wipers, lights, seats, seat belts, and so on.
- Ask the clerk to show you how to work the jack. (This is a good

way to make sure there is one and that it works.) Check the spare
tire: take it out and look at it carefully.
- Give the car a quick check to make sure all fluids are up to the
Full mark. Don't assume anything.
- Get a good road map.
- Have the car filled up. (The factory will give you just enough gas
to let you get to the pump outside, and sometimes less.)
- Ask for directions to the road leading to your first destination. This
one step can save you an hour or more of aggravation!

Car Insurance

- Insure your car through the factory for the shortest time permissi-
ble. For longer trips abroad, extend the coverage through a private
European insurance company. If you're on a short trip, accept the
fact that insurance will be a rip-off: you have no choice, anyway.
- You'll need a permanent address abroad if you want to extend
coverage through a private company. The permanent address can
be that of a friend or relative.
- Check your insurance company's Green Card, which is a kind of
folder consisting of many sheets of green paper. At the bottom of
each sheet, you'll see abbreviations for European countries. If any
of these has been crossed out, your insurance will not be valid in
that country.
- If you'll be traveling in any of the Scandinavian countries (Denmark, Finland, Norway, Sweden), make sure that none of their
names has been crossed out. If one name has been crossed out,
your insurance will not be valid in any Scandinavian country
because of a reciprocal insurance agreement.

Buying a Used Car

You'll find long lines of car owners carrying placards advertising their
cars in front of American Express offices, especially in the fall.
- Don't look for recent models. They cost the same (or nearly the
same) as brand-new cars when sold on an export basis.
- Make sure that all local taxes have been paid. If you buy a model
slated for export, you won't have to pay them at all.
- If you're buying the car from a private party, make sure that you
can legally have the insurance transferred to your name.
- Buy a car that can be serviced in the area where you'll be traveling.
- Assume that everything's going to fall apart 10 minutes after you
buy the car, and make an offer accordingly.

Renting a Car in Advance

- Make sure that you have the exact address where you are to pick up the car.
- Get a written confirmation of the arrangement in advance.

Renting a Car Once You Arrive

Rent a car where it will be most economical. If you will be traveling extensively by car, plan to start your trip in the country where the costs are lowest (see pp. 60–63). If you plan to travel in Eastern Europe, rent your car there. The car will be better suited to the available gasoline, since pollution control and unleaded gas have not yet been introduced as extensively as in Western Europe.

- Rates are often lower in small towns outside the main tourist destinations.
- During the off-season, you can get substantial price reductions on car rentals from European agencies. Call, or have the concierge call, several agencies to get a few comparative prices. Savings at smaller agencies can range from 25 to 50 percent off the large companies' prices. (Be sure to tip the concierge for his or her efforts!)
- Rent small cars, which are better in every way. They guzzle less gas, are roomy if you're traveling reasonably light, can go anywhere, can weasel into tiny parking spots, and cost less on ferries and toll roads.
- Unlimited mileage agreements at a set cost per week are usually your best best.
- In some areas, there are age limitations on applications for car rental. These vary from age 23 on the low end to age 70 on the high end.

Questions to Ask When Renting Cars

- What is the full car-rental price for the length of time you plan to travel?
- Is there a charge for additional drivers?
- Are there any additional taxes or service charges to pay?
- Is there an extra charge for leaving the car in another city? (Specify where you intend to leave the car.)
- Is there an extra charge for full collision coverage? If so, what is it? Pay it. If full collision coverage isn't available in an area (as in the Azores), do not drive a rental car there. An accident and the ensuing legal hassles could keep you a prisoner in a foreign country for a long time.

- If the car breaks down, who pays for repairs?
- Do repairs have to be done in specific garages, or can they be done anywhere? If specific places are established, get a list.
- Who pays for oil, gas, and lubrication?
- Is there a documents charge?
- How much is the deposit?
- Can you pay the bill in dollars? (Great if you can.)
- What will the charge be if you return the car later than the agreed-upon time?
- If you cut the trip short, what will the charge be?
- If time and mileage come out to be less than the amount of your unlimited mileage agreement, will you be allowed to pay that smaller amount?
- How much is the charge per gallon for filling the car on return? Will you save by filling it yourself?
- Are all the documents (Green Card and registration) in the car?
- Is there a map in the car?
- is the tank full of gas?
- Where's the jack? (Have them show you how it works.)
- Is there a spare tire in the car? (Check to see.)
- Are the tires in good condition? (Check by sticking a small coin into the tread to judge its depth.)
- Are the tires fully inflated? (Consider carrying a tire gauge.) This is especially important in parts of Eastern Europe where finding a garage with an air compressor or pump can be difficult (consider carrying a hand pump).

Shipping a Car to the United States

There's only one word to describe this whole process—painful.

- Note that shipping rates vary, but northern ports are generally less expensive.
- Ask the manufacturer about reduced rates from specific ports.
- Make sure that the shipping cost estimate includes such services as draining the gas tank, steam-cleaning the car, and waxing it (for protection against salt).
- Buy marine insurance.
- Arrive at the pier with as little gas as possible, because the gas tank will be drained.
- You'll have to clear the car through customs in the United States or pay an agent to do it. Either way, you'll pay duty and a handling charge.
- If you leave the car in storage for more than 3 days, you'll pay a daily storage charge.

- Brace yourself for a dock strike, which may delay the unloading of your car.

Driving

A car gives you much better access to the undeveloped areas of Europe than other means of travel do. But driving does have its drawbacks. You will have a lot to adjust to, and a lot to remember about driving laws and customs. For the adventurous, though, nothing beats it!

Gas

- On the Continent, gas is usually sold by the liter (a little more than a quart). In Great Britain, it's usually sold by the imperial gallon (about 5 quarts). Prices may be double the pump total in some areas.
- Because gas station hours and days of business are unpredictable, play it safe and try not to get too low on gas.
- Note that European gas stations often charge for services like inflating tires, cleaning windshields, and checking the oil. Do them yourself to avoid charges.
- In warm weather, buy gas in the early morning or late in the evening. You'll get more gas when it's cool.
- Fill up frequently when you're in Spain, Portugal, Greece, Norway, Sweden, or any of the islands. Open gas stations are long distances apart in these areas.
- Do the same in Eastern Europe. And carry a metal can of extra gas, since stations are often closed or out of gas. Carry a map indicating the exact locations of gas stations throughout the country.
- Supergrade gas (95-octane) is generally worth the extra cost.
- Always ask for a specific amount of gas in the foreign currency, or the attendant may try to squeeze every last cent out of you.
- Fill up before crossing a border into a country where gas costs more. The following countries are listed in order of increasing gas prices: Spain, West Germany, the Netherlands, Austria, Switzerland, Norway, Ireland, Great Britain, Denmark, Luxembourg, Belgium, Finland, Portugal, Italy, France, Sweden.

Gas Coupons or Vouchers

In some Eastern European countries you may still have to buy gas coupons or vouchers to get gas at local stations. The situation in regards to these may soon change, and hopefully this will be an obsolete procedure. At present you have to pay for this gas in hard currency. Ask about up-to-date requirements from the appropriate National Tourist Offices (see pp. 247–250).

When the Gas Tank is Empty

- When you're really low on gas and no gas station is nearby, use the mileage marathon technique: accelerate as slowly as possible to 20 miles per hour, then immediately turn off the ignition while moving into neutral gear. Let the car slow down to 5 miles per hour. Start the engine again and repeat the same steps. This technique can double and even triple gas mileage in an emergency!
- If your steering wheel locks when the ignition is off, this technique will not work. It's also not recommended for steep downhill grades—but you may have to take a gamble. Finally, it's illegal in some areas—but, late at night on a deserted road, you won't really care!
- If you have to stop, don't race the engine.
- If the car won't stop running when you turn off the ignition, pop it dead in gear (not very good for the car, but you'll save gas).
- Don't allow the car to sway from side to side: this will save you 1 to 2 miles per gallon.

Road Travel

The only fast roads in Europe are the superhighways. Other roads can be tied up by traffic, trucks (belching diesel smoke), repairs, mopeds, and even herds of goats.

Coastal and mountain roads must follow the natural contours of the hills, meaning hundreds of curves per mile. Passing is virtually impossible on many of these highways. You move as slowly as the slowest link in the chain.

- Start trips early and end them early.
- Try to average no more than 150 miles per day; even that's quite a bit.
- Do just the opposite of what most Europeans do. Instead of taking a break for lunch, drive between noon and 2:00 P.M. Traffic conditions will be better.
- Avoid driving in cities. City traffic is almost always impossible, except on Sundays. If you have to drive in a city on a weekday, avoid morning and evening rush hours.

Maps

Good maps can make a trip an enjoyable rather than frustrating experience. Chapter 3 has tips on where to obtain maps before you reach Europe, but some prefer to buy them abroad.

- Select maps that conform to the kind of travel you are planning. Why buy expensive, detailed maps if you'll only be traveling between major cities? On the other hand, you'll appreciate such detail when you are exploring some rural areas.
- Many of the foreign automobile and touring clubs offer very good maps; those of the Touring Club of Italy are excellent.
- The Michelin maps, available in most bookstores abroad, are reliable. Get up-to-date maps (check date on cover).
- In Great Britain, you can buy ordinance maps, extremely detailed for off-the-beaten-path trips. In Ireland, look for Geodetic Survey maps.
- Maps showing the exact location of gas stations are critical for driving in Eastern European countries. Get these before attempting travel by car in this area!

Driving Customs in Europe

This chart outlines some of the regional peculiarities that you'll encounter abroad. Note that you must wear a seat belt in most European countries and that children under 12 should be placed in the back seat, according to local ordinances.

Country	Driving Customs
Austria	Driving is slow in most areas.
	Have chains for winter driving.
	In the mountains, cars going uphill have priority.
	Don't drink and drive—not even one drink!
Belgium	Exceedingly slow driving.
	You must wear a seat belt.
	Watch for cyclists—thousands of them.
Bulgaria	Roads vary enormously.
	Avoid dirt roads in wet weather.
	Mountainous roads are often dangerous.
	Traffic is light.
	Get map showing exact location of all gas stations.
	Top off constantly.
	Coupons or vouchers may be required for gas purchase.
	If required, jump to head of the line at gas stations.
	Try to pay in local currency (much cheaper) than with vouchers.
	Stopping in unauthorized areas along roads may result in fines (get a receipt).
	Never drink and drive—never.

Czechoslovakia	Get map showing exact location of gas stations.
	Top off constantly.
	Gas coupons or vouchers may still be necessary.
	No cars are allowed in parts of Prague.
	Parking is extremely limited in Prague.
	Never drink and drive—never.
	Give trams right of way.
	Park only in designated parking areas.
Denmark	Slow driving.
	Many ferries.
	Parking on the right side of the road only.
	Fill up frequently—don't get caught without gas.
	Have low beams on during the day from September 1 to April 30.
	Stiff penalties for drinking and driving.
France	Good driving overall.
	Always give priority to cars on the right.
	Watch for mopeds and cyclists.
	Have chains for mountain driving in winter.
	Keep lights on in fog, mist, or poor light.
Germany	Excellent driving overall.
	Gas stations open 24 hours on *Autobahn*s.
	Very high speeds on *Autobahn*s.
	Blink lights if you want to pass someone.
	Slower traffic must stay on the right!
Great Britain	Slow driving overall.
	Drive on the left.
	Leave turn signal on while passing.
Greece	Ignore horns.
	Watch for flocks of goats and sheep.
	Back roads are quite steep.
	Dangerous dirt roads through the mountains.
Hungary	Roads are quite good overall.
	Gas is generally available.
	Top off regularly, nevertheless.
	Avoid night driving.
	Green flashing lights equal yellow lights in the West.
	Never drink and drive—never.
	Always give right of way to trams.
Ireland	Slow driving.
	Drive on the left.
	Tight, winding roads.
	Watch for flocks of animals.
	Fill up frequently.
Italy	Good driving on main roads, very slow on secondary routes (bad along the coast).
	Don't park in green zones or the car may be towed.
	Charges on *autostrade* are steep; you pay when you exit.

Cars are very helpful on Isola d'Elba.
No cars can go to Capri.
Off-season and round-trip reductions on ferries to Sicily.
Chains are required in mountains in winter.

Luxembourg Good driving overall.
Tight, winding roads.
Watch for cyclists.
Wear a seat belt.

Netherlands Good driving overall.
Wear a seat belt.
Watch for cyclists.
Use major roads when in a hurry.
Leave car parked in Amsterdam.

Norway Good, if long, driving overall.
Don't speed excessively (you will lose your license).
Fill up frequently.
A "mile" is 6 American miles.
Don't drink and drive.

Poland Roads are reasonably good.
Avoid all dirt roads in wet weather.
Carry a map showing the location of gas stations.
Top off constantly.
Watch out for horse-drawn carts.
Avoid night driving.
Never drink and drive—never.

Portugal Slow driving.
Narrow roads in many areas.
Cobblestones dangerous when wet.
Frequent road repairs.
Fill up often when off the beaten path.
Watch for flocks of animals.

Romania Check tire pressure (air compressors rarely available).
Poor roads overall.
Avoid all dirt roads in wet weather.
Traffic is extremely light.
Carry a map showing exact location of gas stations.
Top off constantly.
Coupons or vouchers may still be required for gas.
If vouchers needed, you are allowed to jump to the head
    of the line at stations.
Try to pay for gas in local currency (much cheaper) than
    with vouchers.
Avoid night driving.
Never drink and drive—never.

Spain Very slow driving overall.
Stick to major highways for fast driving.
Roads skirting the coast are slow.
Trucks are a real problem.

	Flash lights or sound horn to pass. Right-hand blinker on trucks is the signal to pass (all clear).
Sweden	Good driving overall. Fill up frequently when off the beaten path. A "mile" is 6 American miles. Don't drink and drive.
Switzerland	Very good driving overall. Cars going up the mountain have priority. Yellow postal buses have priority (you must get over on the shoulder, in some cases). Chains are needed to cross passes in winter. Most driving is not in the mountains.

Superhighways

Using superhighways is the fastest and most efficient way to get around in Europe. Superhighways are called *autoroutes* (French), *Autobahnen* (Germany), *autostrade* (Italian), *auto estradas* (Portuguese), and *autopistas* (Spanish). You'll have to pay tolls on many of them, but if you're in a hurry, they are worth the price.

Speed Limits

Maximum speeds are posted in kilometers per hour (kph). Be prepared for the high (in some cases unlimited) speeds allowed on the major freeways.

- To convert speed limits or mileage signs given in kilometers into miles, divide the figure by 10 and multiply by 6. For example: 80 kph divided by 10 equals 8; 8 times 6 is 48 mph.
- In areas designated for high speed, slower traffic must stay to the right. If someone approaches you from behind, you must move over to make way. Often, cars coming from the rear will blink their lights as a warning signal for you to move over. Because speeds in the left lane can reach 120 to 140 miles per hour, you can cause a serious accident if you don't move over.

Parking

- One of the biggest headaches for the motorist in Europe is finding a place to park the car. You can almost always find space in a garage, but the daily charge of several dollars adds up quickly. Most people prefer to park on the street and take their chances with vandalism. If you've got an antenna, push it down. "Bend-the-Antenna" is a favorite European game, "Break-off-the-Antenna" is a popular variation.

- If you do find a parking place, take it and leave the car parked until you leave the area.
- If the place you find has a meter, take it until an unmetered parking place opens up.
- If the meter expires, you may be fined or have locks placed on your tires.
- Some people think parking tickets make good souvenirs—you'll have to decide about that for yourself. If the car is rented, you'll probably end up paying for the souvenir. If owned, it is unlikely you'll ever have to pay, unless your wheels are locked.

Parking Tickets

"No Parking" signs may be placed on the walls of buildings or painted on the walls, and are sometimes very difficult to see. Make sure you're not blocking someone's driveway, which may be closed with an iron gate. However, keep in mind that police in Europe rarely tow cars with foreign license plates unless they're blocking traffic or the commissioner's driveway. But don't expect immunity from the law just because you're a foreigner.

- Do not park in green zones in Italy, especially if you're driving a car with Italian plates. Your car will be towed away at your expense.
- Do pay the Italians who stick tags on your car; it costs about 16 cents to park.
- Do pay the boys in Naples who hover over you like a swarm of gnats. Give the oldest boy in the group about 50 cents, to be divided up as he sees fit. Make a motion with your hand indicating that it's to be shared (try to give him lots of small change).
- You are supposed to use time discs in blue zones of Europe. These discs can be obtained free of charge in many banks, gas stations, and police stations. They may be nuisances to get, but if you don't want a parking ticket collection, you'll need them.
- In Eastern Europe avoid parking in restricted areas where your car might be seen as a security risk. If unfamiliar with local signs, get information ahead of time when renting the car. In many countries police put special wheel locks on cars. You have to pay a stiff fine to get these taken off. Besides, it's a hassle and takes a lot of time.

Moving Violations

- *Don't drink and drive*—particularly in Austria, Denmark, Finland, Norway, and Sweden, where penalties are stiff for having had even one drink. This charge can put you in the clink for 3 weeks, foreigner or not. This advice goes double in Eastern Europe.

- If you're stopped on any charge, stay cool and show your international driver's license. Generally, except for drunken-driving tags, fines can be paid on the spot, and your license can sometimes get you out of a fine altogether. You'll be given a receipt if you must pay.
- If you are driving someone else's car, you cannot cross borders without written permission from the car's owner.
- If you are traveling with a minor, you cannot cross borders without written permission from the minor's parents.
- Follow local customs concerning headlights. Use parking lights in cities (flashing on your low beams as you approach intersections) if others do so.
- Don't get annoyed at the French for flashing their high beams at you when you're on low. Since they're used to yellow fog lights, white low beams appear too bright to them.
- Watch for a trucker's signals to pass—usually a wave or a turn signal. Say thanks with two bips of your horn; otherwise, leave the horn alone.
- To find city centers, look for signs saying *centre ville* (French) or *centro città* (Italian), or head for the highest visible church spire.
- Always yield to traffic on the right (including pedestrians and cows), especially in France.
- Never cross white or yellow center lines.

Motorcycling Strategies

- When passing long lines of cars, watch for the occasional irate motorist, who (in a fit of jealousy) will swing a door open to knock you off the road.
- Since a touring motorcycle can't stop as quickly as a car, leave plenty of space between you and the car in front of you.
- Stay in the center of your lane: this will discourage motorists from squeezing by you as if you were on a bicycle.
- Be wary of skidding on tram or train tracks during downpours—they get very slippery! So do cobblestones.

Car Repairs

Repairs are generally less expensive in smaller towns. In Southern European countries, repairs often cost a fraction of what they'd cost in the North.

- Always drop your car off at night for repair the next day. This allows the engine to cool off.
- Get an estimate in writing.

- Agree on a pickup time. Have the mechanic note it on your estimate.

European Road Service

Country	Procedure
Austria	Use emergency phones placed at 1-mile intervals on main roads.
Belgium	Call local number for *Touring Secours* VAB-VTB (*Wacht op de Weg*) or RACB.
Bulgaria	Call 146 or wave someone down.
Czechoslovakia	Wait for a Yellow Angel (local auto club) to appear or wave someone down. If near a phone, call 154.
Denmark	Call local number for *Forenede Danske Motorejere*.
Finland	Call nearest filling station.
France	Call local number for *Police Secours-assistance*.
Germany	Call local number for *Strassenwacht*.
Great Britain	Dial 01-262-2638. Use phones placed at 1-mile intervals on main highways.
Greece	Dial 107.
Hungary	Call (1) 115-1220 for the auto club in Budapest.
Ireland	Call nearest filling station.
Italy	Use phones placed at 1-mile intervals on *autostrade*. Ask for *Soccorso autostradale*. In other areas, dial 113 and ask for *Soccorso autostradale*.
Luxembourg	*Dial 311031. Ask for* Secours automobile.
Netherlands	Call local number for *Wegenwacht* (patrols from 7:00 A.M. to 11:00 P.M.).
Norway	Call local number for *Norges Automobile Forbund* (patrols from June 20 to September 1 only).
Poland	Phone auto club in Warsaw at 628-6251 or wave someone down.
Portugal	Call nearest filling station. If you break down on Ponte Abril leading into Lisbon, put a white handkerchief on the car door to signal for help.
Romania	Contact the nearest Carpatji office or wave someone down.
Spain	Call nearest filling station.
Sweden	Call local number for *Larmtjonst AB*.
Switzerland	Use emergency phones placed at 1-mile intervals on main highways.

Breakdowns on the Road

- Members of American automobile clubs can be covered for emergency road service abroad by paying small extra fees for tempo-

rary membership in foreign clubs. Contact the AAA or other automobile clubs for full information.
- If you have a breakdown on a superhighway, lift your hood and wait—and wait, and wait. Mobile road service or police will eventually come your way.
- If you're out in the boondocks, wave down a car for help. Or an oxcart, or a moped, or a . . .
- If you rent a car, ask for a list of numbers to call in case of a breakdown. Get numbers for all the areas you'll be visiting (see below).
- If you buy a new car, check the glove compartment for a pamphlet that lists service stations.

Car Ferries

- You can get information on ferries at the American Express office in most cities.
- Watch for off-season discounts.
- Ask about round-trip discounts.
- In the peak season, try to reserve space in order to avoid delays. If you don't have a reservation, you'll be placed on a ferry on a first-come, first-served basis.
- You can make reservations ahead of time through some railroads. Inquire at the train station.
- The smaller your car, the less you pay.

Taking Trains

Whether or not you use a Eurailpass, taking trains can be a great way to travel through Europe. A few pieces of information can really help make travel go smoothly.

Validating a Eurailpass

You will have to validate your Eurailpass at the station where you start your first rail trip. Small slips can cause big trouble at this point, but you can prevent them.
- Before your turn comes, write down the dates your pass will be valid. Before the clerk writes on the pass, compare your dates. This simple double-checking procedure may save you considerable grief, because any erasures on the pass may cause it to be challenged by conductors.
- If a mistake should still occur somehow, ask the clerk to fill out a paper showing the correct validity dates. If conductors cause problems later on, show them the slip.

- If you board a train without getting your pass validated, the conductor will do so for a $5 charge, which must be paid in the proper foreign currency.

Cutting Costs Without Eurailpasses

- Travel second class—it's 33 percent cheaper as a rule. Go first class in Greece, Italy, Portugal, and Spain if you find second class trying.
- Make a point of asking for the least expensive fare. Check into reductions for group travel, round-trip fares, excursion fares, youth fares, one-day fares, one-week fares, one-month fares. Look into circular tours, midweek fares, weekend fares, regional, family, and gross-kilometer fares, seasonal and holiday fares, senior citizens' discounts. . . . Got the picture?
- Avoid taking trains that require you to pay supplemental charges. Their speed or comfort comes at a price.

Insuring the Best Train Ride

- Get reservations for popular trains to avoid waiting in lines (see p. 57). If you didn't make the reservations in the United States, make them as soon as you arrive in a city. Lines are shortest in midmornings, Monday through Thursday.
- Get a nonsmoker seat if you don't smoke.
- Ask for a window seat, which gives you the window and also a foldout table for writing, playing cards, or picnicking.
- When traveling to a city where you don't have a room reservation, plan to arrive on the earliest train.

Getting to Train Stations

In a number of cities, you'll find that there are several stations, so that making connections can become a headache. Of course, you will have to know which train station to go to for which destination. During rush hours, use the underground (subway) whenever possible to get from one station to another. Crossing cities by taxi is both expensive and painfully slow.

Provisions for Train Travel

- If you want to cut costs, bring your own food and drink. You may want to bring your own water: the water in train bathrooms is not drinkable.
- Bring local currency for each country you'll travel through to buy food or drink or to rent a *couchette* (bunk bed) on board. Buy cur-

rency before getting on the train. Note that in Eastern Europe it may still be illegal to import or export more than a small amount of local currency. Find out about this ahead of time. Hopefully, this silly regulation will be obsolete by the time you read this book.

In Train Stations

- Note that European train schedules use the military (24 hour) system of time so that 12.00 means noon, and 24.00 means midnight. The system is designed to keep you from confusing 5:00 A.M. (5.00) with 5:00 P.M. (17.00).
- Ask a native speaker to pronounce the name of your destination in the appropriate foreign language, so that you will be able to recognize it over the public address system when it is announced.
- If you have lots of luggage, look for pushcarts, which are free—but usually scarce. If your cart won't budge, squeeze or press on the handle to release the brake. (Traveling by train with lots of luggage can only be compared to making frequent and unsuccessful attempts at suicide.)
- Don't be fooled by European train designations. "Direct" might mean "direct to the next station." Ask the clerk for the fastest train to your destination that doesn't require a supplemental charge. On the board that lists trains, *Dep* is an international abbreviation for Departure; *Arr* is an abbreviation for Arrival.

In Eastern Europe

- Find someone who speaks English in a local tourist office, travel agency, or major hotel. Ask him to explain the local train system and symbols in the station. Have him pronounce your destination. Write this down phonetically.
- Get the intended date of arrival of the train at your destination. Note whether you leave on time. As you get closer to your destination, begin to ask whether you have arrived, using the phonetic pronunciation. Simply state the name as if it were a question. The reason that you may have to do this is that many stations are so poorly marked that there is no other way to know where you are.

The Super Trains

The nostalgic will be sad to learn that the famous Trans Europe Express (TEE) trains no longer operate.
- The TEEs have been replaced by a network known as EuroCity. The network consists of 56 day trains and eight night trains that connect more than 200 cities. Although Finland, Greece, Ireland,

and Portugal do honor the Eurailpass, they are not a part of the EuroCity system. Like the TEEs, these trains are faster and more expensive than others.

- EuroCity trains offer both first- and second-class tickets. The latter costs about one-third less.
- The TGVs *(trains à grande vitesse)* of France are part of the Euro-City network. Reaching speeds of just under 170 mph, they are among the world's fastest trains.
- A Eurailpass is valid on all EuroCity trains.
- The TGVs require reservations, even with a Eurailpass. These reservations may be made either in the United States or abroad.
- In the United States you can make reservations through agents or directly with the French National Railway. The latter has offices in Beverly Hills, Chicago, Coral Gables, Montreal, New York, San Francisco, and Vancouver.
- Reservations may be made up to 2 months ahead of any scheduled train departure.

Aboard Trains

- Check to make sure the specific car you get on is going to your destination. Trains are often split up en route!
- If you have to get up for any reason, leave something on the seat—a newspaper, magazine, inexpensive hat, or handmade sign that says "occupied."
- If you stretch out, be sure to take your shoes off. This will prevent encounters with the conductor.
- Think twice before renting a *couchette* (a bunk bed in a compart-ment). If you do rent one, the conductor will give you a sheet (something between a hospital gown and a shroud), a blanket, and (if you beg) a pillow. The compartment will be noisy; and it will be either too hot or too cold. Whether your luggage remains out-side or goes with you in the compartment, it will be vulnerable to thieves while you sleep.

Getting off Trains

- Never get off a train until you've reached your final destination, unless you're sure the trains will be in the station for a specific amount of time.
- Never throw away a ticket until you've passed through the exit gates of your destination train station.
- Get information about the next train you'll be taking before you leave the station. If you find out this information right away, you won't have to make an extra trip or phone call to the train station.

- To save on washroom fees, always find a nearby hotel or restaurant and use the bathroom there.

Hitchhiking

Hitchhiking in Europe is far safer than the alarmists would have us believe, and many dangers can be avoided by traveling in pairs. Hitchhiking is illegal on superhighways—but that's where you get the long rides—so be prepared for occasional exchanges with the police. Be friendly and don't argue.

Prearranged Rides

- Try to arrange rides before you even hit the road. Look at the American Express office to see whether anyone is heading in your direction. Check the bulletin boards at student halls and other youth-oriented places.
- Post your own notice, indicating where you want to go. Make it easy to read and eye-catching—if it's funny, all the better. Use color to make it stand out. Tell people reading the notice how to contact you.
- Be willing to share gas costs with drivers. It will be less expensive than a train fare. Note that organizations have been set up to get drivers and passengers lined up with each other. Ask locally about an agency named Mitfahrzentrale in Germany. Another company, Eurostop, has offices throughout Europe for the same purpose. It is expanding, but presently has offices in Amsterdam, Barcelona, Brussels, Copenhagen, Florence, Milan, Paris, Vienna, and Zurich. I have only read about these agencies and not used them personally, so I can not tell you how efficient or helpful they will be.

Where to Hitch

- Use public transportation to reach the outskirts of a town and stand by a stoplight or stop sign. Don't bother trying to get a ride from a city center to the outskirts, since Europeans rarely pick up short-haulers—except for women hitching alone.
- Try standing near gas stations, rest stops, restaurants, and ferries.
- Don't hitch where there are truly inexpensive alternatives (as in Spain) or where it's generally disliked (as in southern France).

Before you Hitch

- Make sure you have a map with you so you will be familiar with towns en route to your final destination.

- Make big, easy-to-read signs. Write down your destination and the name of the next major town in order to pick up either long or short rides.
- Write the name of your destination in the appropriate European spelling: Athens *(Athina)*, Brussels *(Bruxelles)*, Copenhagen *(København)*, Florence *(Firenze)*, Geneva *(Genève)*, Lisbon *(Lisboa)*, Munich *(München)*, Naples *(Napoli)*, Rome *(Roma)*, Venice *(Venezia)*, Vienna *(Wien)*, and so on.
- If there is room on the sign, include the word *please: s.v.p.* (French), *bitte* (German), *per favore* (Italian), *faz favor* (Portuguese), *por favor* (Spanish).
- Stay as clean as possible. If your clothes are not fresh, splash on some cologne.

How to Hitch

- Try to be either the first or the last person in a line of hitchhikers.
- Carry as little gear as possible, and place what you've got behind you. Motorists don't like to pick up people who are carrying a lot of baggage.
- Take off your glasses (or your sunglasses) so that drivers can see your eyes, and hold your sign in front of you. Face the traffic. Extend your arm with your open palm toward the oncoming cars and your thumb up.
- If you can get someone to stop and talk to you, you've got a ride. Be polite but assertive.
- When you arrive in any large city, ask the driver to let you off near a tourist office or central train station (for easy access to information and room-finding services).

Hitchhiker's Success Rates

When hitchhiking, it's not who you are but who you're with that determines how quickly you will get a ride.

Combination	Results
One woman	Immediate success
Two women	Quick success
One woman, one man	Short wait
Three women	Slightly longer wait
One man	Long wait
Two men	Long, long wait
Three men	Join the army

Cautions for Hitchhikers

- Stay away from curves. Place yourself on a straight stretch of road.
- Stop only in areas with good shoulders.
- If you are hitching after dark, wear something light colored. Stand under a reflecting sign.
- Get well off the road to sleep or eat.
- If you notice that someone is a poor driver, ask to get out right away. No ride is worth a collision.
- Travel with a companion: the ideal team is a man and a woman. You'll avoid robbery and rape this way. Do not allow yourselves to be split up (the woman in the front seat, the man in the rear of a truck).

When to Hit the Road

- Sunrise is great, sunset is almost as good, and nighttime is good but dangerous.
- Midday, particularly in Southern Europe, is awful, as are weekends, particularly Sundays in religious areas. Holidays are a bust.

Hitchhiking Etiquette

- The people already waiting at a hitchhiking area have the priority in choosing a spot, such as the front or back of a line of hitchhikers.
- If a car stops at the middle of a line of hitchers, it's every person for himself or herself. Generally, the person closest to the car will get the ride.
- You should entertain the driver, not go to sleep or sit silent. But don't demand attention—be sensitive to the driver's interest in conversation.

Bicycling

Whether you're using a standard bike or one with a small motor (moped), here are a few tips:
- Many motorists will honk at you. They are doing this for safety purposes. Still, it's extremely annoying.
- Always get far off the road when you stop. If you want to have a picnic, do it away from the road. It is safer there, and you'll avoid a potential fine.
- Never leave a pump on your bike. It is easy to steal. Lock your bike every time you leave it. Use the best lock money can buy.
- Learn how to repair a flat before you begin to travel. Carry a spare

inner tube with you and all appropriate tools necessary.
- All gear should be in a waterproof bag. This way it will stay dry in a downpour.
- Wear a good helmet for safety purposes.
- Gear your pace to the slowest member of the group.
- Each day agree on a planned meeting place in case the group somehow gets split up. Sometimes people take the wrong road or have a flat or just get lost.

Taking Public Transportation and Taxis

The easiest way to learn about the ins and outs of public transportation is to ask the concierge or someone who speaks English at the hotel to explain it to you.

You can also ask the help of many people on the street in Austria (with some communication problems), Denmark, Finland, Germany (with some problems), Gibraltar, Great Britain, Iceland, Ireland, Malta, Netherlands, Norway, Sweden, and Switzerland (with some problems). In other countries, you may have frequent problems communicating. When you do, go to the nearest large hotel and ask the person at the front desk for help. Just remember that people usually like to help other people.

Public Transit Questions to Ask

- What is the best way to get from A to B?
- What is the least expensive way?
- Where do I get tickets or tokens? How much are they?
- Can I get a reduction for buying a pass or a set number of tickets?
- How do I get onto the bus or tram? (You must board some vehicles from the back.)

Public Transit Bargains

- *Amsterdam*. Packets of tram tickets at discount prices are available at cigarette shops displaying Amsterdam Transportation Company emblems.
- *London*. Find "Go As You Please" tickets at the Travel Enquiry Office at Piccadilly Circus.
- *Munich*. Get a 1-day tourist card (*Turistenkarten*), at the Central Railway Station.
- *Paris*. Booklets or *carnets* of 10 tickets are available at subway (*métro*) ticket windows.

- *Rome*. Buy a 1-week pass at Central Station.
- *Stockholm*. Buy a 3-day pass at the tourist office.

Public Transit Tours

By using public transportation, you can often take tours at a fraction of the cost of organized tours. A few examples (more exist):
- *Amsterdam*. Pay for circular tours from and back to the Central Railway Station.
- *Helsinki*. Public transit tours cost a pittance.
- *London*. Take bus No. 15 from Selfridges or on Oxford Street with panel marked "Aldgate"; or take No. 11 east from Victoria with panel marked "Liverpool Street."
- *Rome*. Take bus No. 30 from Central Railway Station.
- *Paris*. The *bâteaux-mouches* on the Seine cost less in the morning.

The Subway in Paris

In Paris, the best way to get around is to take the subway (*métro*). It will take you quickly and inexpensively to all major attractions.
- Get a pocket *métro* map from an information office on arrival or ask for one at the hotel. Have someone explain the system to you.
- Buy tickets for each trip from a booth in front of the station. These are cheaper in packets (*carnets*) of 10 tickets.
- Find the platform for the train heading in your direction. Always carry the pocket map with you because it can be difficult to read the maps in the cars.
- If you get lost on the *métro,* go to the nearest mechanical map and press the button for your destination. The whole route will light up. The name of the route is in bold print. You might have to move from one subway line to another to go all the way.
- Be careful not to go through the wrong gate when you get off a subway. There are two kinds of doors: one for connections (*correspondance*) and one for street exits (*sortie*). If you take the wrong gate, you will have to pay another fare.

Taxis

In all but a few countries, such as Spain, Greece, and Portugal, taxis are extremely expensive. Try to avoid them by taking advantage of inexpensive, very good public transportation, including subways, buses, and trams.
- If you have to take a taxi, find out the approximate cost of the trip ahead of time by asking at the information desk or the front desk

in a hotel, or by asking the cabdriver. Find out also if there are minimum charges—perhaps the walk will be worth it.

- Be wary of asking a hotel to call you a cab, especially if you're staying in a more expensive hotel. Many of these establishments are served by special cabs—ones that offer extra comfort at an extra price. The less expensive cabs have already been warned to stay clear of such hotels unless they are called by the hotel itself (a problem in Vienna). Insist on an ordinary metered cab!
- Always try to share the cost of a taxi with other people. This can be easily done on rides to major cities from outlying airports.
- Accept the fact that taxi rates go up late at night when public transportation is not available.
- If you think a cabdriver has swindled you, threaten to take down the number of the cab and report him or her to the central transportation authority or the police. If the driver has in fact duped you, he or she will probably lower the fare on the spot.

Taxis in Paris

No system is more complicated than the taxi system of Paris. Here are the basics to help you out.

- The cab must have a meter. No meter? Skip the cab.
- There are three basic rates listed as fares A, B, and C on the meter. A covers central Paris on weekdays. It's the cheapest (but still expensive) fare. B covers suburbs at any time and central Paris from 8:00 P.M. to 6:30 A.M. weekdays, and on Saturdays, Sundays, and holidays. C applies only to suburbs in the evening.

Taxis in Eastern Europe

Paying the correct fare for a taxi is always a problem. In Eastern Europe there are certain idiosyncrasies worth knowing about ahead of time.

- Not all cabs have meters. They may be legitimate drivers. Get the fare in writing. Hand the driver a piece of paper and a pen. Have him write the fare down. Get your pen back.
- In some areas you pay for the trip to and from your destination, even though you travel only one way. When in doubt, ask ahead of time about local custom.
- Fares may double if you leave the city proper. Again, ask locally about reasonable rates and local customs in regards to longer rides.

The main point is to ask, then ask again. If you get two people telling you the same thing, then they are telling you the truth.

Communicating

Americans are often scared away from going to Europe because of the "language barrier." Naturally, you can become better acquainted with Europeans if you can speak their languages, but you can still have a great time in Europe with practically no foreign vocabulary. For one thing, you'll be surprised at your sign-language fluency.

Another thing that concerns travelers is losing touch with the folks back home. These days, though, you're as close as a phone to your family and friends, and mail delivery is quite reliable.

So relax—read this chapter—and enjoy!

Speaking

You'll have little trouble communicating in areas where there's heavy tourist traffic. You'll usually find someone who can help you out in hotels, restaurants, banks, shops, and travel terminals. Off the beaten path you will probably run into a language barrier, but even if you can't speak a word of a foreign language, you'll still get by.

Basic Expressions

- Because it takes years to learn a foreign language, many people don't even try. However, you should take the time to learn a few basic expressions and how to count to ten, not only because it will prove helpful but also because it's the right thing to do.
- No book can show you how to pronounce foreign words correctly! Have a native speaker pronounce them for you (and don't be afraid to ask).

Asking Directions

If you get lost, you may have a problem getting directions to your destination. When asking directions, the most important word is *to*.

- Open your mouth and say "ahh," as if you were in a dentist's chair. Follow "ahh" by the name of the place you're going. "ahh Paris," "ahh Trendelburg," and so on.
- If you point to a map as you do this, most Europeans will understand, even if you use English in the rest of the sentence. You can say, for example, "I would like to go ahh Madrid."

- Remember that many cities are spelled differently in foreign languages. If someone doesn't understand you, maybe it's because you're not speaking his or her language! What good does it do to ask for Venice in Italy, when Italians call the city Venezia? Here are the major cities and their correct foreign spellings.

A Few Foreign City Names

Athens	Athina	*Lisbon*	Lisboa
Brussels	Bruxelles	*Munich*	München
Copenhagen	København	*Naples*	Napoli
Florence	Firenze	*Venice*	Venezia
Geneva	Genève	*Vienna*	Wien

Tricks for Communicating

- Speak simply. Say "Menu," not "I would like a menu, please."
- Repeat statements only once—slowly and without raising your voice. No go? Smile and say "Thank you" in the foreign language.
- If your vocabulary is limited, try to communicate in writing. Carry paper and a pen, and get waiters and clerks to write down prices for you.
- Drop your inhibitions and give sign language a try!
- Note that in Bulgaria and Greece a nod indicates "no" and shaking your head back and forth indicates "yes." And you wonder why the taxi turns left instead of right? Cultural differences take a little getting used to.
- Still, don't be intimidated by the language barrier. Don't let it stop you from venturing into remote areas that have barely been touched by modern tourism.

Writing

Letters from home and the postcards you send can be especially important while you're traveling. No news may be good news, but news is still fun when you're far from home.

Staying in Touch

- Duplicate your itinerary to give to friends and relatives with whom you'd like to keep in touch. Airlines sometimes can reach travelers for urgent messages if they have information on flight plans. But don't count on it.

BASIC EXPRESSIONS

English	Bulgarian*	Italian	Czech*	Polish*	French	Portuguese	German	Romanian*	Hungarian*	Slovak*	Spanish
hello	zdrahVEHYteh	buon giorno	DOHBreeden	janeDOHbrih	bonjour	bom dia	guten tag	boonazeewa	YOHnawpoht	dohbreedyen	buenos dias
good-by	doughveezdahneh	arrivederci	nahSKHLEDahnoh	dohvyehDZEHnyah	au revoir	adeus	auf wiedersehn	lahrevedereh	VEEsontlahtahshraw	dohveedenyah	adiós
slowly	BAHvno	lentamente	POHmahleyyee	pohMAHWwoo	lentement	lentamente	langsam	eehseteesohr	lahssahn	POHmalsheeh	lentamente
please	MOHLyah	per piacere	PROseem	PROHsheh	s'il vous plaît	faz (faça) favor	bitte	vuhrawg	KEHrem	PROHseem	por favor
thank you	blahgodarYAH	grazie	DYEHkooyee	janeKOOyeh	merci	obrigado (a)	danke	multsumesk	KUsunum	DYAHkooyem	gracias
how much	KAWLkohSTROOvah	quanto	koleektawstoyee	eelehtohkoshSHTOOyeh	combien	quanto	wieviel	cheetkosta	MENyibeKERewl	koltotawstoyi	cuánto
yes	dah	si	AHno	tahk	oui	sim	ja	dah	EEgen	ahno	si
no	neh	no	neh	nyeh	non	não	nein	noo	nem	nyeh	no
I don't understand	nehrahzBEErahm	non capisco	NEHrahzoomeem	nyehrohZOOmyeh	je ne comprends pas	não entendo	ich verstehe nicht	eunewintseleg	nemehrtem	NEHrohzumeehm	no entiendo
how are you	kahksteh	come sta	YAHKsehMAHteh	yahkSHEHmosh	comment allez-vous	como esta	wie geht es ihnen	chemayfahchetsee	hodiyahn	YAHKohsahMAHtyeh	cómo está
how do you say	kahkKAHZvahteh	come si dice	YAHKsehZRKAAH	yahkshehMOOvee	comment dit-on	como se diz	wie sagt man	kumspoonetsee	hodijkellmondahknee	YAHKsahZRKAA	como se dice
" "	_____	_____	_____	_____	_____	_____	_____	_____	_____	_____	_____

* These basic expressions are written phonetically. They are not easy to pronounce. Ask a local person to help you pronounce them correctly. It will be an amusing experience. If you buy a dictionary for Eastern Europe, get one with pronunciation included, or it will be next to useless.

NUMBERS

English	Bulgarian*	Czech*	French	German	Hungarian*
one	ehDIN	yehden	un	eins	edj
two	dvah	dvah	deux	zwei	kettoer
three	tree	tzhi	trois	drei	HAHrom
four	CHEHteery	CHTEEZRhee	quatre	vier	nehdge
five	peht	pyeht	cinq	fünf	ert
six	shehst	shesht	six	sech	hwat
seven	SEHdehm	SEHdum	sept	sieben	heht
eight	OHsehm	OHsum	huit	acht	nyohits
nine	DEHveht	DEHvyeht	neuf	neun	KEElents
ten	DEHseht	DEHseht	dix	zehn	teeze

Italian	Polish*	Portuguese	Romanian*	Slovak*	Spanish
uno	YEHDden	um	oonoo	YEHdehn	uno
dos	dvah	dois	doy	dvah	dos
tres	tchih	tres	tray	tree	tres
quattro	CHTERIh	quatro	pahtroo	SHTEEree	quatro
cinque	pyench	cinco	chinch	pet	cinco
sei	shesht	seis	shahseh	shehst	seis
sette	SHEHDdem	sete	shahpteh	SEHdehm	siete
otto	OSHem	oito	opt	OHsehm	ocho
nove	JEHvyench	nove	nowah	DEHveht	nueve
dieci	JEHshyench	dez	zecheh	DEHsaht	diez

*Phonetic spelling. Other languages in original spelling.

- Ask correspondents to write "hold for arrival," followed by the approximate date you'll be arriving, on all mail they send to hotels.
- Ask friends to *type,* not write, the address on the envelope. A typed address increases the odds that you'll get your mail.
- Ask friends to address each envelope to an individual person, not to a couple. Otherwise, the couple may have to show up to collect it.
- Tell all people to capitalize and underline your last name. This will help the clerk file the letter in the right alphabetical order.
- Tell people to send all letters airmail and to allow a week for delivery. Surface mail reaches Europe in 6 to 8 weeks.

Alternative Mail Drops

If you have an exact itinerary but don't know where you'll find lodging, you can choose any of the following methods of receiving your mail abroad.

- Have the mail sent in care of American Express in the cities you'll be visiting. If you have either an American Express credit card or some of their traveler's checks, this service is free. Expect long mail lines in the peak season at these offices. Your mail will be returned to the sender after 30 days. Note that for a charge you can have mail forwarded from any American Express office.
- Have mail sent to General Delivery in central city post offices abroad: *poste restante* (French), *postlagernde Sendungen* (German), *fermo in posta* (Italian), *lista de correos* (Spanish), *posta-restante* (Portuguese). There's usually a small charge at General Delivery, and letters will be sent back after 10 days. But the lines are usually short in comparison with those at the American Express office. Do not do this in Eastern Europe.
- When having mail sent to *poste restante,* have your friends write "1" after the city name so that the mail will be sent to the main post office and not a branch. This will stop you from post-office hopping once abroad in a major city.
- In Eastern Europe have your mail sent to the Canadian or U.S. embassy. Frankly, embassies don't like this or consider it part of their duty. You may end up with a lecture along with your letters, but *poste restante* is not reliable in the East.
- An alternative, which also works well in Western Europe, is to send your mail to a major hotel, preferably one related to a chain in the West. Follow the steps outlined above as if you were staying in the hotel. When you arrive, ask for your mail and tip the clerk for the service. If you aren't staying in a hotel and don't tip, the hotel will stop doing this for other travelers in a similar predicament.

Sending Mail Home

- Stamps are sold at tobacco and stationery shops and in most hotels.
- Aerograms are the least expensive way to write letters to the United States. You can buy them at the post office or in some stationery stores.
- Postcards are nearly as expensive to mail as letters, but they are fun to receive.
- You'll often find inexpensive postcards in department stores and at street stands. They are cheaper than the ones found in hotels and are just as nice.
- Note that most hotels provide free envelopes and stationery. If you find none in your room, just ask.
- See pages 236–237 for advice on sending packages home.

Phoning and Cabling

The telephone can do so much for you as you travel—help you book rooms and seats, hunt bargains and compare prices, and, of course, let you talk to people long distances away. European phone systems are sometimes idiosyncratic, but you can make good use of them with a few hints.

Local Calls

The simplest places to make local calls are the hotel and the post office, where operators can help handle your calls.
- If you make local calls in a hotel, check on possible surcharges ahead of time. You can also use public pay phones, as in the United States.
- There are no such surcharges at central post offices. You pay only for the call. Payment is often based on time alone.
- Note that many public phones require tokens, which you can buy in tobacco shops, post offices, bars, newsstands, and wherever public telephones exist.
- Note that in some areas you deposit coins or tokens *after* your party answers—and in some cases, you keep dropping them in throughout the call!
- If you have trouble locating a name in a foreign telephone book, ask for help. Note that some alphabets have extra letters, such as å, aa, ö, Ø, and ồ, which come at the end of Scandinavian alphabets.

Long-Distance Calls from Hotels

Many hotels add their own charges to long-distance calls made from their rooms. In recent years, these charges have sometimes been three times the cost of the call—and the practice has sent warning ripples through the tourist industry.
• Never, never make a long-distance call from a hotel room without checking on the hotel surcharge first. Note: hotels often lie.

Avoiding Hotel Surcharges on Calls

• If you can dial directly to the United States from your hotel room, play the "call back" game. Dial your friends, give them the number of your hotel and your room number, and ask them to call you back immediately. Since you pay only for the actual length of a call in Europe, your charge should be for a minute or less. Even if the hotel adds a surcharge of 100 percent or more, the total shouldn't break your bank.
• Note that U.S. telephone credit cards are accepted in many European countries and cut the cost of surcharges.
• If you don't have a telephone credit card, call collect. The overall rate for a collect call is quite high, but surcharges are lower. Collect in five languages: *P.C.V.* (French), *R-Gesprach* (German), *pagamento a carico del destinatario* (Italian), *a cobrar* (Portuguese), *pago revertido* (Spanish).
• Note that some hotels are raising surcharges on collect calls—ask ahead of time. You may not get a straight answer.

Using Public Telephones to Avoid Surcharges

• Avoid surcharges of any kind by making long-distance phone calls from the main telephone terminals in central post offices and in some railway stations and airports. The operator will tell you how long you should expect to wait to get a connection: times vary from a minute to several hours.
• Because these main telephone terminals can be packed in peak hours, avoid the crowds by going at unusual hours. Remember that it's many hours earlier in the day in the United States.
• You'll be asked to write down your name, address, telephone number, and the number, full name, and address of the person you're calling.
• You can call person to person, as in the States, but it's more expensive. Person to person in five languages: *préavis* (French), *Foranmeldung* (German), *personale* (Italian), *persona a persona* (Spanish and Portuguese).

- Get information from your long-distance phone company giving specific directions on how you can make a call from a phone booth abroad. The big advantage of this is that you don't have to worry about excessive and common hotel surcharges, which are often hidden in final bills.

Cables

A cable often costs as much or more than a telephone call. It's paid for on a total word basis, which includes the name and address of the person to whom you're sending it. You can send a cable from central post offices in most major cities.

- Compare costs before you cable someone. A phone call may turn out to be more economical than you had expected.

Little Black Book

- Carry a small book to keep addresses and contact information. It's surprising how often you'll use it.
- Business cards are often useful.
- Better are postcards from your hometown with your address already on them (use gummed labels). Foreigners appreciate these cards, and you'll often receive them in the mail at the most unexpected times!

Doing Things

There are so many wonderful and fascinating things to see and do in Europe that you can never do them all in one vacation. Below are just some suggestions—pick and choose the activities that appeal to you.

Shopping

If you are one of those people who enjoys shopping and loves every minute spent in fashionable stores, street markets, and boutiques, you will find Europe a delight.

Bargain Hunting Abroad

- Since many articles you can buy in Europe are also for sale in the United States, study American prices before going abroad. Otherwise, you will not know whether you're really getting a bargain.
- Unless a European item is much lower in price or of much higher quality than you can get in the United States, don't buy it. You'll lose on the currency exchange, you'll have to lug or mail it home, and you may even have to pay duty on it. If you can't save 40 to 50 percent off the U.S. price, don't buy!
- Shop around before you decide to buy something in Europe. By checking out several stores, you'll often save many dollars. Ask local people the cost of specific items in advance.
- Ask what each shop's exchange rate is right away. If the rate is better in a bank, pay in local currency. If the rate is better in the store, you're being offered a subtle discount. At times this discount can be as much as 10 percent.
- Never buy American items abroad (this applies to everything!). Domestic brands are just as good.
- Never buy items in shops catering to crowds of tourists. Such items will always be sold at inflated prices.
- Ask about airline discounts; Air France offers discounts at Le Printemps in Paris. All you have to do is show your ticket.
- You can find superb bargains by settling for goods that have barely visible flaws, particularly in the case of porcelain and glass products.
- Always say "hello" and "good-by" to shopkeepers, even if you don't purchase anything in the store. This is basic courtesy in Europe.

Good-Buy Guide to the Best in European Goods

The following chart will help you find some good buys in Europe, as it lists products that are typical of each area. Most of the good buys included in this chart will be less expensive in Europe than in the United States.

Country or Island	Good Buys
Andorra	Cameras, crystal, dolls, leather, porcelain, stamps, watches, and wood products.
Austria	Antiques, art, Austrian jade, ceramics, costume jewelry, crèches, enamelware, fashions, figurines, guns, handbags (*petit point*), handmade blouses, knitwear, lace, leather, lingerie, porcelain (*Wiener Augarten*), skiwear, wood carvings, wrought iron.
Azores	Local handicrafts.
Belgium	Antiques, ceramics, chocolate, copperware, crystal, diamonds, glass, handmade shotguns, lace, leather, linen, paintings, pewter, silverware, wrought iron.
Bulgaria	Carpets (from Bansko, Chiprovtsi, Kotel, Panagyurishte, Rhodopes villages, and Yambol), copper, dolls, embroidery (reds prevail), eye glasses, filigree (silver), gold, leather, linen, perfume, pottery (Troyan), shoes, wood carvings, wrought iron (check into Corecom shops for assorted goods and keep all receipts. Seek out any shops sponsored by the Union of Bulgarian Artists in many towns).
Canaries	Local handicrafts, liquor.
Cyprus	Copper, lace, rugs.
Czechoslovakia	Art books, Bohemian crystal, china, garnet jewelry, lace, maps, musical instruments, wooden toys (check into Tuzex shops for assorted goods and keep all receipts).
Denmark	Ceramics, china, food products, furniture, furs, Georg Jensen silver, glass, linen, pewter, Royal Copenhagen porcelain, teakwood, toys, watches.
Finland	Brass, ceramics, crystal, glass, jewelry, leather, pewter, wood products.
France	Alençon lace, antiques, Daum crystal, high-fashion clothes, gloves, Lalique glass, leather, lingerie, paintings, perfume, scarves.
Germany	Art books, beer steins, binoculars, cameras, comforters (down-filled), cuckoo clocks, cutlery, furs, leather, Meissen china, music boxes, pewter, prints, Rosenthal porcelain, toys, watches, woolens, wood carvings.
Gibraltar	Cameras, crystal, luxury items, perfume, tobacco.
Great Britain	Antique jewelry, antiques, books, cashmere, china, fabrics, glass, high-fashion clothes, pewter, pipes, shoes, silk, suits, tobacco, tweeds, Wedgwood china, woolens.

Country or Island	Good Buys
Greece	Antiques, crocks, embroidered blouses, furs, leather, olivewood candlesticks, patterned coats, pottery, rugs, silver jewelry, skins, tote bags, wood carvings.
Hungary	Art books, ceramics, dolls, embroidery, lace, porcelain (Herend, Kalocsa, Zsolnay), pottery, tapestries (check into Intourist shops for assorted goods and keep all receipts).
Iceland	Ceramics, pony skins, sheepskins, silver filigree, whalebone items, wool sweaters.
Ireland	Antiques, china, crystal, knitwear, lace, linen, rugs, silver, tweeds, whiskey.
Italy	Glass, gloves, gold jewelry, high fashion, leather (Florence), prints, shoes, silk, silver jewelry, straw goods.
Luxembourg	Ceramics, crystal, jewelry, lace, linen.
Madeira	Lace, local handicrafts, Madeira wine.
Malta	Baskets, brass, ceramics, copper, dolls, embroidery, filigree, lace, perfume, pipes, pottery, wrought iron.
Majorca	Leather goods, Majorcan pearls.
Monaco	Dolls, jewelry, perfume.
Netherlands	Antiques, blankets, books, cheese, china, crystal (Leerdam), Delft porcelain, diamonds, figurines, gin (*genever*) in stone bottles, oriental rugs, pewter, pipes, posters, prints, silver, tobacco.
Norway	Ceramics, glassware, pewter, sealskin boots, silver, skiwear, sweaters, Swiss watches, wooden salad bowls.
Poland	Amber necklaces, art books, ceramics, dolls, embroidery, glass (painted), lace, paper cut-outs, pottery, rugs, silks (hand-painted), silver jewelry, tapestries, wood products, woolens, wrought iron (check into Baltona, Cepelia, and Pewex shops for assorted goods and keep all receipts).
Portugal	Azulejo tiles, book covers, china, clay roosters, copper, cork, embroidery, filigree, furniture reproductions, guitars, handicrafts, lace, pewter, port wine, pottery, rugs, Vista Alegre porcelain, wrought iron.
Romania	Ceramics, embroidery, handicrafts, rugs (with floral designs) (check into Comturist shops for assorted goods and keep all receipts).
Scotland	Cutlery, Scotch, silver jewelry, sweaters, tweeds.
Spain	Gloves, high-fashion clothes, jewelry, lace, leather (Barcelona), mantillas, pottery, saffron, Talevera porcelain.
Sweden	Cutlery, handicrafts, Hasselblad cameras, modern furniture, Orrefors glass, pottery, silver jewelry, suede, steel products.
Switzerland	Cameras, cheese, chocolate, cuckoo clocks, embroidery, fondue sets, lace, music boxes, ski gear, steel products, toys, watches.
Turkey	Copper, *kilims* (primitive rugs), Oriental carpets, pipes, samovars.

About Purchasing Goods in Eastern Europe

Regulations are changing rapidly on a country-by-country basis in Eastern Europe in regards to what may or may not be exported. Limitations on the value of exported goods is also up in the air at this time. Before purchasing anything in any country make sure that the item can legally be exported and will not be liable to a surcharge at the border. Get this information from the appropriate tourist office before going abroad (pp. 247–250). Do not expect someone trying to sell you something to know the regulations or to tell you the truth.

- Special tip: When you buy anything in hard currency (dollars or Deutschmarks), get a receipt as proof that you paid for it in this manner. This may allow you to leave the country without paying duty.
- Note that in some shops you must have a basket or cart in order to enter the shop, especially in Czechoslovakia. If no baskets are available, you must wait until one is returned to enter the shop.
- If certain stores are only open to foreigners willing to purchase goods in hard currency, then you may be approached by locals to buy special items for them. The legality of this is questionable, but it is certainly true that a number of foreigners have made money buying and selling hard-to-find items on this basis. Personally, I hope that such stores will soon be out of business and that all goods will be sold on an open-market basis to everyone for local currency. Perhaps this will already be a reality by the time you travel to this area.

Value Added Tax (VAT)

- In most European countries you pay a luxury tax on many goods. Tourists are allowed refunds of this tax.
- Always ask if you can get a refund and what the procedure is.
- Many shoppers use credit cards as a way to get an immediate refund. You ask the clerk to make out one for the purchase, another for the VAT refund—the simplest method of avoiding this stiff tax.

Duty-free Shops

- Avoid most duty-free shops in airports and train stations, as they are now classic rip-off establishments. Prices there are often higher than comparable prices in quality stores.
- You can pick up truly duty-free goods on all international ships and ferries. Everyone else knows this also, which means that the lines will be long.

Bargaining

It's actually improper for you to pay the asking price for goods in Spain, Portugal, Greece, and on most islands. It's equally improper in almost every European country when you shop at open markets, small owner-operated shops, antique shops, art galleries, and flea markets. Bargaining is not only accepted in these settings, but it is also expected. If you're not used to bargaining, here's a chance to learn how.

Basic Bargaining

Bargaining is an attitude, a position, a style. The attitude is wariness; the position is, "I won't buy unless it's a fair price." The style is tough but breezy, with a good sense of humor.

- Dress casually. Avoid wearing expensive clothes, jewelry, or watches. Women should not wear perfume.
- Take your time and comparison-shop first. When you've decided on what you really want, begin the bargaining game. Frivolous bargaining is unfair and a waste of the merchant's time.
- Ask for the price. Propose your own, undercutting the stated price by whatever you think you can get away with. Carry a pen and paper with you in areas where language is a problem. An inexpensive pocket calculator is effective as well. Sell it before you come home.
- State the U.S. cost in fair and accurate terms. Tell the merchant that you have no intention of buying unless you can make a substantial saving—of at least 40 to 50 percent. Shopkeepers respect this simple, honest approach to buying.
- State that you'll have to shop around because you want to come up with the best price in town and are willing to spend the time to do it. Prices will often slide down on the spot!
- Let a missing person play the bad guy. "Oh, I think it's beautiful. But my husband (or wife) would be very upset if I spent that much."
- Be complimentary but shrewd, saying, "It's one of the finest pieces I've seen, but I really think it's overpriced."
- Evoke the expert. "I've got someone who really knows about these things. I'd better ask his advice before I spend all that much."
- Find a flaw. Almost everything has one, especially high-quality, handmade articles. I don't like this approach myself, but it does work. Try it only as a desperation ploy.

Advanced Bargaining

- Play the add-on game: "I'll pay your price if you'll throw this extra item in." That so-called extra item may be exactly what you were after in the first place!
- Play the lump-sum game: "I'll pay you this much for this, that, and that." You play the lump-sum game after finding out the prices for the individual items. Naturally, you shave off a fair percentage for buying them as a group.
- If the price doesn't come down to what you're willing to pay, keep cool, thank the merchant, and be on your way. You'll be surprised how quickly this brings on a new round of negotiating. You'll sometimes be a block down the street before it starts!

Luxury-shop Bargaining

Polite bargaining is very effective in places where you don't want to be too aggressive. Don't let anybody tell you that it doesn't work! It does work, even in so-called luxury shops where you'd least expect to be successful. The following questions are all polite ways of asking, "How far will the price come down?"

- "Will the item soon be on sale?"
- "Is there a reduction for foreigners?"
- "Is there a discount for paying in traveler's checks?" This discount is quite common.
- "Are there professional discounts for writers (priests, teachers, doctors, lawyers, etc.)?" Become a professional for a moment if you think you can get away with it.
- "Is there a discount for cash purchases?" This implies that you will use a credit card otherwise. And, of course, the shop will have to pay a percentage of the purchase price to the credit card company.

Popular Flea Markets

- *Amsterdam.* Head for Waterloopein on Saturday by taking the No. 9 tram or the No. 5, 11, or 55 bus.
- *London.* Go to Bermondsey early Friday morning (catch the bus by dawn) on the No. 1 bus from Trafalgar Square. Also popular but not as good is the Portobello Market on Saturday, reached by bus No. 15 on Oxford Street (panel marked "Ladbroke Grove").
- *Madrid.* Try El Rastro, south of the Plaza Mayor along Ribera de Curtidores, on Sunday. Get there by taking a taxi to Plaza del Cascorro.

- *Paris.* Go to the Porte de Clignancourt on the subway line of the same name, or take the No. 85 bus to rue des Rosiers on Saturday, Sunday (best), or Monday.
- *Rome.* Go to Porta Portesi in Trastevere on Sundays.
- Ask about market days in England and similar days in other countries. Lots of fun!
- In these areas carry small denomination bills, lots of them tucked into different pockets. Never bring out any money until you are ready to buy. Show as little money as possible, almost as if you have to scrape the amount together to pay for the item (see pp. 137–138 on pickpockets).

Sightseeing, the Arts, and Nightlife

Europe offers a fascinating blend of sightseeing, the arts, and nightlife. Since these are often oriented to the tourist, you'll save substantially by being somewhat wary.

Local Tours

- Tours of any city's famous sights are organized by local and large European tour companies. Such tours are well organized but usually expensive.
- Tourist offices often organize and promote local tours. These also tend to be overpriced.
- Student organizations often sponsor similar but less expensive tours—a good option for all.
- You can usually put together your own tour using local buses or trams, for a fraction of the cost of organized tours.
- For free information on suggested sights and routes, pick up brochures, maps, and detailed commentary from local tourist offices and from your hotel. The Yellow Pages of local phone books often list good sightseeing suggestions.
- If you're a romantic and want to try a buggy or gondola ride, expect to pay in spades, not hearts.
- Whenever you're agreeing to pay for a "special" ride, get the price in writing. Make sure that this is not a per-person price. One way to avoid hassles is to pay ahead of time!

Walking Tours

- You can easily walk around the most interesting parts of these major cities: Amsterdam, Antwerp, Athens, Berlin, Bruges, Brussels (the center), Dublin, Edinburgh, Florence, Hamburg, Helsinki (with the tourist tram), Innsbruck, Lisbon, London (the center), Luxembourg City, Madrid (the center), Munich (with the tram), Oslo (with the tram), Salzburg, Stockholm, Toledo, Venice, and Vienna.

- You can walk much of Rome and Paris, although in these cities you'll need to use buses and subways to see all the major sights comfortably.
- Look for booklets, brochures, and special maps geared for walkers in the places you visit.

Zoos

The Berlin zoo, the game parks of Great Britain, and the deer park at Klampenborg 6 miles north of Copenhagen will be of interest to many tourists, particularly families traveling with children.

- For information on any of these, contact the appropriate national tourist office (see pp. 247–250).

Museums and Galleries

Check ahead before making a special trip, because museums and galleries often close at odd times. For example, the Louvre is closed on Tuesdays.

Admission to most museums is free on certain days. The Louvre is free on Sundays and Wednesdays.

- Look for special flat-rate cards, good for admission to many places. Ask at National Tourist Offices (see pp. 247–250) about special flat-rate cards.
- Note that students with student IDs (see p. 8) can often get reduced prices.
- High heels are forbidden in many galleries and museums because of the damage they do to floors. This is particularly true in France.

Theaters, Movies, Concerts, Casinos

- You can often get into a London theater if you show up in person just before show time. This approach works best if you're alone.
- Also in London, ask if a half-price booth is still operating.
- Note that theaters often give substantial discounts for matinee and off-night (usually Monday) performances. If there's a show you desperately want to see, be flexible.
- When an event or festival is solidly booked, try bribery. Go to the gate and slip the controller the equivalent of several dollars in foreign currency. You'll find that they may suddenly be able to find a place for you.

- Arrive at foreign movies on time, because ticket takers may not let you in if you're late.
- To get into a casino, you may be asked to show your passport, and you may not be allowed in unless properly attired (i.e., sports coat and tie, or comparable dress for a woman).

Meeting People

One of the pleasures of traveling in Europe is meeting new, interesting people. Whether you're looking for a pleasant dinner companion or a traveling partner, you will find it easy to make new acquaintances while traveling.

- If you have a choice, consider taking a ship to Europe. Ocean voyages are wonderful settings for meeting people.
- Tours are also a good source of companions. Your mutual destinations will highlight mutual interests.
- It's easy to meet people on trains. If you're game, make a point of being friendly to your fellow travelers—Europeans will usually wait for you to take the initiative.
- Youth hostels, student tours, and similar youth-oriented places are natural meeting spots. Each summer the American Express offices all over Europe become social headquarters for virtually six million Americans. They're excellent sources for finding impromptu traveling companions.
- The lobbies, bars, and dining rooms of the finer hotels are also good places to meet interesting people.

Looking for Romance

- Women looking to meet European men shouldn't expect to meet them as easily in Northern Europe as in southern countries. Greece has perhaps the best prospects for meeting men. Italy is legendary.
- Men looking to meet European women will have more success in central and northern European countries than in the South.

Sexy but Classy Shows

In London, try the Raymond Revue Bar. In Paris, the Crazy Horse or the Lido, which are stylish, sexy shows. See a show at the Lido from the bar: get there by 9:30 P.M., order one drink, and make it last for the whole show—and it will still be expensive.

Photography

Europe is a visual feast for photographers. Be sure you bring enough film to record it! (I'm assuming that you have a 35-millimeter camera; if you have some other type, some of these tips won't apply.)

Equipment

- Be familiar with the workings of your equipment before you go abroad.
- Change all batteries and carry a few spares.
- A broad camera strap makes taking pictures easier and carrying cameras more comfortable.
- Equip each lens with a polarized filter. Leave the filter on at all times, not only to improve photos, but also to protect the lens.
- Bring photographic lens tissue or liquid lens cleaner.
- Don't forget your instruction book if you're not completely familiar with your camera or haven't used it frequently in recent months.

Register Your Equipment

- Don't forget to register equipment to avoid problems coming back through customs (see p. 99).

Film

- Buy your film in the United States before you leave. It costs much more in Europe.
- Avoid any film with "Professional" printed on the label. It requires refrigeration!
- Specify either slide or print film. Slide film allows you to see each picture before ordering prints—a real savings.
- Figure on a 36-exposure roll for each day of travel abroad—at the minimum.
- Get films with different ASAs (ISOs in Europe). These numbers refer to light sensitivity. Use the appropriate film for varying light conditions.
- Since processing costs vary considerably, comparison shop in area stores.
- Try to keep your film cool.

Security Inspections

- Don't have film in cameras when you go through security inspections at the airport. They may be opened.

- The X-ray machines at airports can damage unexposed or undeveloped film, particularly those with an ASA over 400. Moreover, the effect is cumulative, so don't let the film go through these machines.
- Politely ask the inspector at all check points for a visual inspection. If you carry unboxed film in a separate clear plastic bag, this takes only seconds. Inspectors usually cooperate fully with this request with a minimum of hassle.
- Don't put film in checked luggage, which can be subjected to high-level radiation. Even lead pouches are no guarantee that the film will not be harmed. Carry all film on board with you.

Protecting Camera Gear

- Dust can be a problem—bring a plastic bag for each lens and camera to protect them, even if they're already enclosed in a leather carrying case.
- If you carry cameras in plain bags, potential thieves will be less likely to suspect that you're carrying them.
- Always zip up the bag—even if you're nearby. Leave nothing exposed to chance and sticky fingers.
- Hand carry all camera equipment onto a plane or bus. This way you won't lose it if your luggage is lost or crushed.
- Never, never, never leave anything valuable on a plane during a stopover, no matter what the flight attendant may say.
- Wear a camera around your shoulder, rather than around your neck in public places. Thieves snatching at your camera can easily hurt your neck in their eagerness.
- Do not leave cameras in car trunks or glove compartments. Not only are they vulnerable to theft, but the heat of the closed compartment can damage the camera and film.

Photo-taking Etiquette

- Wherever you see the symbol of a camera with a line drawn through it, photography is forbidden. Unless you want to spend 3 days answering questions in the local police station, don't take photos in these areas. You'll encounter stringent restrictions in certain towns in Holland and at various historic and religious sites as well. Observe them.
- In Moslem areas you must be especially sensitive, since the Moslem religion discourages photography.
- Many museums forbid photography, especially flash photography. When in doubt, ask.
- Don't sneak photos, particularly of people. If you want to take

someone's picture, be forthright and friendly—it will work wonders.
- Take along someone who speaks the language, if possible. If not,
  a smile rates second-best, but it's still good. Just lift the camera
  slowly, nod your head, and smile. If the person turns away or
  tosses his or her hand at you, don't take the photo. Or just say
  "please" (see p. 196) as you lift the camera to get a reaction.
- Don't be afraid to pay for pictures. You can carry some small
  change for this purpose or plan to pay in a different way. Cigarettes will often cut the ice. Carry American brands, because the
  bland tobacco appeals to many foreigners as a change of pace and
  costs a carload abroad.
- Other thank-you gifts: unusual American coins; flower seeds;
  knickknacks, such as pins or U.S. flags, medals, badges, and
  stamps (some people go gaga over the brightly colored ones).
- If you work with a Polaroid, you can count on instant rapport with
  your subject.
- Don't gush or dawdle once you've taken a picture. Smile, shake
  hands, offer a gift—then go on about your business.

Skiing

Skiing is excellent in Austria, France, Germany, Italy, and Switzerland. If you intend to stay in a fashionable ski hotel, you must make
reservations months in advance.

Ski Packages

Many package deals combine airfare, beds, meals, and lift tickets in
one price. These are available from ski clubs, airlines, and specific
tour operators specializing in skiing. Most tour packages are couple-
oriented, with stiff charges for single supplements.
- If possible, go on a 14-day, rather than an 8-day tour. You should
  allow yourself several days just to get used to the altitude.
- To cut costs, try some of the lesser-known resorts in France and
  Italy, ski before February or after mid-March, and avoid the Christmas and Easter holidays.

Sources of Information

- Always check snow conditions before going skiing. For information, call (212) 757-6336 (Switzerland) or (212) 944-6917 (Austria)
  between December 15 and March 15.

- Get in touch with the U.S. Ski Association, P.O. Box 100, Park City, UT 84060, Tel: (801) 649-9090, for information on ski clubs that might be going to Europe.
- Many airlines offer ski packages. Compare these with British packages offered in the travel sections of the *London Sunday Times* or *London Sunday Telegraph*. You might come up with an interesting trip by combining travel to London with a British ski package.
- Also contact Steve Lohr's Ski Holidays, 206 Central Avenue, Jersey City, NJ 07307, Tel: (800) 929-5647 or (201) 798-3900.
- Consult the appropriate National Tourist Office (see pp. 247–250) as well, though their information is generally less specific than you might want.

Lift Tickets

- If the price of your lift ticket has not been included in the ski package, buy weekly passes only if you're an excellent and hardy skier. Otherwise, buy coupons or point-card tickets, which allow for several runs.
- If you do buy weekly passes, you'll need photos to attach to the pass. Inexpensive ones from a photo booth are fine. Bring some from home.

Clothes and Boots

- Check on dress requirements with the tour operator or airline. Most ski resorts are quite informal, but a few are not.
- Lugging heavy boots is a chore, but it's worth it. Nothing is worse than the blisters caused by ill-fitting rental equipment.

Other Outdoor Activities

Skiing may well be the sport with the broadest appeal to most travelers. However, in this section you'll find helpful hints on other sports as well, even though some have limited followings.

Birdwatching

Bird-watching can be delightful throughout Europe. Here are some of the prime spots you won't want to miss.
- *Austria.* The Neusiedlersee lake, east of Eisenstadt, is best in late spring.

- *England*. Slimbridge, 12 miles west of Stroud in the Cotswolds, is one of the finest wildfowl preserves in the world.
- *France*. The Camargue in southern France, west of Marseilles, is famed for its flamingos. Go in May.
- *Iceland*. You'll find gannets at Eldey Rock, ducks on Lake Myvatn, pink-footed geese at Thjorsarver, and puffins on the Westmann Islands—birds by the thousands. Iceland has many remote and difficult trips for ardent bird lovers.
- *The Netherlands*. Visit the flat coastal area of Zuidilijk Flevoland.
- *Romania*. The Danube (see p. 261).
- *Spain*. The Las Marismas area of the Guadalquivir River in southern Spain is accessible by horseback and filled with ducks (mostly widgeon) in the fall.

Fishing

Some of the best deep-sea fishing anywhere can be found off the Canaries near the coast of the Sahara. A limited number of charters are available in Gran Canaria. Excellent trout and salmon fishing can be found in Iceland, but all the details of the entire trip must be worked out in advance. Be prepared to camp out or stay in modest hotels. The big advantage: many hours of daylight in the summer.

During mid-May the mayflies hatch in Ireland, a country famed for its brown trout fishing.

Some of the finest trout and salmon rivers in the world are found in Scotland. Most stretches are privately owned, which means that a trip should be extremely well-planned and well-financed. Many hotels have their own fishing privileges. While they are generally very expensive, careful research can uncover reasonably priced daily licenses for some streams.

- Be sure to consult local guides or tackle shop clerks about local conditions and techniques.
- Pack only the most essential tackle, because local customs will probably dictate what you can use. Rent or buy what's needed when you arrive.

Gliding

Gliders should head to Great Britain and Germany; both have centers for the sport.

- Both the British Tourist Authority and the German National Tourist Offices offer free pamphlets on gliding (see p. 247 and p. 248).

Golf

During the summer, you'll want to try the famous courses in Scotland. Enjoy golf in southern Spain and Portugal during the winter; many courses are open at this time and are often associated with comfortable luxury hotels.

- If you belong to a private club in the United States, bring a letter of introduction from the secretary as a way of breaking the ice at private Scottish clubs.
- If you stay in certain hotels, you'll have access to their private clubs as well.

Hiking

Hiking is possible almost anywhere in the world, but it's a national pastime in Germany, Great Britain, and Switzerland.

- For information on hiking and available trails, contact the appropriate National Tourist Office (see pp. 247–250) for free pamphlets and maps.

Hunting

Some of the best duck hunting in the world takes place near Valencia in southeastern Spain. A certain number of days are set aside for hunts, and blinds must be paid for and reserved months in advance. It's very expensive and aristocratic!

Many Americans go to Scotland each fall to hunt grouse. Once again, this is an aristocratic pastime with arbitrary stays in ultraexpensive luxury hotels.

- You will hunt with double-barreled guns; no pumps are allowed.
- Bring formal evening attire.

Nude Sunbathing

Europeans view this as a sport.

The Island of Sylt off Denmark turns into a nudists' mecca during the warmer months, as does St. Tropez in southern France.

- Bring sunscreen if you're not ordinarily a nudist—for obvious applications.

Riding

For experienced riders extended rides and even tours, including stays in country inns, are offered in Hungary. Contact the Hungarian Board of Tourism for more information on this incredible opportunity (see p. 249).

Swimming

Swimming is enjoyable and safe in most areas. However, there are spots with strong currents and dangerous undertows. Ask about conditions before swimming. If you get caught in a current, swim with but slightly across the flow until you break free. Stay calm and relaxed (much easier said than done). Someone should always know when you are swimming, just in case something goes wrong. Never swim at night in saltwater areas.

Studying and Working

What better ways are there of getting to know a country (and not incidentally, its language) than to live and learn with its people?

Foreign Study

To enter a foreign university on equal footing with the rest of the students, you must already have completed 2 years of college in the United States. However, you can take many courses (but none for credit) with only a high school diploma.

Courses abroad are considerably less expensive than in the United States, because education has been subsidized by the government. But summer study, geared mainly to foreigners, is much more expensive than the regular courses.

- Arrange for a student visa if you're planning long-term study. Contact the appropriate National Tourist Office (see pp. 247–250) for help with visas and other information.
- Explore low-cost housing and meals for which students are eligible.
- Get someone to translate your school transcripts (with imprinted seals); a health certificate signed by your doctor, which attests to your good health; and your birth certificate (or a notarized copy).
- Get several extra passport photos.

Language Courses

- Note that the finest French is spoken around Tours in central France, while the best Italian is heard in Tuscany, the region surrounding and including Florence.
- You can learn French cheaply in superb, graduated courses for foreigners in major French university towns.
- You can learn German at the Goethe Institutes, found throughout

Germany, which are also set up for foreigners. But they're expensive.
- You can learn Italian and Spanish cheaply in courses for foreigners at universities in Italy and Spain.
- Contact appropriate National Tourist Offices (see pp. 247–250) for lists of schools.

Working Abroad

All in all, it's difficult for Americans to find work in Europe. It's much easier to earn money in the United States. Jobs abroad are scarce, and for long-term jobs abroad you'll need work permits, which are a hassle to get. However, lots of menial work is available illegally, for which you won't need a work permit!
- Women can readily get au pair jobs—a combination of light housework and babysitting. They pay practically nothing, but often include room and board.
- English teachers and tutors are often needed—at low wages. However, in Eastern Europe there is now a high demand, especially in Budapest.
- Athletes can sometimes get jobs on city teams if they're highly skilled and willing to work for a small wage and/or room and board.
- Contact CIEE for job-hunting help (see p. 9).

Staying Healthy

Some health problems come up so frequently when people travel that they become standard jokes. However, for the person suffering the indignities of diarrhea, nothing seems amusing. These hints can prevent and cure some of the most common ailments that may appear in Europe.

Health Care Abroad

Health care abroad can be excellent, but you have to know the ropes to take advantage of the good and to avoid the bad.

Doctors and Drugs

- If you need a doctor for a minor illness, you can trust the concierge of any hotel to come up with a recommendation. If you feel that language will be a problem, you can get the names of English-speaking doctors from American consulates, motor clubs, and medical associations (see p. 19).
- If you can't find an American consulate, try a British one. Or call a representative of an American shipping company or airline. They can usually help.
- To find a pharmacy that's open all night, go to the nearest one. If it's closed, look on the door and you'll see the name and address of the pharmacy open that night.
- Although many controlled substances are available over the counter in foreign countries, do not bring these back into the United States. One of the most common is codeine. It is also not even allowed in some foreign countries with or without a prescription. So be wary, since it's found in many cold medications.

Hospitals and Clinics

- Avoid public hospitals if you are seriously ill. I've found European public hospitals to be inspired by Dante, going so far as to put a cast on a leg that didn't need one. And even that was done badly. Go to a private clinic if at all possible.

General Health Problems

Many discomforts, minor ailments, and major problems that come with travel are easily prevented or cured.

AIDS

Presently, AIDS is incurable. You can, however, easily avoid contracting AIDS by following these guidelines:
- To be totally safe, refrain from sex altogether.
- If sexually active, always practice safe sex, and use latex condoms purchased in the United States.
- Avoid needles.
- If you need a transfusion, call the nearest U.S. consulate for advice on local blood supplies.

Altitude Sickness

In higher altitudes you may experience altitude sickness: loss of appetite, nausea, mental confusion, fatigue, and shortness of breath.
- The simple, but somewhat drastic, solution is to move to a lower altitude.
- Diamox, a medication, can relieve its symptoms.
- Slow down the pace. Relax and let your body get used to the lack of oxygen.
- Avoid alcohol: its effects are tripled at high altitudes.
- Drink lots of liquids—fruit juices, water, colas.
- Eat less and eat your main meal in the middle of the day.
- Sleep more. Here's the perfect excuse for a nap after a tiring trip.

Amoebic Dysentery

You can't do much to prevent getting this disease. If you do get it, it's just bad luck. The symptoms are similar to those of diarrhea, but last longer and often include severe cramping and blood in the stool. There are a number of drugs that will kill amoebae, and they're available abroad and in the United States.
- You may have to submit a stool sample to find out for sure that you've got amoebic dysentery. However, a negative stool sample does not necessarily mean that you don't have it. Some doctors say that stool samples are negative so frequently that they may be a waste of money. They treat for amoebae without them.

Anxiety

It's very common for travelers to experience anxiety in Europe.
- Try to get plenty of rest, have a good meal with a beer or glass of wine, and take a tranquilizer if absolutely necessary.
- Get physical. Exercise relieves stress. It's hard to be uptight after two hours of snorkeling in the Mediterranean.
- Don't feel compulsive about sightseeing and schedules!

Bee Stings

The normal reaction to a bee sting is pain, swelling, and itching. Other less-common reactions to bee stings are hives, rash, swelling in the throat area, spasms, and even breathing problems. Someone severely allergic may even experience shock and falling blood pressure, which can lead to death.
- Reduce pain with aspirin, reduce swelling with ice, and relieve itching with calamine lotion.
- No calamine lotion? Use toothpaste—not as good but passable.
- If you or someone else has a severe reaction, seek medical help immediately!
- If you plan extensive hiking, motorcycling, or bike riding, carry Epipen. Get one of the newer kits with the substance already in a syringe (requires prescription).

Blisters

Nothing can ruin sightseeing or hiking faster than a blister.
- Wear comfortable walking shoes that you've used at home before your trip. Don't worry about how they look. No one else gives a damn. Comfort and convenience should always come ahead of fashion while traveling.
- The minute you feel a blister forming, stop! Try to cover the tender spot with a Band-Aid or some moleskin. If you don't stop, a blister will form.
- If you do get a blister, clean it with soap and water. Rub your foot with alcohol if possible. Keep the blister covered with a Band-Aid until it heals.

Constipation

- Try to follow a routine and get plenty of exercise during the day. Walk whenever possible. Not only does walking help the body, but it is also one of the most enjoyable ways of getting to know a town or city.

- Drink mineral water or mix bran into fruit juice as a laxative if this is a chronic problem. You can get bran at health-food stores and carry a small packet with you.

Diarrhea

This is the number-one problem for travelers. It is not funny, because it can ruin a vacation.

How to Prevent Diarrhea

- Do not premedicate for diarrhea. This will kill helpful bacteria in your system. However, you might want to take freeze-dried acidophilus tablets, made up of the same kind of bacteria found in kefir and yogurt. Many travelers swear by them.
- Acidophilus tablets are sold at pharmacies but are quite expensive. They should be kept cool. For a short trip, they make sense, but for longer trips, forget it!
- Pepto-Bismol both prevents and cures diarrhea in many instances, according to recent independent studies. The product comes in both liquid (most effective) and tablet (most convenient) form, with dosage indicated on the container.
- Drink only tea, beer, wine, distilled liquor, bottled soft drinks, and carbonated bottled water. Noncarbonated bottled water may or may not be safe because it may be tap water placed in a labeled bottle. Be sure the water is opened at your table.
- Carry bottled water at all times, especially onto trains. This is common practice in Europe.
- Avoid tap water that hasn't been purified, even for brushing teeth. Ice for drinks is often made from tap water. Most problems with water occur in Eastern Europe, Italy, Portugal, and Spain.
- If you drink from a can or bottle, wipe off any moisture around the area from which you'll be drinking. Use straws if possible.
- Avoid all water from lakes, ponds, and streams. This water frequently carries pathogens.
- You can purify water by boiling it for 30 minutes, by adding Halazone tablets (fine if fresh, but they break down in time), or by adding 5 drops of 2 percent tincture of iodine to 1 quart of water and letting it stand for 30 minutes. If the water is cloudy, add 10 drops. Alcohol will not purify water!
- You can also use liquid chlorine bleach. If it's a 1 percent solution, add 10 drops per quart and let stand 30 minutes. If it's a 4 to 6 percent solution, add only 2 to 4 drops per quart. The water should have a slight odor of chlorine. If it doesn't, add a few more drops.
- If you want to play the odds, let the hot water run from the tap until it's scalding—then fill up a container and let it cool off.

- Note that purification and boiling will not get rid of chemical cont-amination.
- Coffee often causes diarrhea. If you're a coffee drinker, switch to tea. Some people cannot tolerate tea either, or chocolate or sodas, because these contain caffeine.
- Stay away from foods sold by street vendors, never eat raw meat or fish (including shellfish), and avoid salads. Stick to fruits and vegetables that can be peeled.
- Stay away from milk or milk products unless you're sure they've been pasteurized. This includes local cheeses in rural areas. Milk can carry incurable and sometimes fatal disease. Avoid it altogether if in doubt, especially in Eastern and Southern Europe.
- Avoid precooked foods that have been allowed to stand for awhile.

How to Treat Diarrhea

Diarrhea generally lasts 3 to 4 days. If it goes on for more than 5 days, or if you notice blood in your stool, see a doctor. The following are tips for temporary treatment.

- If you have to travel, resort to Lomotil. It locks in infections, but you don't have much choice.
- As soon as you can, lay off the Lomotil (don't take it for more than 3 days). Switch over to something milder. Your doctor will suggest a prescription. Imodium can be effective.
- Do not buy drugs for diarrhea abroad. Never buy Entero-vioform. This preparation, which cannot even be sold in the United States, is said to cause blindness and other complications.
- The main danger of diarrhea is dehydration. So here's a diarrhea potion: In one glass put 8 ounces of fruit juice, 1/2 teaspoon of sugar, and a pinch of salt. Fill another glass with 8 ounces of puri-fied water and 1/4 teaspoon of baking soda. Alternate swallows from each glass until both glasses are empty. Yum!
- Or, pour salt and soda into a bottle of cola and swill that.
- Drink clear broth, hot, with lots of salt.
- Avoid fatty, spicy foods, and stick to bland foods until you've recovered.

Ear Problems

- If your ears begin to hurt during the landing of a plane, try to yawn. This should release some of the pressure. You may also try chewing gum.
- If you'll be flying on your trip and have a stuffy head, use a decon-gestant before landing. This will make it easier to relieve the pres-sure.

- Babies should be given a bottle to suck on during a landing.
- Sometimes your ears get plugged with water after a swim. If you've tried everything from dancing on one foot to shaking your head like crazy and nothing works, have someone pour warm (not hot) water into the ear. Let it sit there for a minute and then roll over. This often works.
- Bug in your ear? Use a flashlight to draw it out.

Encephalitis

If you are a wilderness type getting off the beaten path in Central or Eastern Europe, be aware of encephalitis. Although genetically very similar, there are two viruses. One is tick-borne encephalitis for which there is a vaccine, produced in Austria and Germany. It is not available in the United States, so get vaccinated in Western Europe. I do not recommend vaccinations of any kind in Eastern Europe. The second type of encephalitis is often named Russian spring or summer encephalitis. The Centers for Disease Control say that the Russians claim to have a vaccine for this, but reliable information on it is not available. Whether this second viral disease can be prevented or not is questionable. Both diseases are incurable and can be fatal. Besides the vaccine, follow the steps for preventing Lyme disease (p. 227).

Exhaustion

Travel, more tiring and stressful than everyday living, may catch you off balance. Exhaustion can lead to more serious health problems as your resistance is lowered. Listen to your body, which speaks in sign language. It will always tell you what pace to keep.

- If you're traveling with people who want to move at a faster pace, split up and plan to meet them at a later date.
- If you're caught on a whirlwind tour, skip part of it. Don't worry about missing something you've paid for—a trip is for fun.
- Match your style of travel to your energy level. If you don't feel well, pamper yourself with a nicer hotel or a more comfortable mode of transportation. Consider making your trip short but sweet.

Exposure to Cold

- Eat more food; drink hot liquids.
- Exercise moderately to increase body temperature, and cover all exposed areas, especially the head, hands, and feet.
- If your hands get cold, shove them inside your clothing against your body.

- Remember to thaw overly cold hands or feet in water only slightly warmer than skin temperature and never rub cold and exposed skin.

Exposure to Heat

- Wear loose clothing, light in color and weight.
- Wear a hat and stay in the shade as much as possible.
- Try following the local custom of eating and napping from noon to four in southern countries during the July and August heat.
- Drink lots of water with fresh lemon and lime juice, and make sure there's salt in your diet.
- Avoid alcohol and smoking.
- Travel in desert areas at dawn or dusk.

Eye (something in it)

Nothing is more frustrating than getting something in your eye and being unable to get it out. Here's the secret:
- Pull your upper eyelid out and down as far as you can. Let go. The irritant will often come out on the first try.
- If that doesn't work, have someone else look for the spot. Have them touch it gently with the end of a tissue. The piece of grit will usually adhere to the tissue and be out of your eye in an instant.

Feminine Hygiene

- Sanitary napkins in five languages: *Bandes hygiéniques* (French), *Damenbinden* (German), *compresa hygienica* (Italian), *absorviente feminina* (Spanish), *absorvente feminina* (Portuguese).
- Tampons may be available only at pharmacies. They are often hard to find and of poor quality in Eastern Europe.

Fever

For mild fever take aspirin, drink lots of liquids, and keep cool. A high fever requires a trip to the doctor.

Food Poisoning

Headache, nausea, vomiting, and diarrhea (often all at once) are the signs of food poisoning, which can only be described as the next worse thing to death.
- See a doctor. Some food poisoning can be fatal. Note that there is little that can be done for most cases except to ride it out.

Giardia

Giardia is spreading and causing problems in water worldwide. Boiling water for 30 minutes will kill these parasites.

- Diarrhea and pain are two symptoms. Doctors now prescribe furazolidone (Furoxone), metronidazole (Flagyl), and quinacrine (Atabrine) for this illness, which often goes undiagnosed—be wary.

Hemorrhoids

- Bring medicine that contains witch hazel to relieve itching.
- Carry your own toilet paper. American brands are much softer than most paper available in Europe.

Hepatitis

Hepatitis is spread by food and drink, as well as sexual contact with an infected person. You can prevent most forms of hepatitis with hepatitis B serum and gamma globulin (see p. 17).

- If you get hepatitis, a good diet and rest are the only cure. No alcohol or cigarettes will be allowed.

Infections

All infections should be taken seriously, even if they seem minor.

- Clean infected areas frequently, preferably with alcohol, and treat them with an antibiotic ointment.

Insomnia

- Exercise, lots of liquids, and a good diet high in protein will help you avoid insomnia.
- Certain foods contain sleep-inducing substances. Drink a little beer to take advantage of its lupulin (a product of hops). Eat a light snack with milk. It contains both L-tryptophan and calcium—both cause drowsiness.
- Take a warm bath just before going to bed. This helps relax muscle tension.
- If noise bothers you, carry earplugs. Try Flents, which can be molded to your ear and block out most noise. You can find them in pharmacies throughout the United States.
- Keep the room dark by pulling down the shades. If that's not enough, use a mask.
- While traveling, follow the same routine that sets up or triggers

sleep when you're at home. For many people this is reading a book or magazine.

- Certain things cause insomnia: heavy drinking; late meals (the norm in Southern Europe); spicy foods (also very common); chocolate and colas, which contain caffeine; and afternoon naps.
- Sleep-inducing drugs work, but they can cause sleep disturbances and other side effects that may do more harm than good.

Jet Lag

- See pp. 104–105.

Lyme Disease (Lyme Borreliosis)

Anyone who does a lot of hiking or walking in wilderness areas should know about this insidious disease, common in the United States and Central Europe. It is often spread by a minuscule tick about the size of a pinhead.

- Exposing as little skin as possible is the first step in prevention. Wear socks over long pants, wear long shirts, and a hat. Spray tick repellent on your clothes where ticks might sneak onto your body.
- It is easiest to detect ticks on light-colored clothes. Check your body carefully for ticks after each hike. If you find a tick, use a tweezers to pull its mouth from your skin. Do not pull on the body as this can force liquid containing disease into your body. Pull firmly and patiently until the tick pops off. If it will not come off, cover it with petroleum jelly. It needs oxygen to breath and will let go. If any part of the tick remains in your skin, see a doctor.
- Clean the bite with alcohol or iodine. Cover it with antibiotic ointment. Save the tick in alcohol. If you notice a rash around a tick bite which seems to spread out in a circular pattern, see a doctor. Or, if you have a flu-like illness after a bite, see a doctor. Having the tick helps in the diagnosis of the disease, most easily treatable in the early stages with antibiotics. It is much more difficult to diagnose and treat in later stages. Symptoms are wide-ranging in people who have had the disease for a long time. For detailed information contact your local health department or the following organization (it asks for small donations to fund publication of its materials).

Lyme Disease Foundation
P.O. Box 462
Tolland, CT 06084
Tel: (800) 886-5963
(203) 871-2900

Motion Sickness

You're either susceptible to this, or you're not. And you know very quickly whether you are. If you don't want to take the chance, there are many medications available, such as Benadryl, Bonine, Dramamine, Marezine, Phenergan, and Scopolamine (Transderm-V). The last is a little pad placed behind your ear. These drugs may have side effects, and some of them must be prescribed by a doctor.

- If you forget medication before getting on a ship, eat frequent but light snacks. Skip alcohol. Walk around in fresh air. If you're on a small boat, lie down away from annoying noise and smells. The diesel smell from an engine is enough to make you ill even if you're not prone to seasickness. The smell of food or tobacco can also be nauseating.
- If you forget medication before getting on a plane, ask for a seat over the wings (the most stable area), recline as far back in the seat as possible, cover your eyes (preferably with blinders), and try to sleep.
- If you forget medication before riding in a car, ask to drive. Drivers rarely get motion sickness.

Sunburn

Sun damage is believed to be cumulative. More and more skin specialists are warning people to stay out of the sun.

- The sun in southern Europe is extremely intense from 11:00 A.M. to 3:00 P.M., one reason why natives eat lunch or take siestas at this time. Consider following their lead.
- The sun is very dangerous at high altitudes. Watch yourself in the mountains.
- Use a sunscreen. Ultraviolet rays are damaging to the skin. The occurrence of skin cancer is mounting rapidly, possibly because of ozone depletion in the atmosphere.
- Sunscreens contain PABA. The higher the percentage of this, the more protection. The number on the container indicates the power of the sunscreen and runs from a low protection of 1 up to 15 for best protection. Although blocks run up to 44, anything above 29 has virtually the same protection as 29-proof brands, but may stay on your skin for a longer period of time.
- Do not use products containing 5-methoxypsoralerv (5-MOP). These are believed to be dangerous, although many Europeans use them.
- Put on all sunscreens at least 45 minutes before going out in the sun. Although some sunscreens claim to be good after swimming, apply them again anyway.

- Wear a hat and good sunglasses to protect your head and eyes.
- Drink lots of water when you're out in the sun.
- Remember that certain drugs, including tetracycline, diabetic medications, sulfa drugs, and tranquilizers, can make you sun-sensitive. If you're taking medications, ask the doctor about sun-sensitivity.

Troubleshooting

Even during the best-planned trips something is bound to go awry. Here's hoping that you never have to refer to this section!

Terrorism

Terrorism is frightening, but it must be kept in perspective. The tips that follow are suggestions by antiterrorist experts, who realize that there is no sure way to predict a terrorist incident. Although in a typical year more Americans are killed in elevator accidents than in terrorist incidents in Europe, threats of terrorism and the vivid images of attacks on innocent travelers have made us all wary of what could happen. Using this wariness to travel more wisely makes sense. Not traveling at all doesn't. If the same risk factors were applied to car, subway, or train travel, no one would be on a freeway or rail line today.

- Choose neutral air carriers in Europe such as KLM (Dutch), SAS (Scandinavian), or Swissair (Swiss).
- Use smaller airports near major cities, such as Gatwick near London, instead of Heathrow.
- Go through security checks and wait in secured, not public, areas.
- Don't flaunt the fact that you're an American or wear flashy jewelry. The latter is an invitation to trouble anywhere in the world.

Losses

No one wants to think about losing something while planning an enjoyable trip, but losses occur with such regularity that you should be forewarned.

Losing your Passport in the United States or Canada

- If your passport is lost or stolen in the United States, contact the Passport Office, Department of State, Washington, DC 20524, immediately. You'll need the information that you've recorded on a photocopy of the original passport.

- Canadian citizens should report lost or stolen passports to the closest Canadian passport office. You'll find one in each province.

Losing your Passport in Europe

- If you lose your passport in Europe, contact the nearest American or Canadian consulate.
- Report the loss to the local police. They will give you a receipt, which you can use as a temporary ID. You must carry it with you at all times.
- Carry two spare passport photos, a notarized copy of your birth certificate, a photocopy of the information on pages 2 and 3 of your passport, and a note listing your passport number to speed up the process of getting a new passport.

Losing Traveler's Checks and Credit Cards

- If you should lose your traveler's checks or credit cards, report the loss to the company immediately. You're liable for $50 at most for unauthorized use of any credit card, but if you report the loss before any unauthorized use takes place, you're not liable at all.
- Make a list of the numbers of your unused traveler's checks. Avis will refund up to $100 in American Express traveler's checks on weekends, holidays, and late nights if American Express offices are closed.

Robberies

- If you are robbed in a restaurant or hotel, report it to the management. Report any robbery to the police. If you follow this procedure, you can get reimbursed by your insurance company. Ask for a copy of the report as proof of your good will.
- Prevent a robbery in the first place by following the hints on pp. 136–140.

Accidents

Accidents do happen. Here's advice on avoiding and dealing with them.

In the Mountains

- Be prepared for an occasional trek into the scrub, in preference to foul (or nonexistent) bathrooms. But never choose the outside edge of a mountain trail. Those innocent-looking low bushes might really be the tops of tall trees clinging to the side of the mountain! This is not a joke: it's a warning from mountain police who have to fetch out the bodies of unwary tourists each year.

Car Accidents

- If another car is involved, if you cause serious damage to property, or if you hurt someone, you should stick to the spot like glue. Take photos if you can.

Summoning Help

- Naturally, if someone is hurt, try to get an ambulance or the police immediately. In rural areas, flag down an oncoming car and ask the driver to get help for you. Administer basic first aid when necessary by stopping bleeding, getting the person breathing, and keeping the person warm to prevent shock. But don't move anyone who is hurt. Let the police or medics do that!
- If someone you know has been seriously hurt, try to have him or her admitted to a private clinic. You may want an English-speaking doctor (see p. 219). If the situation is critical, the nearest hospital will have to do, but public hospitals in some areas can offer cures that are worse than the original complaint.

After an Accident

- Be prepared for lengthy questions and a detailed report. Note that these reports can be used in court. If you're at fault in a serious accident, you may be liable for a prison sentence.
- Expect trouble if you don't have your passport with you. You may spend some time behind bars—even if the accident wasn't your fault.
- Contact your car insurance company. The insurance company will tell you what to do regarding repairs.
- If you own the car and intend to ship it back to the United States, have all repairs done in the United States. The reason: you can collect for the damage done to the car. You can claim a much lower value for it and pay a proportionately lower tax coming through customs. This advice applies only to operational cars.

Emergency Phone Numbers

This list of numbers might prove helpful in an emergency. Note that emergency numbers are often listed in the front of telephone books abroad, as they are in the United States.

These numbers are to be used only in an emergency situation—not for such things as a flat tire or breakdown! You may find that they don't work in some rural areas.

Country	Number
Austria	133 (police), 144 (ambulance)
Belgium	900 or 901
Bulgaria	166 (police), 150 (ambulance)
Czechoslovakia	150 (police), 155 (ambulance)
Denmark	000
Finland	000
France	Local number of Brigade de Gendarmerie
Germany	110
Great Britain	999
Greece	100 or 109 (police), 525555 (ambulance)
Hungary	07 (police), 04 (ambulance)
Ireland	Local number of Garda
Italy	113
Luxembourg	012
Netherlands	222222 (in Amsterdam or The Hague), 94 (in Rotterdam), (03438) 4321 (anywhere else)
Norway	331290 (police), 201090 (ambulance)
Poland	997 (police), 999 (ambulance)
Portugal	115
Romania	955 (police), 961 (ambulance)
Spain	091 (in Madrid or Barcelona)
Sweden	90000
Switzerland	17, 117, 11, 12, 111, 112 (no money needed for call)

Arrests

If you're in doubt about your legal rights, ask to speak to someone from the nearest American consulate. Note that your rights are defined by local law, not American law!

Jaywalking

Follow the locals on this custom. Note in some countries it's considered antisocial, and you'll pay a stiff fine on the spot. This is particularly true in Czechoslovakia.

Drunken Driving

If you get arrested for drunken driving, you might be in real trouble. In many countries, it will mean an automatic jail sentence of a month or more, for locals and foreigners alike.
• Note that the legal definition of drunkenness may mean any sign of alcohol whatsoever in your blood at the time of driving. Never drive after drinking in Eastern Europe—never. Austria and Scandinavian countries are also extremely tight on drinking and driving. If you're drunk and involved in an accident, you're open to criminal charges.
• Take a taxi if you've had too much to drink!

Minor Traffic Violations

If you're arrested for minor traffic violations, you will be asked to pay a fine (see pp. 181–182).

Drug Violations

If you're arrested for smuggling drugs, you have to spend many years in a foreign jail. It might be tempting to bring hash from Morocco into Spain, but a 6-year jail term is hardly worth the risk.
• Never carry illegal drugs, even small amounts, across a border!

Political Violations

Some countries impose fines and jail terms for any activity directed against the state or its political system. This would include insulting behavior and denigration of a national flag.
• Mind your manners—you are a guest.

Duties and U.S. Customs

The brochure *Know Before You Go* provides detailed information on customs procedures. You can get it from the U.S. Customs Service, P.O. Box 7407, Washington, DC 20044, Tel: (202) 927-2095, or from any local customs office.

Duty Regulations

• Products made in some countries can be imported free of any duty. For a list of the countries and exempt products, ask for *GSP and the Traveler,* available free from the U.S. Customs Service.
• You are now allowed to bring back free-of-duty goods with a total retail value of $400. You pay only 10 percent duty on the next $1,000. After that, you pay varying duties, depending upon the nature of the imported article.

Customs Inspections

• Have your registration slip ready for valuable articles that you took from the United States to Europe, or you'll have to pay duty on them if you're over the $400 limit (see p. 99).
• Have all sales receipts at hand to prove the actual cost of things purchased in Europe. Note that customs officials know relative retail values almost to the cent. You're not going to get by with a doctored sales receipt.
• Note that a customs official may ask you to empty your pockets, and will very rarely check your body. If it makes you feel better, you're expected to be slightly nervous. But don't make jokes, jabber, or volunteer information. Answer all questions as politely and briefly as possible.
• Note also that U.S. Customs inspectors carefully check baggage for pornography, plants, drugs, perfume, excess alcohol (you can bring back one quart), and excess cigarettes (you can bring back 200) and cigars (you can bring back 100).

Possible Snags in Customs

• If an official catches you bringing in something that you haven't declared, admit the mistake immediately. Just say that you forgot about it. Avoid confrontations and arguments.
• If an official breaks an item while searching bags, file a U.S. government form SF9-5 with the regional customs office in the state where the damage takes place. You'll be reimbursed.

U.S. Customs Regulations on Packages Shipped Separately

• You can send any personal article home without paying duty, as long as it was purchased in the United States. Mark the package "American goods returned."
• You can send a friend one duty-free gift every day just as long as

its retail value is less than $50. Mark the package "Unsolicited gift (value less than $50)." Clearly state what the gift is on the package.

- You can also send many separate gifts in one large package, as long as each gift is individually wrapped and marked with the name of the recipient. The nature of every gift within the large package must be marked on the outside.
- You must pay duty on all items you send to your home, but not on those gifts sent to friends. Many travelers arrange to send items to friends who will hold them for their return.

Shipping Goods Home

The safest and surest way of getting any article to your home is to carry it with you. The second-best way is to ship it home; the least sure way is to have a shop ship it.

In most European countries you'll pay 8 to 18 percent VAT (Value Added Tax) on all purchases unless they are sent out of the country. In short, you don't pay local taxes for packages shipped to the United States.

Shipping Goods Through Shops

- You may want to oversee the wrapping of your purchase to make sure that the right item is packed and that it is properly protected (which it generally is).
- If you have a store ship your package for you, have the shipping date clearly marked on your bill of sale.
- Ask the clerk to note the cost of any insurance, the value of the insurance, any shipping charges, and the mode of delivery.
- Specify airmail or surface mail. Airmail costs more, but is safer and faster. Surface mail may take months to arrive and increases the odds of damage.

Using Brokers

Goods may come into the United States through a broker, who may or may not inform you of their arrival. Unless it's clearly understood that packages are to be delivered to your home address, they may simply sit in storage in some remote warehouse. Try to avoid using brokers whenever possible.

- Get the name and address of any brokers.
- Be prepared to pay storage fees for any package that sits in the warehouse. If you want your goods, you will pay the charge.

Shipping Goods on your Own

- Check with the post office if you'll be mailing large or heavy packages. Size and weight limitations apply.
- If you find you have to send a package through a freight office, call several and compare costs and service before signing on the dotted line.
- Use twine instead of tape. Twine can be sealed with wax if you want to insure the package. In some countries, you will not be able to insure international mail.
- If you're sending books back, be sure to get the special book rate.
- Fragile items will often be broken in the mail—not because the package was poorly wrapped or mishandled, but because it was unwrapped in customs, only to be poorly rewrapped! Carry fragile items with you or skip buying them altogether. (If you do buy something fragile, try to arrange to pick it up at the end of the trip.)

Appendixes

A. Climate Chart

This chart gives you a capsule picture of each country's weather, followed by a breakdown of its average temperature (in degrees Fahrenheit) and rainfall (in inches) on a month-to-month basis. Naturally, temperatures drop by 10 degrees or so in the evening to rise again by 10 degrees or so over the average at midday—so take these overall averages with a grain of salt.

Nevertheless, the chart does provide a good, accurate idea of what to expect in the way of weather at any time—and might influence your decision on when to make a trip to Europe.

Country or Island

		J	F	M	A	M	J	J	A	S	O	N	D
Andorra. Almost all people go to Andorra in the summer, although late spring and early fall can be quite mild.	rain	1.5	1.5	1.5	1.5	3	2	2	2	1.5	2	2	1.5
	temp.	27	31	37	49	57	63	67	67	60	49	35	31
Austria. Most mountain resorts are open in summer and winter only. Major cities tend to be shrouded in a gray mist during the winter, while both spring and fall can be pleasant in the valleys. Bring a raincoat.	rain	1.5	1.5	1.5	2	3	2.5	3.5	3	1.5	2	2	1.5
	temp.	29	33	40	51	58	64	68	66	60	50	40	34
Azores. Very bleak in the off-season. Try to go in the summer.	rain	5	5	4	2.5	1.5	1	1	1	3	4	5	4
	temp.	57	57	58	59	61	65	69	71	70	66	62	59
Belgium. Off-season weather is poor in Belgium. Occasionally, you'll find mild weather in November, known as "St. Martin's Summer." March is one of the worst months. From April to mid-October you'll find the nicest weather, but it's unpredictable, so bring a raincoat!	rain	2.5	2	2	2.5	2	2	3	3	2	3	3	1.5
	temp.	36	38	43	47	55	61	63	63	59	50	44	39
Bulgaria. Travel to this area is recommended from late spring to mid-fall. The area along the Black Sea is extremely hot during	rain	1.5	1.5	1	1.5	2	2.5	2.5	2.5	2	2	2	1.5
	temp.	29	32	39	48	57	63	66	65	59	47	40	34

241

Country or Island		J	F	M	A	M	J	J	A	S	O	N	D
ing mid-summer and packed with people. The shoulder seasons are quite mild and pleasant. Temperatures vary from the low 20s to mid 80s. Temperatures are on the cool side in the Rila Mountains. Rainfall is higher than average in mountainous areas.													
Canaries. For these isolated islands off the North African coast, good weather is the main attraction. Temperature and rainfall vary from island to island. Lanzarote and Fuerteventura may go for months, sometimes years, without rain, whereas La Palma and Tenerife tend to be lush along the coast. Very mild, even in mid-winter.	rain	1.5	1.5	1	.5	0	0	0	0	0	0	2	2
	temp.	63	63	64	65	67	70	75	76	73	72	69	64
Corsica. Go in the summer. Too bleak in the off-season.	rain	3	2.5	2	2	2	1	.5	1	2	3.5	4	4
	temp.	45	47	51	54	61	67	71	71	71	61	52	47
Crete. Warm and dry much of the year. Mild but not swimming weather in winter. Torrid summers.	rain	4	2	2	1	.5	0	0	0	.5	2	2.5	4
	temp.	53	54	56	62	69	75	79	79	75	69	62	56
Czechoslovakia. The weather is similar to that of Germany, with temperatures varying from the low 20s to the low 80s. Temperatures remain cool in the High Tatras mountains. The shoulder seasons are good times to visit Prague and other cities. The eastern area tends to be somewhat cooler and drier than the rest of the country.	rain	1.5	1.5	1	1.5	2	2.5	2.5	2.5	2	2	2	1.5
	temp.	29	32	39	48	57	63	66	65	59	47	40	34
Denmark. Best visited from mid-May to mid-September, but bring a raincoat.	rain	2	1.5	1.5	1.5	2	2	3	5	2.5	2	2	2
	temp.	32	32	35	43	53	60	63	62	57	48	42	36

Country or Island

	J	F	M	A	M	J	J	A	S	O	N	D
Finland. Best visited late May to early September. rain	2	1.5	1	1.5	1.5	2	3	3	2.5	2.5	2.5	2
temp.	20	19	24	35	48	57	62	60	51	40	33	27
France. Whole country lovely from April to late October. North (including Paris) cold and damp during the winter season. Riviera mild in the off-season, but not warm enough for swimming. rain	2	2	1.5	1.5	2	2	2	3	2	2	2	2
temp.	36	38	44	50	57	62	66	65	61	52	44	39
Germany. Whole country lovely from April to late October. Munich very cold during the winter. Heavy snowfalls in the South and mountain areas, including the Black Forest. rain	1.5	1.5	1	1.5	2	2.5	2.5	2.5	2	2	2	1.5
temp.	29	32	39	48	57	63	66	65	59	47	40	34
Gibraltar. Very hot during the summer, quite mild in winter. rain	6	4	5	2.5	1	0	0	0	.5	2.5	6	5
temp.	52	55	57	61	66	70	75	75	72	67	61	57
Great Britain. Nicest weather in June. Good weather much of the time from April to late October, although you'll need a good umbrella. Cold with occasional snows during the winter. rain	3.5	3	3	2.5	2	1.5	1	1	2	1	3	4.5
temp.	38	40	43	47	51	53	61	60	53	51	43	43
Greece. Scorching hot weather from late May to early September. Mild in spring and fall, so-so in winter—OK for sightseeing, but not for swimming. Very cold in the North in winter. rain	2.5	1.5	1.5	1	1	.5	.5	.5	.5	2	2	3
temp	48	50	32	59	68	76	81	80	74	66	58	52
Hungary. Temperatures vary from the low 20s to the low 80s. As in much of Central Europe, you will experience periods of rain, fog, and cold. The shoulder seasons are excellent times to visit major cities. In mid-summer it can be very hot. rain	1.5	1.5	1	1.5	2	2.5	2.5	2.5	2	2	2	1.5
temp.	29	32	39	48	57	63	66	65	59	47	40	34

243

Country or Island

		J	F	M	A	M	J	J	A	S	O	N	D
Iceland. Basically a summer-only island as far as tourism goes, because that's when the weather is best. Bring rain gear nevertheless.	rain	3.5	2.5	2.5	2	1.5	1.5	2	2.5	3	4	3.5	3.5
	temp.	32	32	34	37	44	49	52	49	47	41	36	34
Ireland. Wet much of the time, even in the summer. Wet, penetrating cold in the winter.	rain	3	2	2	2	2.5	2	3	3	3	3	3	3
	temp.	40	41	43	46	51	56	59	59	55	50	44	42
Italy. Excellent weather in most areas from April to late October. Very mild in the South during the winter, but not mild enough for enjoyable swimming—except in heated pools. Rome, Florence, and Venice can be stifling in the summer heat, and most Italians take a break from noon to 4 P.M.	rain	3.5	3	2	2	2	.5	.5	.5	3	4.5	4.5	4
	temp.	46	48	52	56	63	70	76	75	70	62	54	49
Liechtenstein. Same sort of weather as Austria.	rain	1.5	1.5	1.5	1.5	3	2.5	3.5	3	1.5	2	2	1.5
	temp.	29	33	40	51	58	64	68	66	60	50	40	34
Luxembourg. Often damp and misty, even during the summer. Cold and drizzly in the off-season.	rain	3	2	2	2	2.5	2.5	2.5	3	2.5	2	2.5	2.5
	temp.	32	34	41	47	55	60	62	62	57	48	40	34
Madeira. Noted for its mild off-season weather. A favorite of the British at Christmas. At its best in spring (lush flowers) and fall (wine harvest).	rain	3.5	3.5	3	2	1	0	0	1	1	3	4	4
	temp.	60	60	61	61	63	66	70	71	70	69	65	61
Majorca. Hot and bright sun during the summer, very mild—even in winter—but not mild enough for ocean swimming.	rain	1.5	1.5	1.5	1	.5	.5	0	1	2.5	3	2.5	2
	temp.	50	51	53	58	62	70	75	76	72	64	57	52
Malta. Dry, hot summers with mild winters—again, "mild" in the Mediterranean does not mean ideal for swimming.	rain	3.5	2	2	1.5	.5	0	0	0	1.5	6	4.5	3
	temp.	53	53	56	60	65	73	78	79	75	70	62	57

Country or Island

Country or Island		J	F	M	A	M	J	J	A	S	O	N	D
Menorca. See Majorca.	rain	2.5	2	2	1.5	1	1	0	1	3	5.5	4	3
	temp.	50	51	53	57	59	70	75	75	71	64	57	53
Netherlands.	rain	2.5	2	2	2	2	2	3	3.5	3	3	3	2.5
	temp.	34	35	41	47	53	60	62	62	57	50	43	37
Norway.	rain	2.5	1.5	1	1.5	1.5	3	3.5	4	3.5	3.5	2.5	2.5
	temp.	23	25	31	41	51	58	62	61	50	40	34	28
Poland.	rain	1.5	1.5	1	1.5	2	2.5	2.5	2.5	2	2	2	1.5
	temp.	29	32	39	48	57	63	66	65	59	47	40	34
Portugal.	rain	4.5	3	1	1.5	1.5	.5	0	0	1.5	2.5	3.5	4
	temp.	51	52	56	60	62	68	71	72	70	64	58	52
Romania.	rain	1.5	1.5	1	1.5	2	2.5	2.5	2.5	2	2	2	1.5
	temp.	29	32	39	48	57	63	66	65	59	47	40	34
Sardinia.	rain	2	1.5	1	1.5	1.5	.5	0	.5	1	3	2	2
	temp.	48	49	53	57	62	70	75	75	71	64	57	51

Menorca. See Majorca.

Netherlands. Best weather from mid-April to late October, with frequent showers. Cold in the off-season: you'll need a warm coat.

Norway. Almost all tourists visit Norway from mid-May to mid-September, to take advantage of the mild summer weather and long days of light. Dark and cold in the off-season!

Poland. The weather is similar to that of Germany, with temperatures varying from the low 20s to mid 70s. The High Tatras mountains stay consistently cool. Springtime is lovely, but nights are chilly. Summer is quite hot. Fall is recommended for travel despite fairly frequent rainy spells.

Portugal. Very hot summers from late May to late August, ideal spring and fall weather (bright, dry, mild, breezy). Cool, windy, wet winters, with February the worst month.

Romania. Travel to this area is recommended from late spring to mid-fall. The area along the Black Sea can be hot during mid-summer. Temperatures vary from the low 20s to the mid 80s. Temperatures are consistantly cool in the Carpathian mountains, even in mid-summer. Mountainous areas are rainy. The Danube Delta area is more dry.

Sardinia. Basically a summer-oriented vacation spot, although pleasant in late spring and early fall as well

Country or Island

		J	F	M	A	M	J	J	A	S	O	N	D
Sicily. Noted for excellent off-season weather. Many clear, warm winter days—not hot, however! Very hot in the summer. Nicest in spring and fall.	rain	4	2	2.5	1.5	1	0	0	.5	1.5	5.5	4	3
	temp.	50	51	53	57	64	71	77	78	73	66	58	52
Spain. Madrid is "nine months hell, three months winter," according to a Spanish saying. And so it can be cold and snowy in the highest capital of Europe. Best visited in late April, May, late September, and October. The Costa del Sol offers mild winter weather, torrid summers—very popular with Scandinavians!	rain	1.5	1.5	2	2	2	1	.5	.5	1.5	2	2	2
	temp.	41	43	50	54	60	69	75	74	67	57	48	42
Sweden. Visit from mid-May to early October to take advantage of long days and warm nights.	rain	1.5	1	1	1	1.5	2	2.5	3	2.5	2	2	1.5
	temp.	26	26	30	40	50	59	63	61	53	44	36	32
Switzerland. Lovely from late April to early October. Cold and gray in the valleys during the winter—go to the ski resorts for sunshine. Most mountain resorts open winter and summer only, despite temperate spring and fall weather—which is ideal for visiting the major cities.	rain	2.5	2	2	2	2.5	3.5	2.5	4	3	3	3.5	2
	temp.	34	35	43	50	57	63	68	66	60	50	42	35

B. National Tourist Offices

Always write the tourist office that's closest to you, or your letter may be returned telling you to do just that.

Note that addresses change constantly, with offices bobbing up and down New York's Fifth Avenue like corks. To verify an address, simply call the business section of a local library and ask the person there to look up the address in the appropriate phone book.

An alternative: call an international airline and ask what the current address is. For example, call Air France for the French National Tourist Office, Lufthansa for the German National Tourist Office, and so on. All airlines have toll-free numbers listed in the telephone book.

Austrian National Tourist Offices

500 Fifth Avenue, Suite 2009
New York, NY 10110
Tel: (212) 944-6880

11601 Wilshire Boulevard,
   Suite 2480
Los Angeles, CA 90025
Tel: (310) 477-3332

2 Bloor Street East, Suite 3330
Toronto, ON M4W 1A8
Tel: (416) 967-3381

1010 Quest rue Sherbrooke,
   Room 1410
Montreal, PQ H3A 2R7
Tel: (514) 849-3709

200 Granville Street, Suite 1380
Vancouver, BC V6C 1S4
Tel: (604) 683-5808

Belgian National Tourist Office

745 Fifth Avenue, Suite 714
New York, NY 10151
Tel: (212) 758-8130

British Tourist Authorities

551 Fifth Avenue, Suite 701
New York, NY 10176
Tel: (212) 986-2266

2580 Cumberland Parkway,
   Suite 470
Atlanta, GA 30339
Tel: (404) 432-9635

625 North Michigan Avenue,
   Suite 1510
Chicago, IL 60611
Tel: (312) 787-0490

World Trade Center
350 South Figueroa Street,
   Suite 450
Los Angeles, CA 90071
Tel: (213) 628-3525

111 Avenue Road,
   Suite 450
Toronto, ON M5R 3J8
Tel: (416) 925-6326

Bulgarian Tourist Information Center

Balkan Holidays
41 East 42nd Street, Suite 508
New York, NY 10017
Tel: (212) 573-5530

1200 Bay Street, Suite 604
Toronto, ON M5R 2A5
Tel: (416) 964-9159

Cyprus Tourism Organization

13 East 40th Street
New York, NY 10016
Tel: (212) 683-5280

Czechoslovak Travel Bureau (CEDOK)

10 East 40th Street
New York, NY 10016
Tel: (212) 689-9720

Danish Tourist Boards

655 Third Avenue
New York, NY 10017
Tel: (212) 949-2333

6311-1/2 Orange Street
Los Angeles, CA 90048
Tel: (213) 936-0975

P.O. Box 115, Station N
Toronto, ON M8V 3S4
Tel: (416) 823-9620

Finnish Tourist Board

655 Third Avenue
New York, NY 10017
Tel: (212) 949-2333

French Government Tourist Offices

610 Fifth Avenue, Room 516
New York, NY 10020
Tel: (212) 757-1125

9454 Wilshire Boulevard,
 Suite 303
Beverly Hills, CA 90212
Tel: (310) 271-6665

645 North Michigan Avenue,
 Suite 630
Chicago, IL 60611
Tel: (312) 337-6301

2305 Cedar Springs Road,
 Suite 205
Dallas, TX 75201
Tel: (214) 720-4010

1981 Avenue McGill College,
 Suite 490
Montreal, PQ H3A 2W9
Tel: (514) 288-4264

30 Saint Patrick Street, Suite 700
Toronto, ON M5T 3A3
Tel: (416) 593-4723

German National Tourist Offices

122 East 42nd Street, 52nd Floor
New York, NY 10168
Tel: (212) 661-7200

11766 Wilshire Boulevard,
 Suite 750
Los Angeles, CA 90025
Tel: (310) 575-9799

175 Bloor St. East
North Tower, Suite 604
Toronto, ON M4W 3R8
Tel: (416) 968-1570

Greek National Tourist Organizations

645 Fifth Avenue
New York, NY 10022
Tel: (212) 421-5777

168 North Michigan Avenue
Chicago, IL 60601
Tel: (312) 782-1084

611 West 6th Street, Room 2198
Los Angeles, CA 90017
Tel: (213) 626-6696

1233 rue de la Montagne,
Suite 101
Montreal, PQ H3G 1Z2
Tel: (514) 871-1535

Upper Level
1300 Bay Street
Toronto, ON M5R 3K8
Tel: (416) 968-2220

Hungarian Travel, Inc. (IBUSZ)

1 Parker Plaza, Suite 1104
Fort Lee, NJ 07024
Tel: (800) 367-7878
(201) 592-8585

Iceland Tourist Board

655 Third Avenue
New York, NY 10017
Tel: (212) 949-2333

Irish Tourist Boards

757 Third Avenue, 19th Floor
New York, NY 10017
Tel: (212) 418-0800

160 Bloor Street East, Suite 1150
Toronto, ON M4W 1B9
Tel: (416) 929-2777

Italian Government Travel Offices

630 Fifth Avenue
New York, NY 10111
Tel: (212) 245-4822

500 North Michigan Avenue,
Suite 1046
Chicago, IL 60611
Tel: (312) 644-0990

12400 Wilshire Boulevard,
Suite 550
Los Angeles, CA 90025
Tel: (310) 820-0098

1 Place Ville Marie, Suite 1914
Montreal, PQ H3B 3M9
Tel: (514) 866-7667

Luxembourg National Tourist Office

17 Beekman Place
New York, NY 10021
Tel: (212) 935-8888

Malta National Tourist Office

249 East 35th Street
New York, NY 10016
Tel: (212) 213-6686

Monaco Government Tourist Bureau

845 Third Avenue
New York, NY 10022
Tel: (800) 753-9696
(212) 759-5227

Netherlands Boards of Tourism

355 Lexington Avenue
New York, NY 10017
Tel: (212) 370-7367

225 North Michigan Avenue,
Suite 326
Chicago, IL 60601
Tel: (312) 819-0300

9841 Airport Boulevard
Los Angeles, CA 90045
Tel: (310) 348-9333

25 Adelaide Street East,
Suite 710
Toronto, ON M5C 1Y2
Tel: (416) 363-1577

Norwegian Tourist Board

655 Third Avenue
New York, NY 10017
Tel: (212) 949-2333

Polish National Tourist Office

275 Madison Avenue, Suite 1711
New York, NY 10016
Tel: (212) 338-9412

333 North Michigan Avenue
Chicago, IL 60601
Tel: (312) 236-9013

ORBIS Polish Travel Bureau
342 Madison Avenue, Suite 1512
New York, NY 10173
Tel: (212) 867-5011

Portuguese National Tourist Offices

590 Fifth Avenue, 4th Floor
New York, NY 10036
Tel: (212) 354-4403

60 Bloor Street West, Suite 1005
Toronto, ON M4W 3B8
Tel: (416) 921-7376

Romanian National Tourist Office

342 Madison Avenue, Suite 210
New York, NY 10173
Tel: (212) 697-6971

Spain, Tourist Offices of

655 Fifth Avenue
New York, NY 10022
Tel: (212) 759-8822

8383 Wilshire Boulevard, Suite 960
Beverly Hills, CA 90211
Tel: (213) 658-7188

845 North Michigan Avenue,
   Suite 915 East
Chicago, IL 60611
Tel: (312) 642-1992

1221 Brickell Avenue, Suite 1850
Miami, FL 33131
Tel: (305) 358-1992

102 Bloor Street West, Suite 1400
Toronto, ON M5S 1M8
Tel: (416) 961-3131

Swedish Tourist Board

655 Third Avenue
New York, NY 10017
Tel: (212) 949-2333

Swiss National Tourist Offices

608 Fifth Avenue
New York, NY 10020
Tel: (212) 757-5944

150 North Michigan Avenue
Chicago, IL 60601
Tel: (312) 630-5840

222 North Sepulveda Boulevard,
   Suite 1570
El Segundo, CA 90245
Tel: (310) 335-5980

260 Stockton Street
San Francisco, CA 94108
Tel: (415) 362-2260

154 University Avenue, Suite 610
Toronto, ON M5H 3Y9
Tel: (416) 971-9734

Turkish Government Tourist Office

821 United Nations Plaza
New York, NY 10017
Tel: (212) 687-2194

1717 Massachusetts Avenue NW,
   Suite 306
Washington, DC 20036
Tel: (202) 429-9844

C. The Best of Europe

Andorra

A lovely isolated mountain retreat with superb duty-free shopping.

Austria

In Vienna, you'll want to see the Spanish Riding School (closed Monday and from mid-June to August), the Boys' Chorus (9:30 A.M. mass from mid-September to late June), the Hofburg (free Sunday), the Imperial Treasury (closed Friday), the Museum of Fine Arts, and Schoenbrunn Palace.

In Salzburg, go to the Hellbrunn Palace and underground through the Hallein Salt Mine (hard hats and all).

On a clear day, take the Grossclockner Mountain drive from Lienz to Zell am Zee. Bring enough Austrian currency to pay for gas and the toll.

Seefeld (near Innsbruck) offers a lively casino and resort life.

Skiing in the Austrian Alps—don't go at Christmas or Easter.

Azores

For total isolation and stark beauty. Go in July when the hydrangeas bloom.

Belgium

Fabulous food, from fresh mussels to Ardennes ham.

In Brussels visit the Grand'Place and Royal Palace.

In Antwerp you'll find Flemish masters in the Museum of Fine Arts. Take in the House of Rubens, several of his paintings in the cathedral (they're covered until noon), and the Plantin House.

In Bruges hear carillon concerts at the Basilica of the Holy Blood on Wednesday and Saturday at 11:45 A.M., January to September. The world-famous Procession of the Holy Blood takes place in late May.

In Ghent visit the St. Bavon Cathedral.

Outstanding are the castles of Beloeil and Chimay. Also superb is the

Chateau of Annevoie-Rouillon.

Try to visit a rural inn in the Ardennes region.

Binche's Carnival on Shrove Tuesday is one of the great festivals of Europe.

Bulgaria

This is a picturesque and relatively inexpensive country, still relatively unknown by most Western travelers.

The monastery church of Rila (any travel in the Rila Mountains is recommended).

The Bachkovo monastery.

A stay in a resort on the Black Sea coast (go in late spring or early fall to avoid the crowds)

The historic village of Koprivshtitsa. Also fine is Melnik Nesebâr.

The picturesque town of Veliko Târnovo, outstanding in every way.

Valley of the Roses near Kasanlâk (go late May to early June).

The Baba Vida Fortress in Vidin.

Canary Islands

These offer excellent off-season weather, low prices, and varied scenery, from desert to tropical.

Corsica

Popular offbeat destination in summer with isolated bathing beaches. Rustic.

Crete

Forbidding and dry island famed for the ruins of Knossos. Good off-season weather from March to November and relatively low prices. Rustic.

Cyprus

A stay in one of the local monasteries.

The mosaics at Kato Paphos.

The Byzantine Icons Museum in Nicosia.

A visit to a local *taverna* to hear *bouzouki* music.

Czechoslovakia

This is certainly one of the most popular of the Eastern European countries. Its culture and architecture are fascinating. There are well over 3,000 castles scattered throughout the country.

Karlštejn and Český Krumlov castles are worth a special detour.

Prague is justifiably on everyone's itinerary.

Try to take a trip into the Tatra mountains as well.

Visit one or more villages, such as Bardějov, Kutná Hora, Levoča, Tábor, or Telč.

Denmark

In Copenhagen shop along the Strøget; go to the Tivoli Amusement Park (open May to mid-September and best at night), the Ny Carlsberg Glyptotek (impressionists; closed Monday), the Royal Theatre (September to May), Amalienborg Palace (changing of the guard at noon when the queen is in residence), Rosenborg Castle, the Erotic Museum, and the suburb of Dragør.

In Helsingør you'll find Kronborg Castle.

Stay in at least one country inn (*kro*).

Finland

Excellent trout fishing in summer.

France

Paris, with fabulous food, sightseeing, shopping, and romance. Here are the top 10 sights, followed by the most convenient *métro* (subway) stations:

: • Arc de Triomphe (Étoile)
  • Eiffel Tower (Trocadéro)
  • Invalides and Tomb of Napoleon (Invalides)
  • Louvre—closed Tuesday (Palais Royal)
  • Musée d'Orsay (Chambre des Députés or Solférino)
  • Notre Dame—10:00 A.M. mass (Cité)
  • Panthéon (St. Michel)
  • Sacré Coeur (Abbesses)
  • Sainte Chapelle (Cité)

- Versailles (Pont de Sèvres, then bus No. 171)

The *château* country of the Loire with *Son et Lumière* shows from May to September. Don't miss Chenonceaux.

The Riviera (Côte d'Azur), best in spring and fall. Most lively in summer.

The cathedrals of Amiens, Chartres, and Reims.

The wine road from Mâcon to Dijon.

Mont St. Michel in Normandy.

The medieval city of Carcassonne.

Skiing in the French Alps (don't go at Christmas and Easter).

Prehistory of the area around Les Eyzies-de-Tayac.

Stays in *château* hotels and *relais de campagne* (country inns).

The Foundation Maeght in St. Paul-de-Vence.

The Musée des Beaux-Arts in Dijon.

Germany

Munich offers both sightseeing and beer halls. The technical museum is outstanding, and the Oktoberfest from late September to early October is a lot of fun.

A trip through the Black Forest with stays in Romantik Hotels.

A trip along the Rhine, using Koblenz as a base. Neuschwanstein Castle in the South.

The medieval towns of Rothenburg ob der Tauber and Dinkelsbühl or Meissen and Quedlinburg in eastern Germany.

The Richard Wagner Festival in Bayreuth from late May to September.

Night life along Hamburg's Reeperbahn.

A must—the cathedral of Cologne (Köln).

Stays in castles and Romantik Hotels.

Goethe's House in Weimar.

The buildings of Sanssouci Park in Potsdam.

Hiking along the Rennsteig in Thüringer Wald in eastern Germany.

Gibraltar

The Rock, duty-free shopping for real bargains, and mild weather in spring and fall.

Great Britain

London, with terrific shopping, theater, and sightseeing. Here are the top 11 sights, followed by the most convenient tube (subway) stations:

: • British Museum, Great Russell Street (Holborn)
  • Buckingham Palace—changing of the guard at 11:30 A.M. (Victoria)
  • Houses of Parliament (Westminster)
  • Madame Tussaud's Waxworks, Marylebone Road (Baker Street)
  • National Gallery (Trafalgar Square)
  • National Portrait Gallery, St. Martin's Place (Trafalgar Square)
  • St. Paul's Cathedral, Ludgate Hill (St. Paul's)
  • Tate Gallery, Milbank (Pimlico)
  • Tower of London (Tower Hill)
  • Victoria and Albert Museum, Cromwell Road (South Kensington)
  • Westminster Abbey (Westminster)

Theater at Stratford-upon-Avon from May to January.

Great Cathedrals: Canterbury, Chichester, Winchester, York—to name a few. The well-preserved Roman baths at Bath.

Stonehenge and Hadrian's Wall, for lovers of ruins.

Peter Scott's unique bird sanctuary at Slimbridge.

The college towns of Cambridge and Oxford.

Medieval gems like the town of Chester.

Scenic tours through Cornwall (spring), Dorset (fall), and the Lake Country (summer).

Stays in charming historic inns.

Salmon fishing and upland game shooting in Scotland.

Edinburgh's Royal Mile.

Greece

Excellent value for your travel dollar.

Athens, with a visit to the Acropolis and the National Archaeological Museum (pay the extra fee for the Santorini exhibit).

Make excursions to the temples at Sounion and Delphi.

The Greek Islands—all fascinating. If you're short on time, go to those just off the coast.

The monasteries of Méteora and Mt. Athos (men only) for Byzantine art.

Excellent weather from April to early November.

Greek Orthodox Easter (different date from our Easter).

Ruins in the Peloponnesus, the region southwest of Athens.

Theater at Epidauros in summer (exceptional acoustics).

Dafni wine festival from July to September.

Hungary

Hungary has long been popular with Western travelers and is already a part of the Eurailpass system. Following are things highly recommended to see or do:

Take a trip by steamer or hydrofoil from Vienna to Budapest.

In Budapest visit the Matthias church, the Hungarian National Museum, and the Museum of Fine Arts (noted for its collection of Spanish art).

Take a side trip to Szentendre by boat (or any trip which takes in the Danube Bend).

Go to the north shore of Lake Balaton, staying in Tihany.

Visit the mountain town of Sopron.

The Gemenc National Park and Game Preserve is another highlight.

Stay in a spa, such as Hévíz.

Visit the Esterházy Palace in Fertőd.

Canoe, kayak, or go horseback riding.

Visit one or more of the castles at Eger, Kőszeg, Siklós, or Szigetvár.

Iceland

Fascinating geology: volcanoes, glaciers, faults (visit Eldga).

Lovely falls, including Dettifoss and Gulfoss.

Trout and salmon fishing—the latter requiring advance preparation.

Bird-watching: Eldey Rock and Thjorsarver.

Ireland

In Dublin visit the following sights:

- Trinity College Library (see the Book of Kells)
- The National Museum (closed Mondays)
- Merrion Square (lovely 18th-century architecture)

- Abbey and Gaiety Theaters
- St. Patrick's Cathedral (where Jonathan Swift is buried)
- The GPO, headquarters of the 1916 Easter Rebellion

Shop along Grafton Street.

Take a short trip south of Dublin to the Martello Tower in Sandycove, site of the James Joyce Museum.

Make sure you visit the southwest of Ireland. Spend a day or two on the Dingle Peninsula, gazing out from Slea Head to the Blasket Islands.

The Cliffs of Moher in County Clare.

The Aran Islands, a 3-hour boat trip out of Galway.

Yeats country in Sligo in the northwest, including his famous burial site at Dumcliffe churchyard under Ben Bulben.

Beautiful Donegal in the northwest.

Italy

In Florence, a fabulous Renaissance city, visit these eight highlights:
- Academia (closed Monday)
- The Baptistry
- Duomo
- Medici Chapels
- Palazzo Vecchio
- Pitti Palace
- Ponte Vecchio
- Uffizi Gallery

Milan is famed for La Scala Opera from December to May. See its cathedral (Il Duomo), the paintings by Leonardo da Vinci in the Pinacoteca Ambrosiana, and his Last Supper in Santa Maria delle Grazie (closed Monday).

Rome is a must on any itinerary. While there, see:
- Colosseum (closed Sunday)
- Forum (closed Tuesday)
- Pantheon
- Trevi Fountain
- Vatican with St. Peter's Basilica

In Venice, best visited in spring and late fall, see:
- Bridge of Sighs

- Doge's Palace
- Grand Canal
- San Marco

Excellent and relatively inexpensive skiing in the Italian Alps.

Pompeii (near Naples) and Paestum—some of the most fascinating ruins in Europe.

Superb off-season weather in Sicily.

Elegant summer resort area—the Costa Smeralda in Sardinia. Very expensive.

The catacombs of Naples.

Stunning drives: Amalfi Drive, a tour of the Como Lake region, the Italian Riviera from the French border south.

Famous festivals: the Calcio in Florence in June and the Palio in Siena in July and August.

Liechtenstein

Famous for its colorful stamps.

Madeira

Lush island with good off-season weather.

Swimming is in pools only: the shore is rocky and off-shore currents are treacherous.

Shopping for handmade lace, wicker items, and varieties of the excellent Madeira wines.

Majorca

Hot and dry summer weather with excellent bathing areas.

Low off-season prices (winter weather is mild but not warm).

Malta

The Malta Government Crafts Center in Valetta.

Side trips to the islands of Comino and Gozo.

Monaco

World-famous Monte Carlo Casino and world's largest aquarium.

Netherlands

Amsterdam: sightseeing and world-famous red-light district. Best sights:

- Anne Frank's house
- Rembrandt's house
- Rijksmuseum
- Stedlijk museum
- Van Gogh museum

The red-light district is fascinating and totally safe at night (use common sense and reasonable caution).

Keukenhof (near Lisse), with fabulous beds of tulips in full boom from mid-March to early April—only a 45-minute drive from Amsterdam.

Twenty-one windmills spin on Saturdays in the summer at Kinderdijk (near Rotterdam).

Take in The Hague's Gemeentemuseum, Mauritshuis Museum, and Maduradam (Holland in miniature—open summers only).

Haarlem's Frans Hals Museum (check into candlelight music from April to August).

The ancient villages of Volendam and Monnickendam.

The cheese market at Alkmaar, each Friday from 10:00 A.M. until noon from late April to late September (take the Kaas-Express train from the central railway station—much less expensive than most organized tour buses).

Aalsmeer's Flower Auction at 8:00 A.M., Monday to Saturday.

See the reclamation project at the Delta Expo on the coast.

Norway

Visit the great fjords from May to September—Geiranger is one of the best.

Take the train (Bergensbanen) from Oslo to Bergen—one of Europe's finest railway excursions.

Also stunning: a coastal trip on the Bergen Line's mail boat—make reservations months in advance.

Pulpit Rock, east of Stavanger.

The Munich and Viking Ship Museums in Oslo.

The midnight sun from late May to late July at Kirkenes (far north).

Try Lake Svela in mid-June for trout fishing.

Superb cross-country skiing in March.

The ancient cathedrals of Stavanger and Trondheim.

Poland

This country is very open and warm to Americans, but tourism is still a new industry. Travel with realistic expectations.

The castles and churches of Cracow (Kraków), considered by most to be Poland's loveliest city.

Go to Częstochowa to see the Jasna Góra monastery (try to be there at dawn).

Any trip into the Tatra mountains is highly recommended.

Auschwitz (Oswiecim in Polish), the most infamous concentration camp.

While in Warsaw, don't miss the Wilanów or Lazienki Palaces.

Stay along the Baltic.

Hike in the Bialowieska forest.

Take a side trip to Zamość.

Visit Malbork Castle.

Portugal

Not to miss in Lisbon:

- Alfama (old Moorish quarter)
- Coach Museum (closed Monday)
- Madre de Deus church
- Mosteiro dos Jéronimos
- Torre de Belem

Visit the hilltop town of Sintra (best in spring).

Excellent weather and swimming on the southern coast (Algarve) from late March to early November. Base yourself in Albufeira (lively) or Praia da Rocha (cliffs over the sea).

Don't miss the cathedrals of Alcobaça and Batalha.

Incredible religious processions of Fátima on the eves of May 13 and October 13.

Go to Santarém in June to see colorful bullfights.

Great resorts with lively social scenes: Estoril and Caiscais.

Ancient towns full of atmosphere: Elvas, Estremoz, Évora, Obidos. The Manueline architecture of Tomar, truly unique to Portugal.

The fish market in Sines (go in the morning).

Coimbra's world-famous library.

The colorful spectacle of fishing at Nazaré.

Stays in *pousadas,* charming country inns.

Port wine tasting in Villa Nova de Gaia, across the river from Oporto.

Rhodes

Mild off-season weather and fascinating architecture.

Romania

This is a primitive yet picturesque country. View all travel here as an adventure. Note that many excursions or tours are open to locals only (to stop foreigners from taking advantage of the low cost). Hopefully, this will change by the time you read this book.

The Museum of Natural History (*Muzeul de Istorie Naturala*) in Bucharest, with its collection of nearly 90,000 butterflies.

Sibiu, a must-see medieval city and also a gateway to superb hiking. Don't miss the Brukenthal Museum there.

A stay on the Black Sea in one of the many coastal resorts. Go in late spring or early fall to beat the crowds.

The painted monastery churches and cemeteries of Moldavia.

Birding in the Danube Delta area. Book a room in the Hotel Lebăda in Crişana. Make private arrangements with a local fisherman to tour the area. His smaller boat is much better for birding than larger boats arranged by tour operators, which scare birds away.

See the Bran Castle near medieval Braşov.

Visit the Royal Palace (Peleş Castle) at Sinaia.

Sardinia

Luxury summer resorts on the Costa Smeralda—very fashionable and equally expensive.

Good weather from April to October.

Sicily

Excellent off-season weather and a wealth of ancient Greek temples.

Spain

Madrid's museums, with much time devoted to the Prado (closed Monday).

An excursion to Toledo (give it a full day or more).

Good swimming weather in resorts along the Costa del Sol from April to early November.

Bullfighting in Madrid and Barcelona.

Running of the bulls in Pamplona in early June.

The tourist cities of Córdoba, Granada (The Alhambra), and Seville (Cathedral and Alcazar).

Duck hunting near Valencia by advance arrangement.

The ancient town of Santiago do Compostela in the northwest.

Wine tasting in Jérez de Frontera (go in September).

Las Fallas celebration in Valencia on March 19.

Tennis in Fuengirola (superb in spring and fall).

Stays in *paradores,* inexpensive country inns.

Sweden

Stockholm, for Drottningholm Opera from May to September. Interesting Wasa Museum (sunken ship faithfully restored).

The Göta Canal trip from Gothenburg to Stockholm, from mid-May through August. Reserve space weeks in advance.

Midnight sun at Luleå from late May to mid-August.

Salmon fishing at Morrun in mid-March.

Switzerland

A trip to Zermatt (the Matterhorn) or to the Jungfrau.

Stays in medieval towns like Gottlieben (tiny) or Stein-am-Rhein (a gem).

Outstanding high-mountain skiing in the Swiss Alps (avoid Christmas and Easter).

Stunning lake area in the south known as Ticino (go anytime from late April to late October).

Turkey

The ancient ruins of Ephesus.

Shopping in the Grand Bazaar in Istanbul.

The magnificent basilica of Hagia Sophia in Istanbul.

D. Free Things for Travelers

Dozens of free things for travelers are described throughout this book. They'll save you hundreds of dollars if you make use of them, and so will these.

- Note that you can get a passport with more pages (and more room for visas, etc.) at no extra charge. It is ideal for extensive travel. Ask for it if you'll need it.

- Ask for free maps and brochures if you buy a Eurailpass. You can get them from the French, German, Italian, and Swiss railroad offices or from your travel agent.

- Check with WATS information to see whether there's a toll-free number before calling an airline or company. Dial (800) 555-1212. Get an 800 telephone book to save money.

- Pick up a telephone credit card for free from your telephone company. Use it to make calls home from phone booths to avoid the surcharges in many hotels.

- Ask about special incentives when booking a seat. Many tourist offices and airlines offer "bonus coupons" to foreign travelers. Some of these programs can save you a hundred dollars or more!

- Ask the airline you're flying on to book room reservations for you—many do so without charge. But ask as far in advance as possible.

- If a plane's coach seats are filled, suggest to the airline clerk that you be placed in first class at no extra charge. Airlines "upgrade" passengers when economy class has been overbooked. Your chances are better if you're dressed well.

- If your flight arrives in a city too late to make a connection, you can get a night's lodging paid for by most airlines. But you have to ask for this bargain; the airline cannot advertise the service.

- Find out about the thousands of foreign-made items you can bring back into the United States duty-free. To learn which ones fall into this category, write for *GSP and the Traveler,* a U.S. Customs Service publication, P.O. Box 7407, Washington, DC 20044.

- Request an excellent free booklet on Europe from: Europe, Dept. WA, P.O. Box 1754, New York, NY 10185, Tel: (800) 626-3237 or (212) 307-1200. An alternate mailing address: P.O. Box 9012, East Setauket, NY 11733.

Index

Boldface page numbers indicate charts

Share Your Favorite Tips with Us!
Send to:

> *Best European Travel Tips*
> c/o John Whitman
> P.O. Box 202
> Long Lake, MN 55356